WL Morrison
Sept 17/04.
s/father Anniversary
used to A & E.P. Royal
"Cirest Patins"

IMPRISONED PAIN
AND ITS TRANSFORMATION

Sydney Klein

IMPRISONED PAIN

AND ITS TRANSFORMATION

A Festschrift for
H. Sydney Klein

Edited by
Joan Symington

London & New York
KARNAC BOOKS

First published in 2000 by
H. Karnac (Books) Ltd., 58 Gloucester Road, London SW7 4QY
A subsidiary of Other Press LLC, New York

British Library Cataloguing in Publication Data

A C.I.P. for this book is available from the British Library

ISBN 1 85575 243 3

10 9 8 7 6 5 4 3 2 1

Edited, designed, and produced by Communication Crafts

Printed in Great Britain by Polestar AUP Aberdeen Limited

www.karnacbooks.com

CONTENTS

ACKNOWLEDGEMENTS

First I would like to thank Maria Rhode, without whose enthusiasm and readiness to contact contributors this Festschrift would not have evolved.

My grateful thanks go to each of the authors, all of whom expressed a warm interest in the project and who have generously written new chapters for the Festschrift or else willingly contributed papers previously written.

A number of people were very helpful in providing background details. These include Isabel Menzies Lyth, Leslie Sohn, Donald Meltzer, Kate Barrows, and Iain Dresser. Margot Waddell interviewed Leslie Sohn for this and also tape-recorded the first draft of his chapter.

Special thanks go to Marie Spruth for all her secretarial assistance, including the difficult task of trying to decipher tapes. She has held the book together both in her mind and on her computer.

Finally but not least, I want to thank my husband Neville for his constant good advice and discerning criticism.

Acknowledgements are due to the following:

The Analytic Press, Inc., for permission to reprint Anne Alvarez' paper, "Projective identification as a communication", from *Psychoanalytic Dialogues* 7 (1997, 6): 753–768.

The International Journal of Psycho-Analysis, for permission to reprint Michael Feldman's paper, "Projective identification: the analyst's involvement" from *IJPA, 78* (1997).

CONTRIBUTORS

ANNE ALVAREZ (M.A. M.A.C.P.) is Consultant Child and Adolescent Psychotherapist and Co-convenor of the Autism Workshop at the Tavistock Clinic, London. She is also Scientific Consultant to the Parent–Infant Psychotherapy Research with Children with Pervasive Developmental Disorder at the University of Paris. One of her most recent publications is the book *Autism and Personality: Findings from the Tavistock Autism Workshop* co-authored with S. Read.

Mrs KATE BARROWS read English Literature at Cambridge and later went on to train as a Child Psychotherapist at the Tavistock Clinic and became a Member of the British Psycho-Analytical Society. She had her training analysis with Dr Sydney Klein. She now works in private practice in Bristol.

MARGARET COHEN read philosophy at University College London and trained as a Child Psychotherapist at the Tavistock Clinic. Dr Sydney Klein was her analyst. She has worked at the Tavistock Clinic, the Hospital for Sick Children, Great Ormond Street, and at the Whittington Hospital in Highgate. She has trained in adult psychotherapy at the Tavistock Clinic and has a private practice in London. Her writing in the last few years has come from her particular interest in premature and sick babies and the work and experience of the staff and parents of neonatal intensive care units. More recently she has been working with the families of children who have leukaemia.

PATRICIA DANIEL is a psychoanalyst in private practice in London and a training and supervising analyst of the British Psycho-Analytical Society.

MICHAEL FELDMAN is a Training Analyst and Supervisor of the British Psycho-Analytical Society. He also worked part-time for many years as a Consultant Psychotherapist at the Maudsley Hospital in London. He co-edited (with Elizabeth Bott Spillius) the Collected Papers of Betty Joseph under the title *Psychic Equilibrium and Psychic Change*, and his own written contributions include a number of chapters and papers on psychoanalytic theory and technique.

SILVIA S. OCLANDER-GOLDIE was born in Argentina, where she qualified as a Clinical Psychologist at the University of Buenos Aires and became interested in the impact that social turmoil and violent social changes can have on the inner world. Subsequently she trained as a Child and Adolescent Psychotherapist, then as an Adult Psychotherapist at the Tavistock Clinic. At present she works in private practice. She teaches regularly at the Tavistock Clinic and has also taught in Spain and Argentina. She was analysed by Sydney Klein.

GABRIELLA GRAUSO trained in England, both at the Tavistock Clinic as Child Psychotherapist and at the British Institute of Psycho-Analysis, of which she is an associate member. She was analysed by Sydney Klein and worked both in institutions such as the Hospital for Sick Children, London, the Adolescent Department of the Tavistock Clinic, the Richmond Child and Family Psychiatric Clinic, and the Cassell Hospital and in private practice. She now lives in Milan, where she works both with adults and with children. She is a full member of the Italian Psychoanalytical Society and a training analyst of the Italian Child Psychotherapy Association.

MAURO MORRA is a full member and training analyst of the Italian Psychoanalytical Society and an associate member of the British Psycho-Analytical Society. He is an infant observation seminar leader in the Italian Child Psychotherapy Association. Formerly he was Consultant in Child and Adolescent Psychiatry at Edgeware General Hospital and Burnt Oak Child Guidance Centre, London. He used to be Assistant Professor in Psychodynamics of Adolescence at Genoa University.

EDNA O'SHAUGHNESSY trained as a child psychotherapist at the Tavistock Clinic when Esther Bick, Mattie Harris, and Donald Meltzer were there. She had supervision with Betty Joseph and Hanna Segal. Sydney Klein—a genial and encouraging man who had a great interest in children—was also an external supervisor. There was a particular ambience there at that time, with great enthusiasm for psychoanalysis and many new ideas being developed. Later she trained in adult psychoanalysis at the Institute for Psycho-Analysis in London and became a training analyst. She has published numerous articles on psychoanalytic work with children and adults.

GABRIELE PASQUALI, psychiatrist and psychoanalyst, worked for several years with children and adolescents in London, where he did his analytic training. Since returning to Italy, his home country, he has practised full-time as an analyst as well as giving consultations to hospital staff. He is a member of the Italian Psychoanalytical Society and the British Psycho-Analytical Society. His interest in clinical work and the enhancement of psychoanalysis has led him to hold a number of positions in the Italian Psychoanalytical Organization. He lives and practises in a village on the Italian Riviera, near Genoa.

MARIA RHODE trained as a child and adult psychotherapist at the Tavistock Clinic in London and was analysed by Sydney Klein. She is co-editor (with Margaret Rustin, Alex Dubinsky, and Hélène

Dubinsky) of *Psychotic States in Children* (Duckworth) and works as Consultant Child Psychotherapist at the Tavistock Clinic and in private practice.

RUTH SAFIER was born in South Africa, where she studied medicine. After migrating to Australia, she qualified as a psychiatrist, child psychiatrist, and psychoanalyst. She is in private practice as an analyst in Sydney. She is director of a Child and Family Clinic with a special focus on early parent–child difficulties and is a consultant to an Early Intervention Programme.

LESLIE SOHN is a training analyst of the British Psycho-Analytical Society. He is an Honorary Consultant Psychotherapist with the Maudsley Hospital Forensic Academic Unit and also Honorary Consultant Psychotherapist at Broadmoor Hospital. He has numerous publications on psychoanalysis and psychosis.

JOAN SYMINGTON is a child psychiatrist and psychoanalyst. She was Consultant Child Psychiatrist at the Royal Free Hospital, London, for ten years. Having trained at the British Psycho-Analytical Society, she now works in Sydney and is a training analyst of the Australian Psychoanalytical Society. She has published articles on infant observation and psychoanalysis and she is co-author with her husband Neville of the book *The Clinical Thinking of Wilfred Bion*.

INTRODUCTION

This book has been compiled as an expression of appreciation of Sydney Klein by his analysands, supervisees, colleagues, and friends. A majority of the chapters were written especially for this Festschrift.

Sydney Klein is a practising psychoanalyst and a training analyst of the British Psycho-Analytical Society. He qualified as an analyst in 1953 with a group who included many well-known analysts such as Isabel Menzies Lyth and Leslie Sohn. He also worked closely with Donald Meltzer, who for some time rented a consulting-room at Sydney Klein's house. It was a time of great enthusiasm for psychoanalysis, when patients with psychosis and with psychosomatic illnesses were being treated with considerable success by analysis. For many years he was Consultant Child Psychiatrist at the Belgrave Hospital for Children in London (Kings College Hospital). On two occasions he was the visiting analyst to Australia and Sydney, where he was much appreciated.

His papers cover a wide range of clinical topics, including children, groups, psychosomatic illness, delinquent perversion, manic states, and autistic phenomena in neurotic patients. All are rich in clinical material and admirably concise in language. Although a Kleinian analyst by training, he has carved quite an independent position within that school. He has a particular interest in Bion, whose discussion groups he attended with Betty Joseph and Roger Money-Kyrle. His writings also reflect his appreciation of insights derived from infant observation, child analysis, and Tustin's work with autistic patients. For example, although isolated psychotic islands had been described previously, Sydney Klein, through his familiarity with the findings from analyses of autistic children and from infant observation, recognized that autistic mechanisms created a hard shell that encysted these psychotic areas, making them difficult to contact.

Sydney Klein is noted for his great interest in children, his quick intuitive perception, his warm bluntness of expression, his down-to-earth realistic approach, and his encouragement of attempts to think independently.

One could say that imprisoned pain is what underlies most problems confronting the psychoanalyst. The pain remains imprisoned because of intolerance of the conditions that would enable transformation towards meaningfulness to occur. Bion spoke of that aspect of the personality which is exceptionally alerted to and persecuted by psychic reality and all its qualities. Hostility to growth of the mind ensures that the pain associated with growth is of a particular intensity. It is in the avoidance of this peculiarly intense awareness that pain becomes imprisoned and hidden. Hence the pain is not suffered. It is lodged within the personality, but it is not experienced emotionally. The patients referred to in Sydney Klein's paper on autistic phenomena in neurotic patients had all had previous analyses, indicating that the pain can remain imprisoned despite analysis.

Transformation of imprisoned pain involves its elevation to thinkable ideas. This means a new exposure to one's psychic reality, like a newborn's raw exposure to the shocking and astonishing world. This step requires an accessible, thinking object so that the new experience can be tolerated and explored in becoming part of the mind.

This book is arranged in such a way as to try to reveal the multi-faceted nature of imprisoned pain. Many chapters describe the deprivations and traumata of infancy and childhood that played a part in rendering the pain intolerable. A major focus is on people in whom pain was not at first experienced as such but, rather, as some disabling behaviour or symptom. The transformation of this in analysis into experienced pain that is manageable depends on the way in which the analyst is able to understand and to speak to the patient about it.

CHAPTER ONE

Moral imperatives in work with borderline children: the grammar of wishes and the grammar of needs

Anne Alvarez

In this chapter Anne Alvarez describes how supervision with Sydney Klein played a decisive part in transforming her understanding of the importance of the grammar of interpretation—that not all interpretations have to unmask hidden desires on the negative side but, rather, can help the evolving process of growth and understanding. This is particularly important in borderline patients in whom such unmasking interpretations may be ego-depleting in that they do not take into account the immediate meaning of the child's communication.

I first came in contact with Sydney Klein's supervision in a clinical seminar organized for qualified child psychotherapists sometime in 1969 or 1970. At one point I presented some case material from a usually depressed, rather cut-off boy named

An earlier version of this chapter was first read at the Bridge Foundation, Bristol, England, in 1989. The present version was read at the International Psychoanalytical Association Research Conference on Borderline Patients, London, March, 1994. It was first published in Symposium on Child Analysis, Part I, *Psychoanalytic Dialogues*, 7 (6): 753-768, 1997.

"Stephen", who had returned from the summer break somewhat excited: walking on the moors during his holiday, he had found the skull of a sheep. I reported that I had explored with Stephen what I saw as the rather disturbing idea of his fascination with the skull. I had linked this with possible destructive phantasies connected with anger about the break from treatment—that is, why and how, in the transference, might I have "been turned into" a skull instead of a live object? Dr Klein listened, I think with some impatience, and then offered several other possibilities: perhaps Stephen was not *indulging* his aggressive phantasies; perhaps he was, on the contrary, disturbed by them, and indeed even afraid that they had been realized—that his object had been stripped down or denuded in some way. Or, he added, perhaps Stephen was fascinated because he was relieved and moved at the evidence of the skull's—and his object's—survival over time. What Klein said made me appalled by the narrowness and meanness of my own thinking, and eventually I managed to have individual supervision with him.

A few years later, he referred a little boy called "John" to me, telling me with some sympathy about the child's despair about not being able to fly paper aeroplanes. He seemed to take for granted that I would understand that one could see flying—in this case, at least—not as a manic defence against depression, but as a natural and desirable expression of exuberance, hope, life, and ambition. Again I was appalled—where had I got the idea that ascent to the heights should be equated with mania and remaining in the depths with gravitas and mental health?

This chapter describes the psychoanalytic psychotherapy of a 10-year-old boy, "Richard", whom I treated from 1967 until 1973. The supervision with Sydney Klein began in 1971. All good ideas seem to go through a period when their range of application is over-exaggerated, and some elements in Melanie Klein's theories are no exception: her concept of the power of unconscious envy, of manic processes as defences against depression, and her related technical recommendations regarding the importance of putting the patient in touch with his deepest anxieties, his deepest guilts, and his deepest hatreds may have been among these. Spillius (1983) has pointed out that in the 1950s and 1960s the Kleinian Membership papers for admission to the British Psycho-Analytical

Society were inclined to "emphasize the patient's destructiveness in a way that might have felt persecuting to the patient" (p. 324), but that destructiveness gradually began to be interpreted in a more balanced way.

My patient had, after the first four years of treatment, become less psychotic, but was by now intensely preoccupied with phantasies of sadistic attacks on small animals. Indeed, he had begun to act upon them. Other colleagues and supervisors had suggested that this was a not unusual development in a previously psychotic patient. Dr Klein, however, asked why I was persecuting Richard with such cruel interpretations; he added that the child probably felt that his vulnerable infantile self was feeling very attacked by this, and that he was probably in identification with a persecutor when he was attacking small animals. I soon stopped persecuting Richard, and he began to soften very quickly! Sydney Klein seems to have been among the earliest analysts to breathe clinical and technical life into Bion's ideas about the normality and neediness of some projective identifications and to show the humanity and breadth (I use that word advisedly instead of "depth") that lay in them. I feel I have spent the last three decades trying to understand the implications of this radical change in theory and technique.

This chapter, then, presents material from work with a borderline psychotic 10-year-old boy who started intensive treatment with me over thirty years ago. Over that period, the impact of Bion's (1962b) extension of Melanie Klein's (1946) concept of projective identification, and the consequent implications for technique explored by Rosenfeld (1987a), Joseph (1989b), and others, have made a tremendous difference to the work with these patients. I was using a technique with Richard that was uninformed by these developments and was more appropriate to work with neurotic patients. For a period I think it was positively harmful to him. The technique, which I shall try to illustrate, had elements of an unmasking quality designed to reveal the depression and loss that underlay what I thought of then as his manic, omnipotent, and paranoid defences. I think now that these so-called "defences" were desperate attempts to *overcome* and *recover from* states of despair and terror—they carried, that is, elements of basic developmental needs: for protection, preservation, for a sense of agency and potency, and even for revenge and justice. Richard was full of violence, bitterness, and persecution, but unlike patients who have a more psychopathic accompaniment to their borderline problems, he was filled up with violence, rather than being dedicated to it or excited by it. And unlike neurotic patients, he had little ego functioning. His "defences" were inadequate to manage his overpowering feelings. He needed, for example, to be able to project, to split, and certainly to repress and forget. I shall consider the difference, in the neurotic patient, between a desire that things could be, or could have been, otherwise and, in certain borderlines, a desperate need that things *should* be, or *should have been* otherwise.

The major theoretical change to which I am referring concerns ideas about the purpose of and motives for projective identification processes. [It has some areas of overlap with the reformulations of Anna Freud and Sandler (1988), Kohut (1971), and Stolorow and Lachmann (1980) on the difference between ordinary defences, and early structurings, protective manoeuvres, or prestages of defence.] Racker (1958, cited by himself, 1968) had emphasized that countertransference was the expression of the analyst's identification not only with the id and ego of the patient, but also with those of his internal objects, and should be used as such. Bion (1962a) also made the connection between countertransference and projective identification when he pointed out that the psychoanalyst may play the part of the patient's lost self not only in the patient's mind, but in his own mind too—that is, the patient may project so powerfully that he may not only feel that his analyst is frightened or depressed, he may make him *become* frightened or depressed. But in the 1950s and still in the early 1960s, Bion (1957) and others were still describing the projective identification as arising from destructive or defensive and pathological motives. Bion (1962a) then went further: his concept of the analyst as receptacle or container of these projections began to carry the implication that the receptacle could be inadequate, sometimes making the patient project even harder. [Grotstein (1981) has pointed out that this introduced the concept of deficit in the object long before Kohut (1971)]. Bion (1962a) suggested that some projective identifications *expressed a need to communicate something to someone* on a very profound level: he compared the analyst's "containment" and "transformation" (1965) of the patient's feelings

and thoughts to the primitive but powerful pre-verbal communications that take place between mothers and tiny infants. This, he
suggested, is how feelings become bearable and thoughts become
thinkable. This—in a way—more democratic two-person psychology leaves room for either term in the equation to affect the interactions. There is more room in such a model for the object, *external*
or *internal*, to have an impact on the system. (I shall use the term
"internal object", with which I am familiar, for what others would
call the representational other or internal working model.)

The technical implications of this increased attention to inadequacies of the object have been profound. Rosenfeld (1987a)
emphasized the dangers of interpretations to borderlines that
over-valued the analyst's contribution. He stressed the importance
of the health that could lie in resistances, and of not breaking down
idealization too quickly. Money-Kyrle (1977) thought the issue of
distinguishing a desperate projective identification from a destructive one a matter of great technical urgency. Betty Joseph (1989b)
has spent a life-time working on this problem. She has expanded
the notion of the communicative use of projective identification
both technically and theoretically, and she has drawn attention to
how very pressuring projections may include a need to communicate something that may require lengthy containment and exploration in the analyst and should not be shoved back too prematurely
at the patient. It is often better for the analyst to hold and explore
the experience in himself—for example, "you feel that I am stupid"
(without adding that it is the patient's projection of his stupidity).
The patient may need to feel, she points out (Joseph, 1978), that
you are willing to carry the projections long enough to experience
the missing part of the patient, or else to experience his previously
unexamined internal object. A disappointing or fragile parental
object, say, whose weakness has always been denied, may need
gradual uncovering, not explaining away—a move one could describe as a move from a grammar of explanation to a grammar of
description. Steiner raises the issue in his discussion of analyst-
centred versus patient-centred interpretations (1993).

Bion (1962a) stressed the normalcy of the need for a container
of such communications as a very early infantile human need to be
in the company of a mindful mind. An implication is that these
communicated emotions are not necessarily emotions the patient

wants rid of—they may be emotions that he needs his object to have on his behalf. They may be emotions he needs to explore in us and only gradually own himself. Furthermore, these need not be negative emotions. Positive states of mind can be conveyed, however confusedly and crazily, through this process of unconscious communication just as powerfully as Bion's earlier examples of fear and murderousness can. Bion said that the psychotic has pain but does not suffer it: one might add, the psychotic also has pleasure but does not enjoy it. Preconceptions need turning into conceptions in both areas for normal development to proceed.

I would now like to explore the idea that such unconscious projective communications may, like more ordinary verbal communications, have a grammar. This grammar's variations may bear some correspondence to where the patient is on the neurotic/psychotic continuum—that is, to his level of ego development and also to the level of urgency and desperation of his needs. Both the neurotic and borderline child may boast in a manic or grandiose manner, or protest and complain of injustice. We may be pressured to admire or sympathize. The countertransference may be similar in both cases, but the motivation of the child may be vastly different in the two situations. In fact, we may be driven to be even more unmasking with the borderline child, whose immaturity may make his boasts sound ridiculous and silly. Yet our interpretive response needs to be carefully structured in grammatical terms that take account of the difference between a desire for omnipotence and a need for potency (Alvarez, 1992). The normal or neurotic child may wish or even demand that things be otherwise, but he can just about bear to acknowledge the way things really are, in external reality and in his own heart. He can usually juggle and compare two realities (Stern, 1985), manage a dual perspective (Reid, personal communication 1989) or binocular vision (Bion, 1950) and two-tracked "thinking in parentheses" (Bruner, 1968). He can hold a thought in reserve and consider the thought within the thought and the thought beyond the thought. He can manage meta-cognitive processes (Main, 1991) and self-reflective functions (Fonagy, Steele, Steele, Moran, & Higgitt, 1991) and some degree of symbolic functioning (Segal, 1957). Borderline patients, on the other hand—in their psychotic moments, that is—are concrete, one-tracked, overwhelmed by the singularity of their state of mind, and in danger of symbolic equations and massive splitting and projection. Are *we* in danger of producing premature integrations when we refuse to stay with their urgent imperative single-minded states? Could it even be that there is, at certain very early stages of emotional development, a need for something like a symbolic equation, the nearly perfect fit?

There has been much work by developmentalists on how the baby's mind grows and how intersubjectivity becomes internalized as intrasubjectivity (Stern, 1985; Trevarthen, 1978). It is a fascinating moment when autistic or other mindless children begin to discover that they like doing something, then that they *like liking* doing it. (When they go further and finally get a dual perspective that there are two different ways of looking at the same toy, for example, language and pretend play can begin.) Mothers follow their babies' direction of gaze long before babies begin to follow theirs (Collis, 1977). Infant observation shows us time and again the way in which mothers light up as they see what has caught a baby's glance—"Oh, it's the movement of the tree!" Both developmentalists and psychoanalytic observers seem to be agreed that if a mind is to grow, it requires a meeting of minds and not too many "missteps in the dance" (Stern, 1977) between infant and caregiver—but also not too few—mismatch, disillusion, and separateness are fundamental too to learning about reality. Yet the balance between match and mismatch in our interpretive work needs to be carefully tuned to the developmental level at which the child patient is functioning at any given moment. Easier said than done!

This brings me back to grammar. I shall suggest that interpretations that stress separateness and difference from ideal objects or ideal self—that is, that make use of the language of wishes and wants—may be appropriate for patients with some ego development, some sense of trust in their objects, and some sense of worth in themselves. However great their anxieties and angers and depressions, such patients have sufficient ego equipment with which to examine the gaps in the fabric of the universe. In Latin a verb containing doubt (you wish, you fear, you think, you hope . . .), would be followed by the subjunctive or conditional. An "I may go" is weaker than "I am going" or "I will go". For instance, the language of "You wish, but we both know that you cannot or did not or will not" is tolerable where the real alternative is just bearable. I found that if I said, "You are afraid that you will die without me on the weekend", the neurotic patient could hear the implications and the alternative possibilities implied in such statements (namely, that he would probably not). From his dual perspective he can think about both more or less at once. I learned to my cost that the borderline patient often cannot. His panics, and even his manic denials, may express a need for us to understand that he should have—that is, he has a rightful need of—assurance, safety, protection, and even justice. He may need to hear something along the lines of "It's hard for you to imagine that you might make it through till Monday" or, "You feel I should not be leaving you at this time". This need not involve collusion or seduction or false promises. [See Kut Rosenfeld and Sprince (1965) of what is now the Anna Freud Centre on the ease with which interpretation of anxiety can escalate anxiety in borderlines.] The child's rightful need for assurance needs understanding, and—except under the most dire of emergency conditions—reassurance should not be necessary. Interpretations of anxiety or loss to an already despairing child can weaken him. Other grammars, the grammar of imperatives, may enable his ego to grow stronger.

Case study: "Richard"

"Richard" was referred to me in spring 1967, when he was 10 years old. The referring psychiatrist found him a very mad boy with a suspicious, strained appearance and bizarre hand gestures, as though warding off blows to the head. Richard's mother was a manic-depressive psychotic and had beaten him often when he was a baby. She left abruptly when Richard was 18 months and his younger brother 4 months old. She had visited very seldom. When Richard came to me, he was not learning much in a sort of nursery school. After his mother left, he had lived with his paternal grandmother for a few months, then with his father and a Nanny, to whom he was very attached. When she left, his paternal grandmother moved into the father's house to take care of the children. Father and grandmother were very kind and intelligent people, but very genteel, and I suspect they would have found it difficult to take the grief and horror and outrage that was in Richard, had it ever displayed itself when he was an infant. His aunt, a warm and sensible woman, also had some hand in the children's care.

I started seeing Richard twice a week in May 1967 and soon increased this to four times per week.

I am going to go through the early sessions in some detail. It seems a rather masochistic and pedantic exercise, because I was pretty green at the time, and the work is not good for lots of reasons. But I want to look at the grammar and the theoretical and technical implications behind the grammar, and so I hope you will forgive the piecemeal approach.

There were painters in my house when we started. At the start of the first session, Richard went on past the playroom door, straightway encountering one of the workmen, who kindly showed him the way. He was a blond, blue-eyed, slightly plump boy with a very robotic walk. Every step was placed terribly cautiously, as though he were walking blindfolded. He looked terrified, but after a few comments from me and explanations about the therapy, he looked at the wall and said: "I know what that is; that's paint." A bit later, he said: "That's a wall!" Later, when he seemed frightened by a noise from the workmen upstairs, he asked, "Why are they here? Is the house all in bits?"

After a while, he seemed a little less frightened and began to paint in big sweeping strokes—rather like the painters upstairs. I said so now he was painting like the workman, and perhaps he was showing me how he would like to be able to paint like the grown-up workman. I added that perhaps he often wanted to do what Daddy could do. He said—and it all poured out in a jumble, with the words and thoughts tumbling over each other: "Yes I do, I do want to, but I *do* work, this is what I do, you see!"

I invite you to note my interpretation: "You *would like to be able to paint. . . .*" And note his desperate correction. I took it as an omnipotent defensive identification, a desire, but could he have been communicating a desperate need to be seen by me as being

capable of being, or at least of becoming like, a potent and reparative father? I think he may have experienced my interpretation,
and many subsequent ones like it, as a crushing reminder of lifelong impotence and maybe lifelong humiliation. He had, after all,
been abandoned by two caregivers and beaten by one. Supposing I
had said: "Well, I think I should notice that you can paint too, not
so differently from those fellows upstairs!"

Later, when he had calmed down a little, he gave a slightly
nervous start after some more noises. I interpreted that he was
still frightened here, and he said: "No I'm not scared. David
[his brother] gets scared." I took it that he was using David now
to be the scared one in order not to be the scared one himself. I
added that, after all, this was a strange place and I a new
person.

But there had been a general calming down, which I could have
underlined by seeing the fear split off into David not as a projection and split that should be returned and reintegrated, but as one
that needed acknowledging and respecting. That is, I could have
said something like, "Now you are feeling a bit less scared and you
can think of someone else as the scared one"—that is, to register
the *other* half of the split—the non-scared half. I could also have
acknowledged even earlier that he felt "at least I recognize something in this madhouse—that's paint and that's a wall". Splitting
and projection have healthy functions, not only pathological ones.
The need—and the ability to put one's fear at a distance—is not
only defensive. It may permit the beginning of a little trust to
develop and therefore preserve and protect a tiny bit of ego
growth.

In any case, Richard went on to explain that it was his conscience that made him scared—and then he reassured us both
that he hadn't broken Granny's alarm clock. I linked the clock
with the feeling of my house all in bits, and that maybe there
was a feeling inside him that something was all in bits, but he
didn't know what it was. (I was finally not rushing to over-
explain.) And at last, he began really to relax. He took out the

glue, looking through his box. Then he said, disappointed, "But there's nothing to mend!"

I wonder now if he was talking there about his tragic situation, where there was not a reparable container: the mad violent mother was not only in bits, she was also gone. Here, I think one is faced with deficit in the internal object that needs addressing just as much as the conflicts and defences towards more highly developed objects. This means letting the transference rewrite history for the patient and not rushing to remind him of irreparable painful reality. I needed, perhaps, to let him feel he could be like or could become like the painters upstairs.

> In the second session he feared it would be shorter and was delighted when I told him it would be just as long, and that maybe he hadn't liked the wait between sessions. He agreed eagerly and said he liked things with no end—forever and forever. I, I am sorry to say, began to talk about his mother. I said I knew his mother didn't live with them now and asked if he saw her. He said in a panicky voice, "Yes, forever". I said, I wondered if he didn't have to feel it was forever because he felt it was too sad if it wasn't. He felt he must have a forever Mummy, just as he felt he should have a forever Mrs Alvarez, not just a twice-a-week Mrs Alvarez.

There, although probably under pressure from my countertransference feeling of terrible pain for him, I did convey some understanding of his needs, but I think I was still using an unmasking model. I treated the insistence on foreverness as a defence against sadness, instead of seeing it as a rightful need for continuity. Secondly, by introducing painful and irreparable external reality just at the point when the child had arrived with some hope of a new internal reality via the transference, I was pushing him back down into panicky despair and rejecting him. I could at the beginning of the exchange have said something like: "You like the feeling that this treatment is going to go on for a long time. A nice forever feeling." The infant needs an experience of duration and durability of good experience before he can learn to tolerate interruptions and endings. Grotstein (1983) points out you first have to be bonded before you can be weaned.

> In the seventh session he told me about his hallucination of the terrible cogwheel going round in his head and seeing the clock with all its works falling out. I again linked it with his mother and me and in later sessions began to take up his fear that he had bunged up his mother's works and mine.

> In fact, I became pregnant twice in the course of his treatment, and he showed more and more of a powerfully intrusive sexuality and got more and more into the idea of enjoying destroying my "works" and, over the years, of murdering babies. I and others saw this clock in bits, or the drilling cogwheel, as a destroyed object, which he felt he had created as a result of his attacks. He conveyed that his other nightmare or delusion was that "Mother Goose had died of grief because she had produced a rotten egg".

This was the late 1960s and early 1970s, when the full impact of Bion's ideas about containment was not yet explored. It was easy to see Richard's increasing sadism as having been freed to come more into the open. This was in part true, but I did not understand the degree to which it was driven by desperation about an irreparable object, and how my interpretations escalated this by seeming to accuse him of being totally responsible for this state of affairs. I think there was an idea around, which was a parody of Melanie Klein, that people got the bad objects they deserved. He did become less frightened and less psychotic (his hallucinations disappeared), but he also became violent and full of sadistic phantasies. I think I could have helped him far sooner to develop restraint if I had conveyed that I understood his object to have some responsibility for being in bits. (I do not think this would have helped if the apparent psychopathic element had been genuine.) If I had helped him to explore his mad irreparable and violent internal object, I might have reduced his guilt rather than increased it. Had I explored the object in whom there was nothing to mend, I might have allowed his preconception of a reparable object (which was clearly there in his reference to its lack) to grow, and also his capacity to identify with a repairing father.

There were periods when his desperation and hatred knew no bounds—for example, when he sang bitterly, "Gotta get a message to you" and then took faeces from his bottom and shoved it up his nose. Another time he said, "I've just got to make you shed tears and then I'll stop". I did not see this as a rightful need to project and communicate his horrors: I continued to take it as sadism—but at times I was overwhelmed with pity and despair, and so perhaps I shared and contained something. He did begin to learn but became obsessed with phantasies of murdering small animals and indeed did kill one or two. I interpreted sadism and jealousy, instead of revenge and a sense of terrible betrayal. After all, I had two babies in the first four years of his treatment, and his real mother had really betrayed his trust.

He complained that I didn't know what it was like to be near a light-bulb that is going to explode, and he was right, I was not getting the message. But I did begin to observe that some of my interpretations seemed to make him madder. Eventually, in September 1971, I took his material to Sydney Klein, who was very influenced by Bion. Richard's sadism towards babies began to diminish. By December he was able to talk about the coming break in a very different way. He sang "Jesus loves me" very sweetly (not in a syrupy way) and spoke about a man on a rope crossing Niagara Falls to Canada. He knew I was Canadian. I have not had time to go into his goody–goody voice which, in the beginning, I saw as denying his hatred, but which I finally came to understand also masked real love. In the last two years of his six-year—but interrupted—treatment, he became far more collected and together and civilized. It is still painful, however, for me to read these early notes.

Discussion

I shall discuss four considerations, which I now think may be important in the treatment of certain paranoid borderlines in whom the psychopathic element is not marked. These are considerations only, because the complexity of the human mind—even the child psychotic mind—ensures that there can be no manual:

the patient can move back and forth between neurotic and psychotic levels of functioning, or from a 3-day-old infant to a 6-month-old infant to a 10-year-old child, in the course of a few seconds, and the level of work needs to change accordingly. So, although I shall speak about a certain type of paranoid borderline as forming a group, it is clear that this is a terrible oversimplification. Also, the stress on grammar is a way of thinking about, structuring my own understanding of, such patients—there is, of course, no magic in the words themselves. If we get the emotional understanding right, our patients forgive us the grammar.

Developmental delay

The first point is that psychotic illness in children, however temporary or however much only a threat from beyond the border, almost always interferes with normal psychological development and produces developmental arrest and deficit. Disturbance and disorder may be accompanied by delay and deficit in any or all aspects of the personality: in ego function; in the self and its sense of identity, its capacity to love, to enjoy, and to feel self-respect; and in the superego and internal objects. The positive side of the patient's personality may be just as *under*developed as the persecutory side is *over*developed. There have always been clear developmental implications in the assertion by Melanie Klein (1952) and Hanna Segal (1964) that it was the *strength* of the ideal object and of the individual libidinal impulses that enabled the integration of persecutory object relations and thus the move from the paranoid–schizoid position to the depressive. In many borderline children this strength, however, is exactly what cannot be taken for granted. The process of the introjection of the ideal object and the building up of a sense of the loving or loveable self is a long, slow process, yet it is vital to mental health. Splitting and projective identification can be seen to be in the service of development rather than as a defence, because they may enable new introjections to take place under conditions that should be described as protective rather than defensive. I am sorry to say that I believe that for many years my work with Richard may actually have interfered with this introjective process. As I have shown, I often interpreted tiny increments in the belief in an ideal self (him as painter) or ideal object (a forever Mummy), or new attempts to split or project badness off into someone else (David, who was scared, or the me who should cry), as defences against persecution and despair. Now I believe that they could be seen as tiny developmental moves—that is, as attempts to overcome, rather than defend against, persecution and despair. A surge of hope or pride or a sudden feeling of relief is different from a manic state used as a defence. A recovery is not a denial, though of course it may be accompanied by denial. In certain profoundly depressed children, apparently grandiose omnipotent boasts, which seem like manic assertions, in fact *communicate a highly tentative question* about whether or not the object could see them as potent. Not all ill-fitting shoes are stolen: some are simply new and need wearing in. But it is unfortunately evident that in the late 1960s, prior to the technical impact of Bion's work, I was still suffering too much from an either–or mentality, where the shoes are either yours or mine.

The distinction between defences and overcomings in the paranoid position

Melanie Klein herself (1935) introduced the fundamental meta-theoretical differentiation between defences and overcomings in relation to reparative processes in the depressive position. She insisted that true reparation, unlike manic reparation, was not a reaction formation to guilt, but an overcoming of guilt. I would add that we may also need this meta-concept of "overcoming" for developments *within the paranoid–schizoid position*. What is at issue in the paranoid–schizoid position is the overcoming of fear and despair rather than of guilt and grief. If love has to be stronger than hate for hatred to be overcome in the depressive position, what, for example, has to be stronger than fear to overcome, as opposed to defend against, persecutory anxieties? What enables fear or despair to be reduced so that good feelings can begin to emerge? Relief from the overwhelming pressure of anxiety can initiate such healing processes, and notions such as Bion's (1962a) concept of the containing functions of the maternal object, Sandler's (1960) "background of safety", Bowlby's (1988) "secure base", and many others outline a major way in which such relief from unbearable pressure may be obtained.

Rectification:
imperative phantasies of vengeance

This involves an elaboration of Joseph's (1978) point about holding and exploring projective identifications in ourselves rather than returning them prematurely. In this instance I am referring to the moments when the patient may be projecting or externalizing an internal object of an extremely bad kind. A psychotic adolescent boy wanted to strangle a seductive but patronizing woman relative. Interpretations of his hatred and anger seemed to escalate them. Interpretations of the fact that he felt *she deserved death for the way she treated him, however*, seemed to calm him, rather than to turn him into a homicidal maniac. This involves important and often dangerous questions of whether we push it all onto patient with a "you" interpretation or let it be contained elsewhere in us or even in some other object. The relieving, calming effect seems to have to do with an understanding that badness needs to *stay out there*. Otherwise humiliation, despair, shame, and revenge can lead to explosive and dangerous eruptions in patients who may have been very heavily projected into. Kundera, in his novel, *The Joke* (1982), pointed out there are two kinds of rectification—forgiveness and vengeance. He writes describing how a person's whole inner balance may be disturbed when a lifelong object of deserved hatred innocently avoids your plan for revenge and decides to make friends with you and cease to be hateful. He asks, "How would I explain I couldn't make peace with him?" . . . and, "How would I explain I used my hatred to balance out the weight of the evil I bore as a youth. . . . How would I explain I *needed* to hate him?" (p. 229). This kind of desperate, embittered hatred has to be carefully distinguished from the aggression of the more casually brutal or more coldly murderous psychopath, who could, of course, experience such interpretations as collusion (see Alvarez, 1995).

Further rectifications:
justice and other moral imperatives

I have suggested that the various kinds of pressures patients put us under carry different underlying grammatical forms and require a different grammar of interpretation. Phantasies may not only be about wishes and imperative demands, but about that which may be, that which could be or can be (hope and possibility), that which will be (confidence and conviction, not necessarily omniscience), and that which should be (justice). The sense of justice involves a different kind of imperative from the psychopathic bullying imperative, but it is nevertheless an imperative. Where there is little ego to start with and perhaps a cruel depriving superego, the interpretive grammar of wishes may carry all-too-cruel implications; rather than help the child to think about deprivation, it actually succeeds in depriving him further. Rather than allowing him to begin to identify with ideal objects, we may be perpetuating the "disidentifications" (Sandler, 1988). We may need, therefore, a different grammar, a grammar of rightful need, one that allows a good object and a good self to grow. I heard one wild demented borderline child from a very dangerously violent family finally insist, after a period when he was becoming slightly calmer, that the therapist, of course, would not be cross if he took some food into the session. Then he corrected himself and said, "Well, she *should* not!" He had moved from manic denial of his fear to a moral imperative. The sense of how things should be is connected, I think, to a deep sense of order, justice, and rightness; when the abused or deprived child indicates a longing for us to adopt him or rescue him, an interpretation along the lines of "You wish, but we both know that you can't" may increase despair and weaken the ego. "You feel I should rescue you or you feel somebody should rescue you or you feel your mother should not have abandoned you" may actually strengthen the child, so long as it is not done as though containing a promise of actual rescue. Zbigniew Herbert, the great Polish dissident poet, wrote (1977, p. 79):

> and do not forgive truly it is not in your power
> to forgive in the name of those betrayed at dawn.

My argument here is that the paranoid position has its own logic, its own grammar, and its own sanities, and it is at some cost to our egoless patients if we try to hasten their journey to more "mature" levels.

Summary

The chapter distinguishes between the grammar of wishes in neurotic patients and the grammar of imperative needs in borderline patients. The first years of treatment of a borderline psychotic boy over thirty years ago was uninformed by subsequent developments in technique arising from the theory of projective identification as a communication rather than as an attack or a defence. Issues that need addressing in borderline patients, especially those who are children, include: (1) developmental delay; (2) the distinction between defences and overcomings in the paranoid position; (3) rectification phantasies of vengeance; (4) rectification phantasies of justice and other moral imperatives.

CHAPTER TWO

Unconscious phantasy and knowledge: a case study

Gabriella Grauso

Gabriella Grauso describes the gradual untangling of the painful psychic constellation locked inside the symptom of body dysmorphic disorder in an adolescent girl—namely, a hatred of the appearance of her eyes and nose. The analyst describes the gradual transformation of this obsession with release of pain in emotionally meaningful experience expressed in the transference through both drawings and language. This involved much work on the patient's hatred of parental sexuality and the relation of that to the wish to cut off various bodily structures.

The case of Little Hans (Freud, 1909b) certainly changed Freud's thinking, so much so that he included a whole new section, "The Sexual Researches of Children", in his 1915 version of "Three Essays on Sexuality" (1905d), in which he states that the instinct for knowledge in children is closely linked to sexual problems.

Later Melanie Klein also linked curiosity with sexuality when she spoke of the epistemophilic instinct focused first on the mother's body and its phantasied content. For her, the child's capacity to symbolize and therefore to know is proportional to his capacity to work through his most primitive and persecutory anxieties within his relationship to his maternal object.

Case study: "Mary"

The link between unconscious phantasy and knowledge underlies the conflict that led to severe impairment in "Mary", a 17-year-old girl.

In Mary's case, the unconscious phantasies, mainly related to the oedipal constellation, seemed blocked and initially experienced as concrete bodily facts or parts of her body. She was obsessed by the shape of her nose; she felt that her eyes were swollen, and she wanted to tear them off.

The analysis fostered a process of transformation of this concrete level of the experience towards a more symbolic one. In the initial phase she used the analysis to evacuate into the analyst all the dirty things she felt full of. She could not take in what the analyst tried to give her, because it was experienced as pushing the dirty things back into her. She also evacuated the good parts of herself in the process, so that she was left feeling empty and overdependent. This was the time when psychotic anxieties and the fear of losing her identity and of madness came to the fore. At this stage she concretely used first drawings and then paintings to express herself. The central phase was characterized by a deepening of the transference relationship and an increasing capacity to verbalize her feelings and to work through her infantile conflicts. In the final phase, characterized by an abundance of dreams, she developed an impressive capacity to learn and to carry on accurate self-observation, which led to increasing ego integration within the context of a more normal life, better relationships, and sexual maturity.

Three elements seem particularly relevant in trying to explain the patient's developmental breakdown: her actual experience with a confused and fragile maternal object, the instinctual pressure that bursts out at puberty, and the psychosomatic symptoms.

H. Sydney Klein, in his 1980 paper, gives evidence of the relation between psychosomatic features and a defective primary object relation, and he describes how the lack of a good stable container led his patient to use her body as a container instead, with a consequent production of psychosomatic symptoms.

In trying to understand my patient's experience of her own body and the violent self-destructive pull, I also found useful Peter Fonagy's and Mary Target's (1995) conceptualization of how, in the absence of a conception of an object at a psychological level, the patient may seek identifications or create representations of mental states via the body, as well as Moses and Eglé Laufer's work on developmental breakdown and psychotic functioning in adolescence (M. E. Laufer, 1997).

History

Mary was referred for analysis by a colleague, with a diagnosis of borderline psychosis, body dysmorphic disorder, and bodily hallucinations, when all other attempts to cure her, including drugs, seemed to have failed. Other professionals were involved, and there was a fear of an impending breakdown.

My experience of the parents, when I met them, was of an almost anorexic, quite fragile, depressed mother and a rather intellectual, cold, detached father. Later I would learn that he is a particularly rigid Catholic. Mary, now 17 and in her penultimate year of secondary school, is the third of their five children. She was born 13 months after her 18-year-old brother. There are three more sisters, aged 19, 14, and 11.

Her mother told me that when Mary was born (the third pregnancy in three years), she had had a breakdown, contained by her own mother's move to live with them. All the children were described as problematic and unhappy. Mary, described as a "very beautiful and very good" baby, became very isolated and withdrawn around the move to secondary school, had acute panic attacks, and refused to go to school. She complained that other children would tease and bully her, as she was afraid of odd noises coming out from her bowels. She became excessively preoccupied with her physical appearance and clinging towards her mother.

While consulting my colleague, the parents also contacted several other types of professionals, including allergists and surgeons, in the hope of finding a solution. Drugs, which were administered by the mother, were used as a concrete bulwark against breakdown.

At the time of this meeting, the situation was quite dramatic, and the picture the parents gave me was the following: Mary was obsessed (their word) by her eyes and the shape of her nose. She was constantly complaining that her eyes were swollen, and she couldn't stand them. She could suddenly develop a rash all over her body or have her face and arms covered with red spots. She obsessively asked to have surgery to remove a slight hump on her nose, which resembled her father's nose. Often during the day or night Mary became violent, ran away from home, and drank heavily. Aiming at her mother's head, she broke every possible thing around the house. More than once she climbed on the sixth-floor window-sill, threatening to throw herself out. Once she actually opened her father's car door while he was driving fast and tried to jump out.

When she was not behaving in this extreme way, she refused to go out on her own. She constantly wore dark sun-glasses and a plaster on her nose. She left the ordinary school to join a convent school, where she was given special attention.

Although the parents claimed they were prepared to do everything for Mary, I could not get their agreement for me to see her five times a week from the start, but we left it open that I would increase the number of sessions, if necessary, so I offered four. (Four sessions is the most usual number of sessions for psychoanalysis in Italy.)

As I would discover later, sexuality seemed to play a major role in Mary's symptoms. Her torments, the swollen eyes and her nose, which, as a deformed penis, must be hidden or operated on, were related to the Kleinian formulation of the "combined object". Her eyes—and not only the external ones—had become terrified spectators of the persecutory fantasy of two parents fused in an endless sexual intercourse.

I have questioned in my mind to what extent mother's passivity towards father, whose rigid Catholic principles could justify the recurrent pregnancies, and the persecutory and confused experience she seemed to have of her own sexuality could have affected Mary's development. I think it is important to relate an episode referred to both by mother, in the initial interview, and Mary often during the analysis. At the time of Mary's first breakdown, the family was involved in a violent car accident apparently caused by father's inattention, which had very serious consequences for the mother and the younger child. This accident epitomizes, at a very concrete level, the breakdown of father's supportive function. It also represents, again at a concrete level, Mary's experience of her parents' sexuality, with its tremendous impact derived from feelings of intense rivalry and jealousy, both for her father and her siblings.

This formulation, with its constellation of unconscious phantasies, is central in the classic literature on child analysis, particularly in Melanie Klein's description of Peter's play with the little cars in the 1932 paper, "Technique in Early Analysis".

In the final stage of her analysis, Mary would often refer to this car accident, and one day she would say: "Because my mother and my little sister were almost dying and all the others too were badly injured except me and Daddy, I was feeling tremendously guilty and wanted to go to church and pray to God not to punish me and to save them."

I think Mary is now capable of acknowledging and verbalizing her emotional response to the Oedipus situation, as described by Ron Britton: she (Melanie Klein) adopted the term "oedipal situation" and included in it what Freud had referred to as the "primal scene"—that is, the sexual relations of the parents, both as perceived and as imagined (1989).

Clinical vignette

The first contact

I have asked the parents to give Mary my telephone number, against father's suggestion that I should not do that. Mary rings the following morning, and I give her an appointment in two days' time. She rings again in the evening to say that that is too long, and she cannot wait. I firmly confirm the appointment, and we meet briefly on the fixed day to discuss the practical aspects.

She is a nice-looking, pale-blonde girl with delicate features. She is wearing dark sun-glasses and a plaster on her nose. She sits in the armchair opposite mine, completely bent over towards me. The first communication is immediate and powerful: "I can't wait any more. I am afraid I will exaggerate!" She looks tense, with her elbows pushed against her tights and her fist clenched. I feel a tremendous pressure on me and say she wants me to help her with her frightening thoughts about committing suicide.

Reflecting back on my answer to Mary's pressing request, I think I felt that I had to hold the dreadful anxiety her parents had not been able to contain, which had forced them to ask for my help. I will come back to this element of "exaggeration", which has been very much present in Mary's analysis and has brought back to my mind Freud's first hysteric patients. I also think that Mary experiences the transfer to me as a failure of the previous therapy, and this reinforces in her some conviction that there is no object capable of standing her most disruptive emotions.

The first phase

During what I have called the first phase, it looks as if Mary is using the analysis to evacuate into me a constellation of sensations, fantasies, and thoughts she experiences as most disturbing. My attempts to talk to her are violently rejected, as she feels I am pushing back into her what she wants to get rid of.

The first weeks are characterized by massive acting-out. She rings in between sessions. Mother rings to describe terrible crises, threats of suicide, and rushing to hospitals. Mary spends most of her time shut in her room, going to the mirror to see if her eyes are swollen. In the session she obsessively complains that her eyes are swollen, she screams she wants to tear them off, she screams at me and shouts "Do something !" again and again.

I feel under strain not only in trying to contain and understand Mary's anxieties but mainly in establishing and protecting a setting that could become a common tool for our work. It is within that function of the analytic setting which I would define as "paternal"—setting limits, barriers, a widening and strengthening of the containing space—that at the end of this first month I decide to increase the sessions to five.

I want to clarify that, as an analyst, together with a rigorous adherence to technique, I consider central to what I have defined as the "paternal" function of the setting one's own analysis, whose process I would describe as follows: to be in close contact with an attentive and understanding mind long enough to be able to introject some of its growth-promoting qualities, such as inner strength, patience, and goodness.

While Mary's parents accept the fifth session immediately, Mary reacts with an escalation of psychotic and paranoid anxieties. The following day she arrives triumphantly announcing that the allergist has eventually found that she is allergic to *graminacee* (weeds). To my suggestion that "*graminacee*" have to do with the increase in the sessions and my words, which, she feels, are filling her up with bad things, she responds with an account of an infantile memory of mother trying to kiss her on her mouth and father watching her while she was taking a bath. While, at a rational level, the fifth session is for Mary the sign that she is mad ("If you want to see me more often, this means I *am* mad") in the transference it is experienced as an attempt to seduce her.

All the links I have tried to make so far between the swollen eyes and some frightening fantasy she cannot face get destroyed. She shouts at me, and the concrete level of the experience becomes more acute. She begins to complain that there is sand in her eyes. It is not only that they are swollen, they actually hurt, and no drops or rushing to the ophthalmologist can alleviate the pain.

It seems as if the beginning of the analysis and the increase in the sessions are reinforcing her symptoms. Mary seems terrorized by the possibility that the analysis can help her to "open her eyes" to what is happening to her. During this phase, my words are like "sand" in her eyes, and our inability to communicate is part of our dilemma: If I speak, my words hurt; if I don't, I am useless, and I often find myself questioning what I am saying or not saying. The "sand" Mary feels is filling her eyes with the underlying oedipal anxieties is reminiscent of Freud's "Sand-Man" in "The Uncanny" (1919h).

> When Mary is able to tolerate beginning to explore her fantasies and feelings within the transference relationship and can "listen" to me if I say something that she feels to be good or useful to her, she starts to utter a guttural sound of assent followed by a short silence—a sound similar to a baby swallowing—and this experience of being able to "feed" her mind can allow a moving moment of contact between us.

> The first and only dreams during this time are: "*Mother is on the brink of being swept away by a waterfall*" and, coinciding with an extra session on a Saturday morning, offered to contain a dramatic telephone call, a dream where "*Grandmother was mending her knickers*".

The first dream illustrates Mary's fear that I can be overwhelmed and swept away by her powerful emotions, while grandmother mending her knickers can be linked to my function to contain and, moreover, to *accept* her fantasies related to my sexuality, the parents' sexuality, from which she feels excluded and which is felt to be devastating over the weekend.

* * *

> Towards the end of the first year Mary begins to refer to some pencil drawings she tries to do at home when she feels her anxiety mounting, and she expresses her wish to bring them to me. I want to clarify that Mary has always used the couch. From a technical point of view, although I accepted that she would bring her drawings and later her paintings to her sessions, I have never kept them. I would put them on a stool by my side so that we could both look at them, and at the end of the session I would give them back to her.

In this way I can communicate to her that the most important part of their significance for us is working through the emotional elements that are emerging. They can then became "symbols" and not substitutes of an emotional experience that belongs to her and that she is slowly discovering and working through in the relationship with me. I am thinking here of Hanna Segal's distinction between symbolic equation and symbolization (1957).

Mary's first drawings represent very strange figures formed by mixed parts of the body. The emphasis is on the genitals, and they are always shapes without eyes and with holes instead of mouths—mostly contorted bodies and disfigured faces. Mary feels tremendous pain in showing them to me. She keeps them for a long time folded in her hands saying that she feels ashamed, and we can proceed in our work only after my interpreting her fear that the drawings represent her fantasies about my sexuality, the parents' sexuality, which she experiences as violent and dirty, and, more importantly, her fear that this can destroy our relationship.

Mary is quite disturbed by the often "pornographic" quality of these drawings, but they give us the opportunity to talk about her confusion between different parts of her body and their functions, the parents' bodies, and violent, aggressive emotions, which can eventually find expression for her through that means. Gradually, through these drawings, we can begin to "communicate" and get to "know" the terrifying world she has not been able to explore so far. She begins to develop an interest in painting and different pictorial techniques and is fascinated by the work of Munch and Francis Bacon. The landscapes she begins to paint now take the place of the previous more disturbing images. I think this represents a gradual evolution from fragmentary and splintering states of mind to a kind of communication that is increasingly integrated at a verbal and symbolic level.

The central phase

At the end of the second year, there is a general feeling of improvement. Acting out—including a dramatic episode shortly before the second summer holiday, when Mary, before the end of the session, storms off and, in the waiting-room, throws a heavy crystal vase full of flowers on the floor, with such violence as to break two tiles—seems to lose its intensity. The need to act out is, however, still present, and both the plastic surgery on her nose and father's peremptory request to reduce the sessions from five to three can be considered in that light, but Mary's wish to reduce the drugs and her capacity to do so indicate that the analysis is beginning to offer a better containment for her more psychotic anxieties.

As for father's request, I have to be firm enough to re-negotiate four sessions and re-establish some mutual collaboration with both parents. (Mother had been strongly against the reduction.) Since then, I have never had any interference in my work with Mary, which proceeded with four weekly sessions until the end.

To go back to what I have called the "paternal" function of the analytic setting, I think it interesting to report Mary's dream the first week after the reduction. She dreams that *Kurt, of the Nirvana group, has committed suicide, leaving his little two-year-old little girl bereft. In the dream, the little girl is asking: "How can I live without Daddy", but a voice in the background says: "She will cope."*

The dream refers to recent news then in the media but, I think, is also indicative of Mary's experience of the reduction in the number of sessions linked to my function for her.

* * *

At the end of the third year, Mary, now enrolled at University in the faculty of Foreign Languages, starts showing a deep commitment to her studies, and slowly, during this year, she gives up all the medication. Painting remains a true passion for her, but it has lost its "desperate" quality as it is no longer her only means of communication. Very often she has to "renounce" her desire and the pleasure she takes in it to concentrate in her studies.

During this central phase of the analysis the obsessive quality of her complaints and the acting out disappear. There is no reference to her eyes, and a growing capacity for independence and new relationships outside the family is apparent. (For the first two years, Mary has been driven to her sessions by mother.) The desire to have a boyfriend and explore her own sexuality emerge forcefully, but it is not a linear process.

The space in the transference relationship has widened and deepened, but the more primitive and infantile level constantly re-emerges. Within this painful process of integration Mary still evacuates and projects parts of herself, and in doing this she is left empty, and often anxieties linked to fear of losing her identity or of madness re-emerge.

The element of "exaggeration" to which I have referred earlier loses its quality of desperate communication of a desperate need and finds expression, at a more symbolic level, in dreams characterized by the presence of actors or well-known public people.

With regard to this, I have found very useful Ruth Riesenberg-Malcolm's (1996, pp. 681–682) formulation of how the patient's need to exaggerate can be linked to the experience of a baby who cannot have its emotions recognized. "The use of exaggeration aims at communicating to someone, to getting rid of, emotions that are felt not to be received by the object and therefore impossible to manage in any other way."

* * *

I would like now to present some detailed clinical material that, I think, illustrates Mary's conflicts and how she attempts to work them through in the transference relationship.

We are in the fourth year of analysis, shortly before the summer break. On the Wednesday Mary has unexpectedly brought some of her old drawings. One in particular—a man pointing a knife at his own head—has given us the opportunity to talk about the relentless attacks she makes on her own mind and thinking.

Today, Thursday, she starts by complaining that she is tired. She has had a nightmare: *She was in her aunt's home—Aunt Rosy and Uncle Tom. She was in their building, inside the lift, pressing the button to reach the sixth floor, their floor. She went past it. The lift did not stop. It was going faster and faster.* She woke up in panic.

She remembers that when she was a little girl, she and her family would go there on Sundays for lunch. The lift had a mechanical door. She describes the door accurately. It is different from the one in her building and similar to the one in my lift—an old-style one, she adds. She felt it was suffocating to be in there, she was afraid to be trapped inside. She then remembers that she has already had dreams in which *she was in some lift, going up and up or down and down without stopping,* and she would wake up in panic. She did not like to go there for lunch; she especially did not like the thought that Aunt Rosy was preparing the food. She was old, and Uncle Tom used to pat his wife on her bottom, and Mary did not like that either.

In the dream *Uncle Tom is reading the newspaper. Mary asks him: "Do you understand?" He replies: "Yes, I do."* (In reality Uncle Tom cannot understand, as he has Alzheimer's disease.)

After a while Mary says she thinks Uncle Tom is connected to her—the part of her that is ill and may now not be as ill any more. She goes on to say that this morning, at University, an old friend of hers said: "What is the matter with you, you look older since I last saw you!" "He was joking", says Mary: "Maybe I was tired, but I did not like this remark. I thought he was saying I was looking more grown-up, more mature." I comment that at a previous time she would have reacted with a bout of anxiety, losing her capacity to think. Mary replies with emphasis: "I would immediately have gone to the mirror, to look at my eyes, to see if they were swollen."

I say that there is still something she does not like to see—the lift in the dream going up and up, the sexual fantasies about me, the old disgusting couple, the tantalizing exclusion during the weekend. Mary interrupts me: "My anger, the rage that increases and that I cannot control. . . . I hoped I would meet Emily [her friend] this morning. She was not there. I felt abandoned, disappointed. . . . Then I began to translate the essay on

Jane Eyre. Next Monday I have the exam. I wish somebody could correct it for me. My father doesn't know much English. Maybe some older student in the faculty. I thought of you. I thought maybe I should bring it to you, you may correct it for me. Then I thought I cannot do that, I must talk about my rage, my fantasies, what makes me feel so bad." I suggest that there seems to be something else that needs to be "corrected".

Mary goes on: "It is a tremendous effort. . . . I feel so angry to have to make such an effort to translate." I say that what is difficult to translate has to do with her emotions. She cannot let them go out any more as she used to, she must struggle to put them into words. Mary says that yesterday it was useful what I had said about her fear that something similar could still happen. [She is referring to my comment on the drawing representing the man pointing a knife at his own head.] Maybe she could deal with that anxiety in a different way. . . . She adds: "In bringing my old drawings here yesterday I wanted to ask you if all those sensations could go away, disappear, that I could get rid of all that without having to struggle. . . ." She stops. Quite a few seconds go by. I observe that she has stopped. After a couple of minutes she goes on: "I was losing the thread of my thoughts. . . . It is like yesterday. . . . The same voice, saying: 'It is so pathetic to talk about when you were a small child.' I remember when they took me to the nursery. I could not stand colours. The children's toys—fuchsia, green, yellow. . . . I did not like the place—the little coloured toys they gave as a present to my little sister when she was born. I was bothered. Mother did not allow me to touch her. She would say: 'She is fragile, do not touch her, she is sleeping, leave her alone!' But I was curious, I wanted to hold her. I thought, why do they think I could let her fall or hurt her. I hated her also because they did not allow me to get close to her. . . ." I say that there seems to be an old grudge about the fantasy of a baby I will look after when I am not with her, and which makes her feel pushed out.

Mary goes on about feeling lonely and anxious. "I feel you are annoyed because I struggle and I find it so hard. . . . I wish I did not have to make any effort, but I must go on. . . . I remember another dream: Andrea De Carlo, the author of a book I borrowed from the library. . . . In the dream *he was refusing to meet me, while I was wanting so much to meet him*" [an emerging young writer, who is very popular amongst young people]. "Last weekend I saw his photo in a magazine with some gossip about him being in love with an actress. In the dream I felt very frustrated. I will never be able to meet him. I wanted him to be with me so much. I don't know why I am now thinking of the monster, the drawing of the monster I tore off yesterday and did not bring to you."

I say the monster has again something to do with her aggressive sexual fantasies and her fear that I cannot stand them. Mary says: "It reminds me of when I was 11 or 12 and went into my parents' bedroom; they were making love, it was dark, it was disgusting, the bad smell, something dirty, squalid. I thought of blood, something violent. I remember a mole I had on my thigh. I felt it was disgusting and tried to cut into it with scissors and cover it with a plaster." I make a link with the plaster she used to wear on her nose, the hated nose, the nose like her father's, and suggest there seems to be something dirty, disgusting, that she doesn't want to see, linked with father's penis, father's potency.

Mary continues: "After I saw my parents together, I was afraid Daddy would do something to me. I tried to push that thought away. I said to myself: 'He is a religious man, a Christian, it would be against nature.' This thought would reassure me. When I cut into the mole, there was blood. I thought it was dirty, I had to get rid of it. Now I think of the drawing with the monster, I tore it into pieces, and I think of the other drawing, the knife pointed at the head. . . ." I say that we are now at the very end of the session, and she is talking of her fears of attacking her mind, her fears of madness, and I link it with the hostile fantasies about me and my couple over the weekend and during the next summer break.

Discussion

I think in this session it is possible to follow the movement from the obsessive thinking and the concreteness of the experience "my eyes are swollen", used as a defence against psychotic anxieties, to the working through, in the dream and the associations, of these infantile fantasies.

Ignés Sodré (1994) links obsessional states of mind to triangularity and the presence, in the patient's mind, of the parental couple with whom he is, unconsciously, excessively involved. The detailed description of the cutting into the mole suggests the concrete attempt to attack father's penis, possibly the nipple in the breast, and ultimately her own capacity to think. It seems to represent, on a concrete and part-object level, what I experienced, during the first phase of Mary's analysis, as a relentless attack on linking between the parents in terms of my own thinking and the experience of me as a persecuting object (Britton, 1989; Sodré, 1994). It also indicates how the most primitive level, intertangled with omnipotent fantasies, interferes with some awareness of separateness from the object. I have found Dana Birksted-Breen's (1996, p. 656) differentiation between "phallus" and "penis as a link" very useful in understanding Mary's anxieties. I quote: "While the phallus belongs to the mental configuration that allows only for the 'all or nothing' distinction, hence the domain of omnipotence, and is an attempt away from triangulation, the penis as a link, which links mother and father, underpins oedipal and bisexual mental functioning and hence has a structuring function which underpins the process of thinking."

The reference to the "monster" offers a vivid illustration of what Melanie Klein called the "combined object"—an image of a threatening uncreative parental couple, endlessly stuck in sexual intercourse, which is contaminated by the child's feelings of hate and jealousy, which in turn generates paranoid and persecutory anxieties.

The dream about the writer and the actress introduces that element of exaggeration or "hyperbole" often present in Mary's behaviour, words, and tone, which seems linked to the urgency of her needs. It is now expressed at a more symbolic level. The moaning tone, at times so irritating for me, is now much less present.

I would now like to compare two dreams that indicate some further development.

The first one belongs to the week following the session I have just reported. She arrives at her session (Thursday) with a new short haircut. She has been to the hairdresser, feels more comfortable and thinks she looks better. Last night she had a nightmare: *She was sick. She had a tumour in her throat.* She woke up in panic. She said to herself: "It is only a dream, it is only my fear." Mary associates to her previous therapist, who kept her hair long. She seems disturbed by the image of a highly sexualized maternal image. We link the haircut to her wish to get rid of disturbing fantasies before the weekend. The session develops with a wealth of infantile memories linked to exclusion from the parental couple but also to the actual experience of a contact, in the transference, with an object with parental *and* sexual qualities, which she still experiences as dangerous and invasive (the tumour in her throat).

The session ends with Mary complaining: "I do not want these links. I am fed up. I think of your anorexic patient. [She is referring to the severely anorexic patient who comes before her.] I think she listens to you. She needs you more than I do." Here Mary splits and projects the part of her that finds it still very difficult to be fed by me. On reflection, I think the haircut in which I have recognized defensive elements could also be seen as a developmental step, a space in which she can work out and develop her own feminine identity.

The second dream is one year later:

She is in hospital with some children with tumours. They have no hair and are sick. She feels great pain.

Mary links the children in the dream with illness and her rage when she feels excluded. Slowly, in the course of the session, the infantile level has emerged as, for her, the children without hair are also babies. It is relevant to note that in her painful process of separation and individuation, the tumour is not in her throat any more but outside her, in the children she looks at with pain.

Conclusion

The developmental striving finds full expression in the final phase of Mary's analysis, which is marked by her increasing capacity to recognize and accept fully her separateness from the object. This process allows her to internalize the creative quality of the analytic relationship.

> When her uncle, Tom, who owned a flower shop, dies, Mary starts to use some ribbons he has left to make, with great skill, silk flowers, and one day she arrives with five beautiful silk roses. "For you", she says, "to let you see them; but", she adds: "I will not ask you to accept them. I know that it is much more important if I keep them in a vase in my room than leave them with you."

Mary is by now doing quite well in her University studies, has succeeded in obtaining her driving licence, is contributing with some little jobs to her expenses, and is more and more aware of her parents' efforts to allow her to have analysis.

> One Monday, towards the end of the fifth year, Mary arrives after having passed brilliantly yet another exam. She lies down and quietly, without excitement, she tells me the news. She then adds: "I feel satisfied, really satisfied." Her voice sounds calm and full. In the long silence that follows I feel moved.

> She then goes on: "Last night I saw an old Charlie Chaplin movie. When I was a child, I was terrified by those movies, especially by the music and that they were black and white. The scene with the assembly line also frightened me. Now I can watch them and see them in their historical context, as documents, and I can appreciate their significance and value as denunciation." I say to Mary that the absence of colours and words in Chaplin's movies and the assembly-line scene take us back to the phase of her "swollen eyes" and the obsessive thoughts, to the time when it was not yet possible to use the analysis to give "voice" and "colours" to her emotions. Now that her life is full of colours, as in her paintings, and emotions

that she can eventually *share* with me, we can look at that time as a document of our work together.

Very recently, Mary has said: "I feel much less possessive towards everything in my life—towards people and towards things but mainly towards my states of mind. This helps me to live better." I think Mary is talking of an internal space, a space where she can begin to detach herself from her own states of mind, "to observe" herself, without risking being swept away. It is the space of the analysis and the introjection of its function.

The last year in Mary's analysis marks a steady development of the integrative process. She falls in love with a young man with whom she has her first intimate relationship. She is now capable of recognizing aspects of her character that prevent further growth. She talks of what she calls "my egocentrism" or "my exhibitionistic attitudes" and links them with difficulties in her relationships. She shares with me concerns for all the members of her family and shows a great capacity to tolerate depressive pain.

On her last session, she goes back to how she felt at the beginning of her analysis: insecure and fragile, incapable of tolerating any frustration. She says she has discovered that it is just the opposite of what she thought initially, and now she knows that the more she will be able to sustain the effort, *any effort*, the stronger she will become. She will miss coming here not only because it is useful to talk to me but also because it is so nice to share some things with me. "It is not like sharing them with somebody else. They are very deep things. It is a bit like sharing—" she stops and sounds embarrassed and adds, "I don't want to sound romantic—like sharing one's own—'anima'".

I think the "anima" Mary is referring to is the very profound core of her strengthened ego, but I also think she is talking of a quality, "animus"—"courage", which she has developed in the painstaking work of analysis and which will stay with her.

CHAPTER THREE

Catastrophe, containment, and manic defences

Silvia Oclander-Goldie

Silvia Oclander-Goldie writes about a boy who had experienced a severe trauma as a young child brought up in a country at war. This experience remained in him, imprisoned and unprocessed, resulting in omnipotent manic defences expressed in apparently unprovoked violent attacks on other children. During the therapy he made a particular comment, which alerted Silvia Oclander-Goldie to the fact that real trauma may have occurred. Following further exploration with the parents, she decided to bring the facts of this experience into the playroom.

The catastrophic destruction of a mother–child relationship occurred during a war situation. It devastated the psychological development of a baby, later producing uncontrollable violence and reliance on massive projective identification and manic defences.

Case study: "Simon"

I observed in great detail the operation of these processes in "Simon", a child whose intolerable and uncontainable manic and aggressive behaviour made it necessary for his parents to bring him for psychoanalytic treatment. They became aware of his problem when he was 3 years old. He was totally isolated in his nursery school, where he attacked other children. They sought help when he could not settle in primary school, refusing to attend or demanding that his mother stayed with him; he could not make friends. His outbursts of intense aggression were apparently unmotivated, and it was impossible for anyone to reach him and calm him down. Very persecuted, he complained that he was hated by everybody.

He was highly intelligent and attractive, although his early experiences had so damaged him that his whole present and future life was at serious risk. Simon was 6 years old when I met him. He is the third of four children. His sister, "Lucy", was born when Simon was 14 months old. He was loved and wanted by everyone in his family. He had been very precocious, having crawled at 6 months and walked at 7, and learned to read when he was 3 years old.

He had been 5 months old when his mother became pregnant, and he appeared overtly upset when his sister was born. At that time, he had started going to a child-minder and, unbeknown to his parents, began hitting and biting other children.

At the time of the consultation he was constantly competitive and aggressive towards his younger sister. He ate little and suffered from nightmares. Often he was frightened to fall asleep and stayed awake in bed for hours, or demanded his mother's presence to be able to sleep. She was extremely overwhelmed by his disturbance, and, having emigrated to England three years before, settling down had also been difficult and demanding. The father travelled abroad frequently. The parents described life at home as warm and loving, but very stormy. In his daily life Simon's own destructiveness was projected, and he had great difficulties in entering new places or meeting children. Even if accompanied by his parents, he would spend long periods outside new places, seemingly terrified.

Following two assessment interviews, I recommended psycho-analytic psychotherapy three times a week.

My first impression of Simon was of a beautiful boy, full of character, of average height, slim and nimble. He had a worried, sad expression. He soon agreed to stay on his own with me, saying that he did not know why he had come to see me. He dived into the toy box and started playing; he chose the wild animals and made them fight fiercely. His play expressed intense violence—there were crashes and death everywhere. He used the whole room very freely and did not seem to want to listen to anything I said to him. Each time I spoke, he quickly talked or screamed over my voice. It seemed that, rather compulsively, he was getting rid of something that he dreaded knowing about. When playing with the animals, well into his hour with me, there was a moment of peace as the lion and lioness were together side by side, and there was some erotic excitement.

The second assessment session was very similar, expressing violence all the time, and brief moments of togetherness between the animals, which were full of tenderness. He willingly agreed to come regularly.

The first months of Simon's treatment were very chaotic. He was curious about every detail of my life. He appeared intensively intrusive, and perplexed at not being allowed to see the whole of my house. The lack of boundaries in his relationship with his parents, particularly his mother, showed in the transference to me. He seemed to expect entry into every part of my mind and body, to occupy and dominate. This alerted me that something quite unbearable and inescapable had entered and occupied him violently and was a constant experience.

He began hitting, kicking, and attempting to bite me, and he became destructive with the materials in his box. As it became evident that he was hearing what I was saying, it seemed clear that he found any interpretation extremely persecuting, and stopped what he was doing.

After four weeks of treatment, following a comment of his that he did not know why he was coming as, he said, "nothing had happened to me!" I sought more information from his parents. I believed that he had experienced something very devastating, which he had never worked through.

His parents recalled an event that had happened when Simon was 13 months old, while there was a war in their country. The city where they lived was subjected to missile attacks. There were fears of the use of poisonous gases, and the population had been provided with gas masks. Being so small, Simon was placed into what his mother called a "small cage". On the first day of these attacks, he spent an hour and a half in it. He screamed, was terrified and profoundly distressed, and could not be comforted. The "cage" did not allow his mother to touch him, and his own screams would have muffled any words of comfort that she offered. This so distressed his mother that she decided not to place him there any more. But during many weeks he was surrounded daily by his family wearing gas masks and hearing sirens and explosions that he could not make sense of. At the time his mother was eight months pregnant, and Lucy was born while the war was still on.

Simon's parents felt surprised that I considered these events to have been very traumatic for him, as at the time he did not show any signs of having been affected by it. They perceived him as "unchanged", and this incident was never discussed.

It seemed to me that Simon's early "constant smile" and happiness hinted at something very fragile in him. It brings to mind thoughts of him as a baby who did not have much experience of expressing distress and anger, and having those feelings dealt with by his mother, like a baby who is not aware that these feelings could be received by her and both of them survive them. It also seems quite possible that any feelings that he might have shown were "not seen", just as his parents were unaware of the biting and hitting of other children at the child-minder's or the attacks at the nursery school. It seems that his parents related only to his outstanding qualities and idealized him, without acknowledging the problems that he had. The "nothing happened to me" was an expression of how he felt perceived by his parents—the space in his mother's mind in which he could relate to her when she was pregnant and preoccupied and could not perceive his distress. There was a space where his distress was "not happening". I understood that the experience of the cage and the bombings confirmed Simon in his phantasies that these were fair retaliation for his destructive and murderous feelings towards what his mother's body contained and towards the parental relationship.

I decided to mention the war and the cage, when appropriate, in his sessions. I also suggested to his parents to talk to him about what had happened to help him make some sense of his history.

In his sessions Simon talked and played intensely and freely. Through his games with animals, he expressed his efforts to separate his wild and fierce feelings from what was genuinely loving in him. But he showed a confusion about them that he could not resolve.

He often refused to leave the sessions at the end when he had finally settled down. He seemed to value the experience of containment that the treatment was beginning to offer him. To the following session he always returned explosive, totally unable to contain himself, and terrified. He seemed to feel quite concretely that he was entering his mother's body occupied by another baby. Handling him was very difficult; sometimes my aim was mainly to survive the session without injury. His attacks were devoid of any feeling of concern, and without external restraint he would cause great harm.

As soon as I started to mention the experience in the cage, he began to curl up in the window of the consulting-room. There is a sliding shutter for this small window capable of creating a space that could be completely closed and be just big enough for him to fit in. He wanted me to close that shutter, which I agreed to do, leaving a gap. From there he started making noises and wanted to know whether or not I have heard him. It seemed to me that he was showing me how his intense wish to get back inside his mother and the nightmare of being locked in the cage have overlapped in his mind. He seemed to me to be communicating his experience of having lost the communication with his mother. He did not know that she tried to speak to him. He wanted to find a safe space where he could express his distress and attack without fearing retaliation or being left in isolation. When his mother put him in the cage, he felt that she wanted to protect herself from his need of her and from his resentment for her pregnancy, rather than protect him from danger.

Simon was always aware that I had cleared up from the previous session and recovered. He began to show some changes— for example, he drew a house, acknowledging that he felt there was now some kind of a safe house with me. His ambivalence towards me could be expressed in insults rather than physical attacks. He could also convey a closeness to me, drawing while sitting on the floor at my feet and looking up from time to time with great tenderness. These moments of affectionate contact were short-lived and were followed by a sudden explosion of violence and insults, still repeating his experience of something catastrophic and dangerous overwhelming him and destroying good feelings.

Eventually he recalled the time of the war. He remembered the sirens but could not say more. An absent look would appear on his face if I continued talking about it. He cut off from what he experienced just as he had needed to do then, and how he felt his parents have done about his feelings.

He seemed obsessed to know whether I was married or not. He reacted with great alarm at any sound around us. I thought of how afraid he seemed to be of being found out, guilty of his desires to invade and posses me completely and the fears of reprisals by a powerful father. However, there was always a part of him that could respond if I restrained him and prevented him hurting me, while I put into words some of his feelings. He could calm down, and his play would show the beginnings of an attempt on his part to control them, a desire to settle down and take things in.

At times he tried to relate in a sadomasochistic way, trying to provoke me to punish or criticize him. There seemed to be in his mind a polarized and extreme object, one that would, on the one hand, be fascinated with him and extremely indulgent, which scared him as it would not be able to control his destructive impulses, and, on the other hand, one that would cruelly restrain him and ignore his need to be helped and his despair.

In his calmer moments, when Simon did something constructive, this quickly turned into an expectation of my admiration. There was no feeling of security in any relationship. His concept of security was of being inside his mother, but this ideal state was confused in his mind with the terrifying cage and led to despair. Increasingly he could recognize understanding and respond to it with evidence of feeling contained. In his treatment his feelings were being addressed for the first time.

* * *

As we approached the first holiday, Simon seemed more integrated, his violence having subsided both in his sessions and in his life in general. In his play he showed fear of the interruption.

His comments at the end of the last session and the first of the following term were concerned with his preoccupation with whether or not I had a husband. He spoke about it, drew a picture of a man, and carefully listened for any sound of his presence. His jealousy of his father and of the birth of his sister became more clear in his play, and it was easier to talk about it with the possibility of developing some of the ideas without having a sudden burst of violence. During one session his play led me to interpret the pain and jealousy of his mother's breasts full of milk for Lucy, while he was still a baby himself. He turned to use Play-Doh and made a baby with it, broke it, and said to me: "Look what you have done." The pain of the deprivation was intolerable, and the hatred was projected outside instantly. Any painful feeling was instantly evacuated.

When brought by his mother, he could hit her hard on her face, and she made no effort to stop him. It occurred to me that if his treatment did not help him, he could later on be capable of killing in a fit of jealousy. His attacks on me were blind and vicious; my safety depended on the speed of my reaction.

His intense wish to be the only baby, to be inside and to be constantly on the watch for any intruder was evident in drawings and associations. It was possible to link up his feelings about the pregnancy, his being placed into the cage, and the war. It appeared clearly how in his mind the cage and the explosions were experienced as a punishment for his feelings about the new baby. All these phantasies and feelings had not been contained, not understood, and never spoken about before. Therefore the excess of his sadism and anxieties did not allow a proper splitting between the good and the bad object. His hatred having abolished the differentiation between good and bad objects meant the loss of the loved object. He might have felt that because of his hatred he had destroyed or devoured his mother when she did not retrieve him from the cage.

As treatment progressed, Simon began to talk more to me about his play in the sessions and about his life outside. He was able to use what remained of his toys to symbolize his violent feelings and was more able to admit that he was listening and to maintain a dialogue.

His conception of his parents' intercourse still appeared as a very violent and destructive one and produced in him intense sexual excitement. This was the result of the projection of his sadism, and the sexual excitement was linked to his triumph. This slowed the progress that we could make, due to his attacks on my own process of thinking as he felt left out of them.

He often touched his genitals during his sessions. This happened when he tried to draw me into a coupling with him. In his mind we would be a couple sharing secrets, telling things to each other as equals, rather than him being the dependent baby with Mummy. I had opportunities to observe how he treated his mother like this and how easy it was for her to be drawn into it. He often added years to his age, and when excited, he liked to lie down on a large cushion and lift his leg, wanting to impress me with it as if it were a large penis erect. When all these manoeuvres failed to achieve the desired pairing with me, his response was of blind and total violence. But sometimes he wanted to hear that he could destroy his toys, if not the room. He struggled to differentiate ways of expressing his aggression from those for which he should exert control. He began to absorb moments of peace when my understanding felt containing and not a persecuting return of what he was evacuating.

Simon showed a voraciousness for objects to replace what he had broken. When the replacement was out of the question, the boundaries between him and me were blurred, and he blamed me for the damage. He could not conceive of ways of repairing. It seemed that when Simon was in the cage, as his mother could not reach him and comfort him, something had been broken for ever. His relationship with his mother showed an anxious clinging and desire to control her, but no real trust. He could not call the father to help either, as this increased the jealousy. He resorted to what Meltzer describes as the "masculine infantile state of mind", where femininity is treated with contempt and masculinity is conceived as tied up with a part-object concept of the penis. It leads to extreme competitiveness and possessive jealousy.

As he had almost nothing left, I added two new cars and some Lego bricks. He became very excited about them, got the bags of Lego out of their box, then turned to the cars and checked whether or not their doors could be opened. He said that these cars were much better than the old ones. After a little while he returned to the Lego, he opened the bags by ripping them, and he poured all the bricks out. He started building with the red bricks, and while doing so he complained that there were not enough of them. I spoke to him about how when he got something good from me he felt very greedy because of fear that he would not be able to have it for long enough. Anything coming to an end felt to him as if I did not want him any more and would replace him by a little girl. He added layers of bricks, complaining all the while that there would not be enough. He feared not having enough time from me for us to understand his intense feelings and his fear of dying. Once again, though more calmly, he was reviving, in the transference, his experience of his mother's unavailability to his anxieties and feelings.

He added further rows of bricks and said that it was a house. This house did not have a door or windows. He built a stepladder and placed it outside, saying that the people could breathe because there was no roof. I said that the moment that he felt understood by me, he felt he had a home for his worries, but then he feels scared to choke in it and die breathless for all his angry feelings towards anybody who is with me at other times. In his roofless house there was no shelter from the rain or cold. His play expressed that when he is away from me he is cold and excluded, and when he is here he is afraid of poisonous fumes. He told me that he had a lot more Lego at home. I interpreted his worry about what he had to rely on until he came back next week. He wanted to leave me being the rich man full of good things, and I should be the little girl left out of all this. He turned to play with the cars, but at the end of the session he tried to stay longer to increase the size of the house. He asked me to keep the house assembled until next time. I thought that he was beginning to conceive of maintaining a good feeling over the weekend.

He returned for the following session, carried in his mother's arms, looking ill and disturbed. He saw the Lego, pointed it out to his mother, and hurried down. He threw his coat down, emptied out the box of toys, and saw the cars. Picking up his favourite, he said that it was still all right, the flaps and doors still opening. His belief in the permanence of good feelings that had not survived the weekend was now recovered. He looked for his house. He said that he wanted to see if it was solid, and he hit the table with it. I spoke of his worry whether I withstood his anger during the weekend when in his thoughts he had knocked me about, insulting me and hating me for being like a house with no doors for him.

To the following session Simon brought in a car of his own and immediately made it compete in a speed race with one from the box. When his did not win, he threw the other one violently, expressing his murderous rivalry. He had once said to me that when Lucy was born, he wanted to kill her. He continued the session demanding more Lego. When he did not get any, he started rolling his own car very fast backwards and forwards, as if winding it. Finally he let it go, but it did not go very fast, as it was not the winding kind. I described this and interpreted how when jealous and upset for not having me all for himself, he touches his penis up and down, and he would like to rush out all the upset feelings that way, but he feels frustrated. In response to this, he took his pencil and put it into the hole of the roll of Sellotape and swirled it around quickly and excitedly. He showed his wish to have an organ with which to enter me, dominate me, and make me do what he wants all the time. He sharpened the pencil very sensuously and used it to pierce the box of Lego. I spoke of his wish to make the baby he believed I had inside me leak out.

In this piece of material a theme developed that makes the content of his desires and phantasies clearer than before. They certainly became more bearable for Simon, due to an incipient feeling that they were not so dangerous, as they were beginning to be understood by me. He perceived that though I was aware of them, I was not damaged by them or retaliating.

With the exception of the cars, Simon generally used objects only once. Something would be made with a piece of Play-Doh and subsequently be abandoned or destroyed. The material would not be used again. This seemed to me to be an expression of having once had something that he then lost for ever. He had no conception of working through, or of the recovery of experiences and feelings in a different form, of transformation and development. He had felt discarded by his mother, like faeces that have to be thrown away.

I heard from Simon's parents of changes and improvements in his life. At home and in his school he was calmer, making an effort to control himself. He began to listen to corrections and instructions for the first time in his life. A child had been playing with him at home and had accidentally broken something that Simon had built with his Lego. Instead of hitting his friend, he cried inconsolably for a long time. He showed an incipient capacity to tolerate depressive feelings and could seek some comfort for them. He could bear to have some hope.

There was growing containment in his sessions. He brought a large red van capable of carrying inside his little red car from the box. When turned upside down, the van could retain the car and not allow it to fall down. I thought that he was beginning to feel remembered by me during the sessions rather than dropped or instantly replaced. Until then, separations had always been like fractures. He started to rebuild his Lego house again. This was the first time that he reconstructed something broken. Not having finished by the time we stopped, he said, "I will finish the house tomorrow"! It was a remarkable step forward that he could think of a secure tomorrow at the time of leaving me.

In the following session Simon finished building the house. He sat on the window sill and talked about the cage for the first time. He remembered being put there and said it was not a cage but a box with a glass top, inside which he could not breathe. I said he might have been afraid that he had been put into it to die. He left the enclosure, pretended to kill some "ghosts", looked at the rebuilt house, and said it looked patchy. He then tried to make it nicer and, reflectively, said that fixing things took much longer than making them.

Simon relapsed when he saw a patient of mine arriving after his session, reacting with ferocious attempts at hurting me. But these relapses were short-lived, followed by efforts at mending broken things.

His moments of emotional closeness were felt to be dangerous to him, and they would be followed by an attack on me or destroying what he was doing. A good mother who could feed him immediately became in his mind one who could betray him and replace him with another baby, leaving him at the mercy of the breathlessness and bombs of his own hatred.

After six months he drew a picture again. In the past he had stopped drawing because he could not control my interpretations. This one was of a happy worker inside a tractor who was lifting concrete to build a proper road to replace a muddy one. There was an acknowledgement that something solid and reliable was beginning to be built inside him.

Two years on there have been many changes in Simon. His difficulties outside the consulting-room have diminished or disappeared to a large extent. His adjustment to school life has ceased to be a problem. After a year and three quarters of treatment his parents moved him to another school, which they thought would be academically more suitable for him. He settled down very well, and two months later he was praised for his "liveliness". His parents describe him as a "changed child". He does not have outbursts of aggression towards other children any more and has made many friends. He is still very jealous of his sister, but he tries to control his aggression, making deliberate efforts not to hit her even when provoked by her, and he can talk to his parents about his jealousy. Though he is able to impress his teachers with his natural brightness and quick grasp of ideas, he has had difficulties in learning when it requires concentration and discipline. It is difficult for him to sustain any constructive effort that does not come from him and that challenges his omnipotent fantasies. He enjoys a range of sports and activities after school, and there are no more problems of fear in entering new places or having nightmares.

The psychotic part of the personality shows an incipient capacity to tolerate frustration. Simon has begun to introject a containing breast and develop a capacity for thinking about his experiences. When his mother had not been able to fully perceive and think about Simon's terror, he had been terrified, and so was she. The absence of detoxification of the fear had led to him experiencing "nameless dread". Therefore the fear had increased. This was a reversal of the thinking process. This still appears in his learning difficulties. He seems to avoid working in order to learn; his imagination and fantasy are quickly blocked, fearing that overwhelming anxiety will follow.

In her study of trauma, Garland (1991) pointed out that the event appears to alter the survivor's capacity for symbolic thinking. In Simon, his capacity for symbolization was hindered by his sadistic phantasies and therefore unavailable for the process of working through. Projective identification became the only way available to him of communicating the helplessness and primitive feelings that he experienced. He expressed his distress through his violent behaviour, making one feel what he felt like.

Initially, Simon presented very violent mood swings, which might suggest the beginning of a manic–depressive illness. H. Sydney Klein (1974, p. 267) explains this phenomenon in his analysis of transference and defence in manic states, linking it also to the failure of containment, producing a "catastrophic fragmentation of the ego". Like the patient described by Klein, Simon had an omnipotent part that did not allow him to feel securely dependent and was tormented by a persecuting superego. Any interpretation that made contact with his feelings, especially those related to his projections, was experienced as intensely persecutory and provoked angry attacks. He felt the interpretations as my rejection of these projections. Having been very idealized as an infant, he could not relinquish the belief that he was all the nurturing and potent objects himself. His treatment attacked his manic defences of believing that he feeds himself. He was filling the absence in him of a good and reliable object with constant activity, often repetitive and not conducive to further development. Instead, he was full of dead objects (the ghosts of his fantasies were dead babies?), which left him in constant danger from his destructive feelings.

The epistemophilic drives in Simon were not inhibited—rather the opposite: his curiosity was voracious. But these drives were not about knowing. They were very intrusive and aimed at controlling his persecution. His nightmares often contained a "robber" or other male intruder coming in and taking him away. He had projected into his father his own wishes to empty his mother of her baby.

Simon could not believe that he had a place of his own in his mother's life, or in my mind when separated from me. The early interpretations had lessened his persecutory feelings towards his father and allowed him to approach him and have a more affectionate relationship. But for a long time he preferred to relate to each parent individually and not as a couple. Britton (1989, p. 7) describes the absence of

a particular mental space within the boundaries of the triangle, which would allow differentiated relationships with each parent, and the recognition of the parents as a couple. He is not able to tolerate the existence of a good container–contained relationship from which he would be excluded.

Hanna Segal (in Britton, 1989, p. 8) adds to the consequences of this process:

> When I think of Dr Britton's triangle as defining the space in which different links can be established between the child and the two parents, I think that space contains the room for the new baby. If a new baby appears inside the mother before such space can be established, and while the little infant is still heavily dependent on the phantasy of getting inside mother, psychotic disturbances can easily ensue.

The relationship between his parents, and its fruit the new baby, were felt by Simon to be destroying his own link with his mother, potentially his annihilation. My interpretations revived in him the awareness of a creative relationship of which he was the product without being part of it. The discovery of meaning in interpretations touched unresolved and frightening oedipal feelings and the conviction that he would be punished again, re-experiencing the fear of death.

Simon had not in his infancy developed an internal object to allow him to have a sense of reality. Sydney Klein (1985, p. 35) describes the consequences of the maternal failure to respond to the child's anxieties:

> Firstly the mother's lack of response leads her to be experienced as hostile, indifferent, narcissistic and inimical to the child's projections. Secondly, the child deals with its initial helplessness by a resort to omnipotence so that the mother's failure leads to increasingly desperate and aggressive projections—that is, there is a hypertrophy of the function of projective identification, going along with excessive omnipotence.

During treatment Simon gradually began to tolerate the frustrations, during which he believed he left room for somebody else.

My own thinking processes about Simon, and the relief that they brought him began to allow the integration in his mind of a couple that took care of him. This removed the conviction that either he has to create everything himself or he feels flooded by violent feelings. The traumatic events began to find their place in the past, in his history. Though his internal violence is still apparent at times, it alternates now with the perception and belief that I am taking care of his difficulties of my own accord, that I want to and am able to contain it and deal with it. Initially the sessions made him feel imprisoned in a place full of his projections. But as we continued working Simon began to experience the containment, and he achieved some self-control as much in his life in general as in the consulting-room.

CHAPTER FOUR

The significance of perversion:
to prevent intimacy

Gabriele Pasquali

In his chapter Gabriele Pasquali shows that a perversion protects against the emotional pain of intimacy. A dream, which was in three parts, each of which described a sexual activity, was crucial to understanding how his patient, a young woman, had not been able to be emotionally intimate because of perverse sexual excitement in three modes. These were represented in the dream and enacted in the analysis. Her fear of intimacy derived from childhood experience but was only combated when the secret sexual fantasies came into the open in the analysis. In this case, her emotional pain was imprisoned by her masochistic excitement with physical pain.

A deep-rooted passion for clinical work leaves Sydney Klein little time for expounding theories: he is first and foremost a clinician. He has conveyed this same passion to me and has contributed to its growth: my chapter describes, through clinical material spanning over a number of years, the emergence of a perversion and its transformation in the course of

57

the analysis. The clinical change has shown up in the transference and resulted in a greater capacity of the patient to use insight.

Case study: "Sara"

In her fifth year of analysis, "Sara", then a woman of 40, who had entered analysis because of depression and a wish to marry and have children, told me the following dream: the dream is in three parts.

> First Sara is in bed, lying on one side of her body with her boyfriend, Rick, in the same position behind her. She feels his penis pass between her thighs and elongate itself up past her stomach as far as her breasts. Sara grips and rubs it against her body and then the penis becomes a plush puppet.

> In the second part of the dream, they are at a wedding banquet; Rick invites Sara to sit on his knees and penetrates her. Sara points out that everyone present can see what is happening, but he insists that nobody notices anything. She pretends to believe him, but just the same tries to cover herself a little with the edge of the table-cloth.

> In the third part of the dream, the two are shut in the bathroom and have sexual intercourse.

Sara, commenting on the dream, says that, on gripping and rubbing the penis against her body, it no longer seem to be a part of Rick any more. It even ceases to be a penis and becomes a plush puppet. Regarding the second part, she points out that she and Rick exhibit their sexual intercourse in public, they tell each other that nobody notices, and yet they know perfectly well that this is not true. In the last part of the dream, the sexual intercourse takes place in the most secret room of the house, the only one guaranteeing complete privacy—the bathroom.

The dream therefore tells us of a secret sexual activity, of an exhibited sexual activity, and of a sexual activity with a part-object, which becomes inanimate, a mocking of the real object, when Sara takes hold of it.

Concerning secrecy, I remind Sara that some time ago she had alluded to some sexual difficulties of hers and then abruptly changed the subject.

After a long pause and with considerable embarrassment, she finally confesses that during sexual intercourse, on occasions she has a strong desire to be inflicted with physical pain. When Rick is hurting her, her mind pictures bound women being raped. Pain has a tremendous exciting power, and Sara yearns for more and more of it. She yearns to suffer. It excites her to feel subjugated to the person who is committing violence on her. The aim and goal of the whole thing is to reach submission. Humiliation is important for the same reason, in that it indicates that somebody is superior to her, that she "is under". This is nothing new. She had this with her previous boyfriends, but she only revealed it to Rick.

Each of her relationships starts with many doubts; each then seems to consolidate itself, and Sara feels full of enthusiasm with life, active, happy, and making plans for the future. Then suddenly everything comes to a halt. She feels she must break off the relationship, she must free herself from it at all costs. Yet she is unable to find any plausible explanation for her behaviour.

But it was for this very reason that she had come to me for help: she never managed to make a relationship last. The one with Rick has lasted the longest—two years. The secret and perverse activity that Sara represented in her dream and described, with a marked sense of shame, during our painful dialogue unearths the deep-rooted causes of her behaviour. The start of the relationship is not easy, although it develops in depth and significance. But then mania and exhibitionism take over. Finally, in the most secret room of the whole house, the relationship is discarded with a crescendo of frenzied excitation and pain caused by the blows inflicted on her by the masochism that makes her the victim of unending, hopeless cruelty. Some of the boyfriends, on suddenly finding themselves rejected for no apparent reason, reacted in a violent physical way at this shattering of their hopes, thus adding unknowingly to Sara's ferocious masochism.

There was such a strong quality of concrete reality in these stories of Sara's relationships with her various boyfriends that I had a lot of trouble in perceiving other meanings apart from the obvious one. I found it difficult to understand the transference, and not infrequently the transference interpretations seemed out of place and irrelevant. But when I managed to reach her and she felt understood, Sara reacted by shutting herself up in silence for the rest of the session or else she would not turn up for the next one. If she did come, however, she would "confirm" the interpretations with ready-made sentences and material tailored to show that I was right. For her, my interpretations had no psychic meaning, and I was continuously led to doubt my analytic instruments.

Sara was not able to stand dependence. Her needs were either thrown on my shoulders, in which case I held the concern about her and ran after her with my interpretations, or they were denied, in which case Sara would imitate some of my qualities and create an atmosphere between us similar to that which develops when two colleagues discuss a patient and pool their clinical experiences.

As we approach a break in the analysis, Sara dreams that *I am giving a party in my home; a lot of colleagues have been invited. Sara is also there walking peacefully round the house and the garden, talking to the guests.*

Through the dream, Sara tells me that there is nothing I can give her: My guests, my garden, everything I have is hers. By going away on holidays, I deprived her of nothing. There is no separation between her and me, between adults and children, guests and patients, my space and hers.

Confusion, projection, denial, mania . . . these we find in every analysis: what is specific to this analysis is that they are at the service of a primitive sexuality that guarantees Sara excitement but does not allow any emotional closeness. The dream I cited at the beginning was explicit on this point.

The first part reveals the fate of my interpretations, which acquire a sexual connotation; they become a penis which from behind her body caresses her skin, thus awaking excitement in her. Then she grips hold of it, separating it from me, transforming it into a meaningless and lifeless object, a plush puppet, and so making a mock of my interpretation.

I would like to underline the sexualization and erotization of the analytic relationship—in particular the link between aggressiveness, destructiveness, and sexual excitement by which Sara, keeps me at a distance. When Sara projects her sexual excitement into me, in her mind my interpretations become excited penises yearningly running after her: it is I who keep chasing her with interpretations that she reduces to ridiculous plush puppets. By these means Sara tells me that my relationship with her remains superficial—an exciting contact spreading in all directions but only skin-deep. My efforts continue to seem completely useless. She tells me, however, that she speaks with enthusiasm of our analytic sessions to her friends, describing them as vivid moments in her life, that I enrich and stimulate her. She portrays me as a competent analyst, full of things to give her: beautiful, unexpected, original, intelligent.

Gradually, as the session goes on, Sara becomes excited, as she had done with her friends: what had started as the sharing of an experience develops into its exhibition. This is just like the second part of the dream—the wedding banquet at which Rick penetrates her, saying that nobody notices. Sara transforms the interpretations that she feels are significant into an excited penis that penetrates her and, at the wedding banquet that ratifies our intercourse, she feels herself exhibited as proof of my sexual powers. At the most crucial and profound moment of the analytic encounter, when my interpretations really mean something and could become the source of insight and growth, Sara is unable to create the intimate space indispensable to get nourishment from the intercourse with the other person. The excitement is too great, and the edge of the tablecloth with which Sara tries to hide it is too small. And so our marriage is offered as food to the guests who, open-mouthed, enjoy the unique scene of the intercourse between a great and overpowering analyst and a patient who can barely manage to hide the humiliation of not having been able to make room in her mind for an intimate experience. In this part of the dream the intercourse is with a whole object, but the little emotional closeness that it has been possible to establish and the little nourishment Sara could make use of is immediately turned into sexual excitement.

This lack of an intimate space—indispensable if an experience is to become a source of growth—gives rise to confusion between orality and sexual excitement which the images of the dream evoke clearly. When I attempt to put her in touch with these mental states, Sara feels reprimanded, humiliated, because she is not making progress. She feels vastly inferior to me, subjugated and disheartened. "That's exactly it", she replies in a little voice as I interpret her drifting away from me and the consequent pain that this causes to both of us. But while I cherish the hope that I am telling her something significant, while I try harder and harder to understand what is going on between us, in her most secret room Sara transforms the pain into enjoyment.

This is portrayed in the third part of the dream, in which *Sara and I have a secret relationship*. From the associations we know that in this relationship she is excited and gets pleasure from my making her suffer. The interpretations are experienced as my hitting her. Under the rain of blows the relationship is flushed away in an orgy of masochistic pleasure.

The various parts of the dream refer to different types of intercourse between Sara and myself at different moments in the analysis. On some occasions I am a lifeless part-object; on others an object that narcissistically excites other people by exhibiting and therefore humiliating her; on other occasions again I am an object used to satisfy her masochism. No matter which type of intercourse, a number of elements remain constant: the excitement, the erotization, and the aggressiveness. I would like to emphasize that the relationships that Sara establishes are void of real emotional closeness. By means of projecting parts of herself into the other person, Sara establishes a false closeness and sometimes even creates an illusion of intimacy. But Sara backs away from a real intercourse, a sharing of emotions: she is terrified of them. Her attack on my capacity to work in the sessions is intended to destroy the possibility of an intimate intercourse with me; Sara is horrified at the thought because she is sure she would become entangled in it—prisoner—in the same way as—and we shall come to this further on—she was a prisoner in her relationship with her mother. Therefore Sara always needs to be in command: even when humiliated and subjugated, it is actually she who is in charge.

Sara's pathology, activated by the analysis, is acted out partly outside the sessions, but above all in the sessions. The detailed work in the transference enabled Sara first to allude to vague sexual difficulties, then to dream of them, and finally to associate them with the dream—that is, to let the destructiveness come out of its secret place, the bathroom. Sara has started to become aware of her split-off destructiveness and to understand the link between it and perversion. The analysis of the transference has allowed her to experience how she projects her aggressiveness, destructiveness, and excitement into the other person, of whom masochistically she becomes the victim.

> One day Sara dreams *that a rather large goose with thick, white and shiny feathers is in her house; a person—a man—approaches the goose and plucks off the softest feathers to make a cushion; he tells Sara that the feathers will grow again. She tries to get hold of the goose to revive it and take it away.* She wakes up desperate.

> She remembers that a few days before, a male acquaintance, "N", whom she had aroused and excited with a story of her friendships with well-known public personalities, had phoned, begging her to speak to one of these high-ranking friends about something he needed very badly; Sara was to intercede with the friend on N's behalf. Sara complains that N telephones rarely, and then only to ask for favours.

Sara allows herself to be stripped of her softest feathers, the friend sits on them so as to be more comfortable, and, if Sara complains and starts crying, he just tells her that they will grow again: the same old story will be repeated. Sara, however, is not excited and experiences no pleasure; on the contrary, she is in touch with her own pain and, distraught, endeavours to free herself of the violence of which she has been a victim for so long.

On other occasions when she had been treated sadistically, Sara had linked the excitement and the pleasure derived from it with the excitement and the pleasure she used to experience when she cursed—quite rightly, in her opinion—the ill luck that dogged her without respite: she had always been badly treated, had always had bad luck. Each time it was always the same story. Sara maintained that she had every right to complain and to demand that which she had never received. At times her claims became her *raison d'être*. Under certain aspects, you could not blame her: the story was repeating itself, always identical. But when Sara made her claims, she was unable to see the role that she had played to cause this repetition.

Sara had not had an easy life, being the only child of parents who did not get on well together but who never managed to separate. As far back as she can remember, she lived in an atmosphere of misery, tragedy, and violence. Her mother lapsed into a state of depression soon after Sara's birth; her father had estranged himself from the family and appeared only in the evenings, and it was her grandmother who took it on herself to look after Sara. As time passed, life between the parents became more and more difficult, and violent quarrels broke out almost daily. Sara's mother tried to commit suicide more than once, and, following one attempt when Sara had just started school, she suffered a severe disablement. A sense of guilt overcame Sara for having left her mother alone at home. The mother now needed help more than ever, but the father ignored her plight completely except to quarrel about money problems. So she turned to her daughter, demanding that she be near her at all times. She also boycotted any friendships the daughter made, rendering it impossible for her to have any boyfriends. She disparaged anyone who showed an interest in Sara, she stopped her going out, and, anguished by the thought of being left alone, would blackmail her. At first, Sara tried to stand up to her mother, but in the end she gave up. Devoured by persecutory guilt, Sara convinced herself that should she decide to have a life of her own, a stable relationship with someone, she would then become responsible for the death of her mother—in the same way as, when small, she had felt responsible for her mother's attempted suicide. Sara is the victim of her mother's sadistic destructiveness, but she is also identified with a mother who destroys from the start the life of the couple.

In spite of everything, Sara had managed to conserve a corner for herself, studying, and it was to this that she devoted all her energy. She excelled both at school and at university, and had equal success in her working career. Her free time is filled with various interests, and she is a keen student of figurative art.

The dream of the plucked goose does not represent another opportunity for Sara to curse misfortune and the sadistic exploitation to which she is subject, and to stake a claim to her own rights; instead, it is an opportunity to understand what a goose she is when she allows the repetition of an eternal story of exploitation and does not summon up courage to rebel, pretending to believe that everything can always be anew.

I am of the opinion that Sara was able to perceive her vicissitudes in a different light only when the perverse activity and fantasies ceased to be secret. Secrecy is crucial for the maintenance of perversion, whereas extracting the perversion from secrecy is crucial for making a contact with the split-off parts. Some form of contact with her own masochism, excitement, aggressiveness enabled Sara to see the dream of the goose—and her behaviour in general—in a new light.

At this point, therefore, we were able to start exploring a series of emotions previously obscured by the violence of the masochism. Sara is now more in touch with her needs, she is aware of her dependence and of the importance of the other person. Now when I tell her something that she feels is useful, she does not shut herself up in silence, and the next day she is not oblivious to the ringing of the alarm clock to the point of missing a session. Missing a session upsets her, a longer separation makes her feel completely abandoned.

When, after a break, we resume the analysis, Sara says she is disturbed by the dreams of the preceding week. She dreamt that *she was in an apartment with someone who then disappeared, leaving her alone abandoned and lost in the streets of an unknown town.* This dream was immediately followed by another one: she dreams that *the previous dream was so important that she must confide in someone about it: so she tells a girl-friend because I am away on holiday. While she is talking, Sara lies down completely dressed on a hospital bed. Then another person, also dressed, lies down beside her and suddenly vomits all over her.*

Sara associates that in the break she had reflected on her masochism with a sense of despair and disgust. She can no longer stand being hurt and feeling pleasure and excitement from it.

On the days when there is no session, I vanish, and Sara suddenly feels she is without a home, thrown out into an unknown and alien world. She has an urgent need of a girl-friend, to be together and sharing with her the experience she has been able to dream about. Unfortunately another woman appears at her side in the hospital bed. It is her twin, who is too ill to dream and to feel the pain of the separation, too ill to share an experience with an analyst friend inside her. The twin can only vomit on her what she cannot swallow—a separation that weighs too heavily on her, with its undigested elements of anger, envy, and despair so untransformed as to make her feel disgusted.

> Sara answers by expressing the doubt that I am really capable of making room for their twin inside me; perhaps she has not given me a complete picture of her internal world, perhaps she is covering it up. If I saw it as it is, I would vomit it up, like the person in the dream. She then recounts that the day before Rick had been late for lunch, and she was furious. Then he arrived with a present, a picture, and she realizes she had been nasty and unjust.

> I interpret that when the interval between sessions is too long and I am "too late", Sara is furious with me; then, at last, the sessions start again, I come back with a picture of her mental state, and she feels guilty and nasty because she sees that in the interval I had not forgotten her. Sara could not have imagined that Rick was late because he was buying her a picture, she was only in a rage at having to wait. In the same way, she is unable to imagine that in the interval she is still in my mind.

> Sara says that she feels insincere in that at the end of the last session before the holidays, she was very moved when saying goodbye, and then became furious; now she will not look me in the eye. And yet when she had said goodbye she was being genuine.

In point of fact, Sara is not insincere. She is unable to comprehend that when she separates from someone, she can be both moved and furious. Either in one mental state or in the other, Sara is divided into two: there is a self who is in touch with the separation from a partner she feels is precious to her, and there is a twin who is full of fury and ill-feelings.

Being together is difficult. It is hard for Sara to keep together the self who pines for the absent object and the self who is enraged. And it is equally hard for her to keep together with the object. I know that Sara does not hold me unfailingly inside her, that at times she has no space for me. But I also know that she has experienced the pain of missing me and has come into contact with her profound solitude without having immediately to transform her pain into excitement. She has had the experience of intimacy with herself and with me.

Sexualization and excitement, the secret perverse activity, have not disappeared but, relegated into the background, leave space for a vast selection of emotions: amongst these the painful and worrying discovery of her destructiveness. Sara realizes that in order to attack the other person, she must rid him of his human qualities, and she herself must do the same. The antidote to losing humanity, and with it the capacity of enjoying intimacy, is to be in touch with her destructiveness and to be able to have that compassion for her twin full of fury, which makes integration possible.

CHAPTER FIVE

Shadow lives:
a discussion of *Reading in the Dark*,
a novel by Seamus Deane

Kate Barrows

Traumata that cannot be spoken about can remain as areas of unresolved mourning. Caregivers in this position are likely to pass on these unworked-through "ghosts" to their own children, who are thus prevented from working through their developmental hurdles and from living their own lives. Kate Barrows illustrates this, using material from the book Reading in the Dark *by Seamus Deane (1997) and also material from a patient. She suggests that lack of containment of the child's aggressive and lively feelings may lead to encapsulated areas of autism, as described by H. Sydney Klein (1980), the lack of containment being linked to ghost-producing traumata in the parents' lives.*

On the stairs, there was a clear, plain silence.
It was a short staircase, fourteen steps in all, covered in lino from which the original pattern had been polished away to the point where it had the look of a faint memory. Eleven steps took you to the turn of the stairs where the cathedral and the sky always hung in the window frame. Three more steps took you on to the landing, about six feet long.

"Don't move", my mother said from the landing. "Don't
cross that window." I was on the tenth step, she was on the
landing. I could have touched her. "There's something there
between us. A shadow. Don't move."
  I had no intention. I was enthralled. But I could see no
shadow.
  "There's somebody there. Somebody unhappy. Go back
down the stairs, son." We were haunted! We had a ghost, even
in the middle of the afternoon.

This is the opening of Seamus Deane's novel, *Reading in the Dark*,
narrated by a child growing up in Northern Ireland in 1945 from
early childhood until he leaves home for university. The child's
interest in the ghost is initially lively, he is "enthralled" and excited. But his excitement drains away when he sees the sadness on
his mother's face as she comes downstairs and cries quietly by the
fireside. He too becomes subdued: "I went in and sat on the floor
beside her and stared into the redness locked behind the bars of
the range." The child's liveliness gets locked up with his mother's
pain, the ghost, and the memories that haunt her.

Sydney Klein has emphasized the importance of being aware of
the patient's vitality and its vicissitudes. In his paper "Transference and Defence in Manic States" (1974), he describes a patient
who had "sufficient vitality to be in touch with reality and hence to
be able to attack it, whenever it aroused painful feelings". He
points out that it may be crucial not to overlook the positive side of
ambivalence, concluding that "technically it is extremely important to realize that what may appear to be aggressive behaviour on
the part of the patient is due in fact to the very intensity of his life
instincts". In addition to constitutional factors in the patient which
may have contributed to his difficulties, Klein suggests that lack of
maternal containment may affect lively and positive feelings as
well as destructive ones. This is illustrated in Deane's novel, where
maternal containment is rendered inadequate by the presence in
the mother's mind of a ghost. This chapter shows how a child's
vitality and sense of self become crushed when he identifies with
his parent's internal ghost.

Each new stage in the child's development entails the loss and
mourning of the previous stage. Similarly, separating from the
parents means giving up the earlier infantile relationship. When a

parent has not been able to come to terms adequately with his or her own bereavements, the child feels that the parent is preoccupied by a dead internal object and is therefore unable to contain the full range of the child's feelings. There is no room for the lively ambivalence that is essential to separation and emotional growth. Instead, the child comes to identify not with his parent but with his parent's unmourned internal ghost; this prevents him from developing a life and personality of his own. Hence an incapacity to mourn can lead to generations shadowed by loss. Freud (1917e[1915]) described how inadequate mourning could lead to "a pathological identification with the abandoned object". He hauntingly and memorably goes on to say that "Thus the shadow of the object fell upon the ego . . . as though it were an object, the forsaken object". However, in the scenarios that I shall describe, it is also the shadow *inside* the object, the shadow of the object's *internal* object, that falls upon the ego.

The narrator in Deane's novel spends much of his childhood preoccupied with finding out about the secrets in his family, the ghosts. The family secrets are complex to unravel and too complex to do justice to here. The narrator gradually discovers that his father's dead brother, Eddie, was set up as an informer, the actual informer having run away to Chicago. The narrator's father believes that Eddie was the informer. When his mother learns that her own father had mistakenly ordered Eddie's execution, she does not tell her husband. She never recovers from this discovery, because she was inadvertently responsible through having helped the real informer to escape to America, deserting her younger sister, whom he had married in preference to her. She becomes intermittently psychotic. She will not talk to her son about the secrets, although she knows that he has found out for himself. The family remains locked in silence until the parents eventually die. It is not just because of the secret of the ghosts but the silence surrounding them that they cannot be laid to rest; they continue to dominate the present.

The idea of the shadow is developed throughout the novel. Early on in the novel the child says: "We slept while the shadow watched." However, his childhood innocence, his capacity to ignore the shadow, gives way to anxious preoccupation. He becomes worried that his family may be living under the weight of a curse.

It is a part of the common folklore that members of blighted families bring bad luck and are to be avoided. "People said no one from those families should ever get married. They should be allowed to die out. That was the only way to appease the ghost. Even if they didn't die, those that remained would always have the presence in their houses. The boys should become monks, the girls nuns. Anything to stop the revenge. Anything." The question of whether his has now become a blighted family has vital implications for his own ability to have a normal life. He pesters his mother and his grandfather with questions about the past, and his mother turns against him for knowing too much. "Now the haunting meant something new to me—now I had become the shadow." The shadow has fallen upon his ego and become his identity.

In a central episode in the book, the narrator and a friend are surrounded by a group of bullies who are about to beat them up. A police car goes by, and the narrator stops it by throwing a stone and attracts attention to the group of children, surprising himself as well as them in a moment of desperation. He finds himself suddenly slipping into identification with the ghost of his uncle, without realizing what has happened until it is too late, until the enactment has taken place. His friends shout at him that he is a "fuckin' stooly, just like your uncle, like the whole lot o' ye". He gives the other children away to escape being bullied and is then furious with his father for continually reproaching him for bringing the police back into their lives.

"Was there something amiss with me? No, I told him, there's something amiss with the family. The police were on top of us long before I was born. If he wanted to blame someone let him blame Eddie, not me. He hit me so fast, I saw nothing. My shoulder felt hot and broken." The child is not allowed to mention, let alone in anger, the family secret. He finds himself being forced to shoulder all the responsibility for the situation and becoming identified in his father's mind as well as his own with Eddie, the supposed informer. He becomes increasingly desperate in his mounting anger and impotent fury.

In a cold, determined rage he destroys the roses that his father grew in the front yard and which had been his pride and joy. He hacks them to pieces and covers them with cement powder, creating a scene of utter devastation. He describes the complete shock and incomprehension on his mother's and siblings' faces; clearly, he has done something to his family as well as to his father. He exiles himself to his room and waits in terror for his father to come home from work.

"He said nothing. . . . I didn't want to look at him, but his eyes held mine and, as he moved again, my head followed him. 'So I know, do I?' I nodded. 'Tomorrow, and the day after and the day after that and every other day that comes, you'll know.' He walked out of the room, slamming the door behind him. I lay there all night."

The child wakes up halfway through the morning to find his uncles and his father cementing over the whole front yard. There is to be no reparation and no forgiveness and, above all, no talking. His father says, "You ask me no more questions. Talk to me no more. Just stay out of my way and out of trouble."

His attack on his father and the rest of the family has been "concretized", and he has been cursed: he will always "know" not only about the family secrets but also about how unacceptable his feelings are. His furious attack came from his desperation about there being no place for his feelings of anger and confusion and his need to be able to talk about the ever-present shadows of the past. His view of himself is blighted by his father's condemnation. There seems to be no hope of him establishing an identity distinct from the family problems. The family solution of concrete, the wall of silence, cannot allow that roses can grow again if they are cut down, or that new feelings can develop if desperation and anger can be contained. There is no possibility of reparation and therefore no place for normal adolescent rebellion, for attacks on the father, mother, and siblings, which might be forgiven. The feeling is that his transgressions are so serious and so unforgivable, with the weight of history behind them, that the negotiation of his feelings in their own right cannot take place, and he can only try to separate by running away from home. It is as though he has become the cause of all the devastation.

At this point in the book the narrator seems near to the edge of insanity. "Walking on that concreted patch where the bushes had been was like walking on hot ground below which voices and roses were burning, burning." The effect of untold secrets and of unbearable guilt about the dead can lead to madness. This is most painful in the case of the narrator's mother, when she discovers that her father ordered Eddie's execution. "That was the beginning of her long trouble." She goes through a psychotic illness. At this stage the child becomes a receptacle for the mother's unspeakable feelings: "I wanted to run into the maw of the sobbing, to throw my arms wide to receive it, to shout into it, to make it come at me in words, words, words and no more of this ceaseless noise." Other characters also suffer mental illness as a result of the secrets. Larry, who, it turns out, was ordered to execute Eddie, has gone into a state of permanent withdrawal and silence. Larry had been engaged to be married, but now he stood, day after day, neatly dressed in suit and tie and never speaking to a soul, gazing up the lane towards the place where he killed Eddie, his own chances of marriage and a normal life long since gone. Crazy Joe, the local schizophrenic and keeper of secrets, was implicated because he had told the narrator's mother who the real informer was. Crazy Joe tells the narrator a tale of how Larry was seduced by a devil-woman, an apparition, and Joe's view of sex is that it is mad, dangerous, dirty. "Copulate if you must", he says. He is not married, but "to live with this condition of his was, he said the great connubium of his infelicity—the condition of being sane married to the condition of being mad; the knowledge that he was mad married to the knowledge that he was sane. And people thought he wasn't married! He was as unhappily married as anyone he knew." In these characters, sexuality has been replaced by insanity, and the development of the child's own sexual identity is threatened.

At one point in the story, the narrator finds himself set up by a girl to be hit and humiliated by her boyfriend. Now he feels identified with Eddie as the one who was set up, who had no control over his own destiny. Unless he can shake off the curse, he could spend the rest of his life imprisoned by identification with the ghosts in his family and by preoccupation with the problems, instead of being able to form relationships with girls and eventually marry and have his own life. This is made clear near the end of the book, when he attends the local dance. Crazy Joe corners him and keeps talking intensely about the ghosts, preventing him from joining in with the other youngsters. Eventually, his father intervenes, and a girl asks him to dance: "I moved gratefully to the floor with her, wanting to hold her tight in my arms." It is important that it is his father who manages to rescue him from Crazy Joe, giving him a push towards a real life of his own and encouraging him to join in the dance. Though his father could not help him to deal with his feelings about the past, he is able to be supportive in the present.

His other support is his older brother, Liam, who helps him at several points in the story. After the police incident, when the narrator has become ostracized by his age group, it is Liam who helps him to engineer a way to get back into the group. The support of members of the living family in helping the child to move on from the dead is crucial.

They also provide some measure of reassurance that the child's feelings have not been too damaging.

Fraiberg, Adelson, and Shapiro (1975), described as "ghosts in the nursery" the figures—remembered or unremembered—from the parents' childhoods who take up residence in the nursery of their own children and dominate the current relationships. Fraiberg and her colleagues found that it was not only the severity of the trauma which led to the ghosts taking occupation in the minds of the new generation, but also the repression of affect: the feelings have not been acknowledged so the ghosts cannot be laid to rest. Fonagy and colleagues (1993) have developed Fraiberg's work, confirming that where the traumas cannot be talked about, where the parent cannot give a coherent and emotionally alive account of his or her experiences, the effects of the trauma will be passed on to the children.

Although Deane's narrator, detective-like, manages to track down the facts of the situation, the most painful feature of his predicament is that what he finds out can never be discussed, and that having knowledge that cannot be shared alienates him from his parents. Knowledge in itself is not enough. After his grandfather tells him who the real informer was, he says: "I left him and went straight home, home, where I could never talk to my father or my mother properly again." He knows that his mother knows, but she will not—or cannot—talk about it, and his father will never know.

"Child—she'd tell me—I think sometimes you're possessed. Can't you just let the past be the past? But it wasn't the past and she knew it." The mother's silence becomes matched by the child's. She turns against him for having found out. "How I had wanted to know what it was that plagued her, then to become the plague myself", he writes. The silence acquires a secondary characteristic, of cruelty. She punishes him for not allowing her to forget, withdrawing from him, presenting him with riddles and conundrums but never actually speaking openly. His fact-finding has been an intrusion, and she asks him to go away. "Then maybe I could look after your father properly for once, without your eyes on me." Having hoped to make things better by finding out the truth and talking about it, he finds that he has only made things worse—the feelings attached to the events that he has unearthed are more powerful than words. It is impossible to share his knowledge with his parents because speech takes on the emotional character of the original trauma, as if talking could cause devastation. The inheritance of the shadow is an emotional inheritance, one of feelings as well as of facts. Secrecy and privacy become confused, as there is no place for the child's feelings in their own right, for distinguishing, on the one hand, between his need to find out about the past and, on the other, the feelings of exclusion and intrusiveness that are an inevitable part of childhood.

Case study: "Miss Y"

The narrator's experience had many features in common with a patient whose autistic features and inability to have a life of her own turned out to be connected to ghosts in her family.

"Miss Y" was referred for psychoanalysis as a last resort and as an alternative to long-term hospital in-patient treatment. She had virtually ground to a halt, was suffering from bulimia and extreme isolation and escalating suicidal thoughts. Like Deane's narrator, she was one of a large family where there seemed to be little space for her feelings and where important things did not get talked about. She had turned to an idealized relationship with her somewhat withdrawn father to avoid a difficult relationship with her mother, whom she felt to be intrusive and hysterical. Her father had died in her teens, and the whole family clearly had great difficulty in mourning his loss.

Early on in her analysis she described herself as a "shadow-person", and she would often say that she felt that she was not meant to have a life like other people, that she thought that she was destined in particular never to marry and have children, as though any possibilities of a fulfilling sexual or family life were blighted from early on. She saw no point in living and resented the fact that her breath carried on, regardless of her wish to die.

Autistic features soon came to the fore. These served the purpose of protecting Miss Y from fears of loss and death (cf. H. S. Klein, 1980). For instance, on one occasion she likened herself to a hermit crab, describing how they lay their eggs in the sand and how when the young hatch out, they have to get to the sea. Only one or two survive out of thousands, and she felt that she was one of the ones who were not meant to survive.

She made considerable strides in her analysis, however, managing to undertake a course of study and to have a boyfriend, as well as recovering from her bulimia and amenorrhoea and participating in a wider range of social situations. Yet she puzzled me because all this felt so insecure, as though it could be swept away in a moment. Her fear of loss was so acute as to render any progress very frightening, because she felt that she would not be able to bear losing whatever she gained.

A dream from Miss Y's third year of analysis threw light on the problem and ushered in a period of further developments. Her boyfriend was living abroad, and she had decided, unusually for her, to miss a few sessions to go and visit him. In a session a few days before her departure she expressed anxiety about missing her analysis and going to see the boyfriend and about contemplating the possibility of having children at some point. When I interpreted her fear that I would be angry or hurt because of this, she was very relieved and told me her dream:

She was stuck in a sort of swamp, trying desperately to get out. There were some figures who were likes ghosts or corpses, she didn't know which. They were trying to get her, to kill her. She was absolutely

terrified that she would be dragged back and killed. Her sister, "Z",
was helping her. Z wasn't affected and could survive this and help her
out of it; her sister was managing to pull her out.

Miss Y was so frightened that when she woke up she had to
have the light on all night. She said that it reminded her of the
dreams that she used to have about *a dead town*, but in those
dreams she used to be attracted to and interested in the dead
places and to like wandering round them, whereas this time it
was terribly frightening. She woke up, but felt as though it
could really be happening. She had always been terrified of
ghosts and had had to keep her light on after her mother told
her and her sister about ghosts recently.

I understood this dream in terms of Miss Y's relationship to me
both as a helpful sister and as a swamp-like mother full of ghosts.
She said that she thought of me as being like the helpful sister, but
her relief when I addressed her fear of telling me about going to
meet her boyfriend suggested that she was also afraid of my holding her back from her relationship and the prospect of having a
family. When I suggested this, she replied, "but I have to have a
life, it can't be helped!" She went on to describe an anxious couple
who held her back from going to a talk that she wanted to hear.
This seemed to express her fear of my anxieties, my ghosts, holding her back from getting the most out of her analysis. It seemed to
me important to be open to taking seriously her thoughts about her
objects—the anxious couple—and not to swamp her with interpretations relating to her own aggression and possessiveness, for instance, which would have been to identify her with the ghosts, to
confirm her idea that she could only have a shadow-life. When this
problem of her relationship to her objects' internal ghosts had been
to some extent worked through, she did gradually become more
able to take responsibility for her own negative feelings, without
feeling that they made her into someone unfit to have a life. Her
ventures became more rooted in the real world, and she said that
she felt that she was at last beginning to have a personality of her
own.

Miss Y's parents had suffered from loss and damage in their
childhoods. Her father had had a younger sister, and she had

drowned when he was supposed to be looking after her. This was never discussed with his parents and only briefly with Miss Y. She was told that her father's father never forgave him and his mother never recovered. Miss Y remembered going to visit these grandparents and feeling that she must sit still and not move, "as though she did not exist". Her father could not tolerate her feelings of loss, saying, for instance, that she should not have pets if she was going to mind when they got ill or died. Her mother had a younger sister who suffered from tuberculosis and was ill throughout her childhood; she never managed to join in life like other people as an adult. Miss Y's mother was scornful about her, and Miss Y feared incurring the same scorn and seemed to identify with the mother's sister in being unable to lead a normal life. The many ghosts in the dream seemed to represent these ghosts inside her parents, as well as perhaps her actual father. Where both parents harbour such ghosts, it is much harder for the child to escape identification with them. [I have described this patient in more detail elsewhere (Barrows, 1999).]

* * *

Sydney Klein (1980) describes encapsulated areas of autistic functioning in some neurotic patients who thus protect themselves from fears of death and disintegration. He connects this both to environmental factors and to the individual's contribution. Lack of containment of both aggressive and lively feelings has led to encapsulation, psychosomatic symptoms, or projection into others. The child may also have been used as a container for parental anxieties. In analysis, the patient clings to an idealized relationship with the analyst, while persecutory fears are denied. I suggest that in cases where the parent has suffered a loss without sufficient mourning, the child may identify with the parent's inadequately mourned internal object and be unable to establish a separate mental life. This is particularly likely to be the case where the parents have been unable to provide containment for each others' feelings. Klein found that all his patients had hysterical mothers and withdrawn fathers, and this was the case with my patient and with the narrator in *Reading in the Dark*. There are also likely to be predisposing factors in the child's psyche, such as the hypersensitivity that Klein described.

When I came across *Reading in the Dark*, I was struck by how much the narrator's predicament had in common with Miss Y's situation and her response to it. Deane's moving capacity to write about this area brought home to me several of the features of people whose childhoods have been dominated by family ghosts. The foremost is the feeling that the child cannot grow up to have his or her own life unless the problem of the ghosts can to some extent be resolved, both by it being recognized and by the child's feelings about it being accepted. Unless the problem has been acknowledged, the child feels him or her self to be a shadow, living under a family curse, not meant to have a life like other people. Ambivalence is felt to be intolerable, negative feelings too damaging, whilst lively ones get locked up and are unavailable for use. There is an underlying threat of mental illness as an alternative to an independent life.

In so far as the child's difficulties in having a life or personality of his own are associated with parental ghosts, other aspects of his character and of his relationship with his parents may have been able to develop more successfully. Deane's narrator was sensitive, intelligent, and well able to express himself. Miss Y had a capacity for finding evocative images to express her feelings and an emotional honesty that helped her analysis to progress. It was central to her analysis to attempt to distinguish between her perceptions of the reality of her object's internal world on the one hand and the part played by her own feelings on the other. Establishing this distinction enabled her to take some measure of responsibility for her own feelings and to disentangle herself from her parents' inner ghosts, and shadows.

The hallmark of Sydney Klein's work is, in my experience, a particular combination of sensitivity and common sense, of intuition and down-to-earth realism. I hope that I have managed to make use of this balance in considering the question of shadow lives.

CHAPTER SIX

On using an alphabet: recombining separable components

Maria Rhode

The adequate function of the psychic skin depends on a part-object union between the parents which precedes normal splitting, as described by Melanie Klein. Autistic children have very early anxieties about the integrity of the skin and other body parts and the boundary between themselves and others. Maria Rhode describes her psychoanalytic work with an autistic boy who confused mental demarcations with bodily damage, resulting in defects in this boundary that made him unable, among other problems, to use letters of the alphabet as abstractions. He felt, rather, that words were bodies that became mutilated if the letters were moved into different words. She suggests that the basis of the capacity to tolerate new experience (Bion's PS↔D) is the ability to split in a way that does not damage the primitive parental link. She explores the qualities of this skin—its permeability and its resilience.

In "Autistic Phenomena in Neurotic Patients", H. Sydney Klein (1980) describes a patient whose 4-week-old baby began to cry when he stopped talking to his wife during breast-feeding. "As soon as he started to talk again, the baby settled down." A few weeks later, the opposite took place: the father's voice, which earlier had been felt as a necessary support, had become an intrusion. "In the context of the session, it appeared that there is a change from an early experience of a good third object which supports the nipple to one in which it becomes hostile and intrusive." This change implies that the capacity for appropriate splitting, which Melanie Klein (1946) considered essential for overcoming chaos and confusion and preparing for later integration, is preceded developmentally by an experience of feeling sustained by the union of the parents on the level of part-objects or of sensory modalities (touch and hearing in this particular baby).

Children with autism characteristically suffer anxieties that antedate splitting (Bick, 1968, 1986) and concern the integrity of the body and its skin boundary. Tustin (1972, 1981) has described terrors of losing parts of the mouth, of being broken in two, of falling, liquefying, losing body contents, burning, or freezing. These are precipitated by a traumatic realization of bodily separateness (Tustin, 1981), whereas being together can be experienced as forming a unit (Tustin, 1990, p. 54: The Symbolon). Haag has elaborated on the fear of coming apart along the midline of the body (Haag, 1985) and of losing limbs (Haag, 1991).

In this chapter, I hope to illustrate how the development of the capacity to split appropriately—to establish useful mental demarcations—can be interfered with by a catastrophic experience of bodily demarcations and by the confusion between mental distinctions and bodily damage. I cite material from the treatment of "Daniel", a 9-year-old boy with autism, who experienced the parental couple as forming a physical unit like Tustin's symbolon (1990) while remaining mentally impervious to his own feelings of physical mutilation. Getting through emotionally—overcoming this imperviousness—could therefore become confused with separating the male and female aspects of the breast that needed to be together to sustain him. The earlier developmental phase described by Klein could not be securely established, and the capacity to split appropriately was constantly undermined, as were Daniel's liveliness and sense of initiative.

In treatment, Daniel developed the notion of a boundary in which male and female elements were associated in such a way as to permit the communication of feeling without damage to the sustaining structure. The emotional interface between the child and other people, which Bick (1968, 1986) conceptualized as a "psychic skin" by analogy with the physical skin, could be thought of as a kind of semi-permeable membrane that allows feelings to be communicated while at the same time offering protection from the loss of a sense of identity and from flooding by unmanageable sensory or emotional input. It needs both to provide a sense of being a separate individual and to allow emotional linking like a kind of interpersonal precursor of Bion's contact barrier. Where this is not the case, the child may oscillate between extremes of experience in the way Sydney Klein (1980) describes, encountering either an impervious brick wall or a boundary that is so yielding as to make the external world seem like the child's reflection, with all the problems in distinguishing phantasy from reality that can ensue from this (P. Barrows, 1999; Britton, 1994).

These issues were illustrated by Daniel's idiosyncratic use of letters of the alphabet. He treated them as though they were parts of the "body" of a word and could not be moved around or shared for fear of damage. For instance, it was hard for him to understand how words with different meanings could begin with the same letter. Later in treatment, letters could be safely rearranged: each one now seemed to be in itself a complete "body" made of parallel lines enclosing an internal space. These developments coincided with the appearance of the capacity to think of being together as overlapping in time rather than in space. Daniel and I could re-member the same event without damage to either of us, and this allowed him to access his memories and capacities more freely.

Case study: "Daniel"

Daniel came from a very deprived background. He did not know his father, and his mother, though loving, was herself very dis-turbed and suffered unpredictable outbreaks of violence. Since encountering a stable setting on being taken into care at the age of 6, he had become clean and dry, but at 9 years he still produced only two-word sentences at best. He had no contact with other children and was described as ineducable, with the absence of eye contact and the frequently echolalic speech characteristic of autism. Any change in routine caused a major tantrum. When he was frightened, he bit the back of his hand, which was badly scarred. However, he had the capacity to evoke love in adults, and his teachers' efforts to get him assessed and bring him on a long journey to therapy were a measure of this.

Daniel brought to the therapeutic relationship a moving sense of wonder that showed his hope of finding a good internal mother in the outside world. Each early session began with delighted recognition: "Green curtains! Three grey radiators!" However, his attempts to make links and begin to play were constantly threatened by an hallucinated monster. Sometimes this was another child or a man who might intrude; sometimes it was Cruella de Vil, the villainess in 101 Dalmatians who pursues the puppies for the sake of their skins. Daniel seemed confused between this terrifying maternal figure and a bad part of himself: he once said "Daniella de Vil" instead of "Cruella". In terms of the boundary between himself and others, it is as though the bad maternal figure were experienced on the physical level as tearing his skin off and on the mental level as being excessively open to being taken over by his projections.

Daniel made rapid progress in once-weekly (later increased to twice-weekly) therapy; he soon learned to read and began to make friends with other children. This progress could be conceptualized in terms of his success, before he came to treatment, in beginning to establish a helpful split that allowed him to look for a good maternal figure in the outside world. However, this split was very precarious. If he came late to his session, I became a terrifying stranger whom he might only recognize after half an hour's work.

In the third year of treatment, at a time when his school was in a state of flux, he showed me a loose flap of skin on his foot. My use of the word "hurt" was enough to send him rushing about the room, shrieking "No" in a terrified frenzy, desperately and unsuccessfully trying to cling with his mouth to the flat light switch. The impact on me of terror and guilt was so hard to bear that I did not realize until later that it was also a communication of the fear of doing damage, linked with Daniel's repeated admonitions to himself, "Leave the light alone! It's dangerous!"

Sydney Klein (1980) writes of the need to protect the nipple from the aggression directed against it when it is felt to take the child's place. Daniel seemed to experience his own damaged skin both as proof that I really was Cruella de Vil, and also as proof of damage to a nipple–light-switch that he could not take into his mouth without tearing it out of the wall. His mouth and the skin of the breast appeared to be deadlocked in a life-or-death struggle for the nipple (see Tustin, 1972, chap. 2): the resulting sense of extreme peril had no doubt been re-awakened by the anxious atmosphere at school.

The struggle for existence: the autistic experience of the oedipal triangle

Often Daniel appeared to feel safe only in relation to what Sydney Klein (1984) calls a placental object—lying on the couch clutching a cushion, thumb in mouth, with his fingers pressing against his eye to produce a visual image. If he spoke, it was in single words for which I was supposed to provide the missing context.

For instance, some play in the sink, accompanied by a timeless atmosphere, prompted me to talk about an underwater world. He said, "Ariel". I thought that this was an allusion to the film of The Little Mermaid, and he confirmed this.

In the story, the mermaid, Ariel, falls in love with a prince and yearns to leave the water and to live amongst human beings. However, the sorceress who slices her mermaid's tail into two legs requires her tongue in payment: Ariel cannot speak, and the Prince marries someone else.

Like some other autistic children, Daniel quoted economically from songs or fairy-tales to evoke a wealth of feeling. The story of the Little Mermaid conveyed the oedipal yearnings of a little girl part of him that was excluded from the parental couple; but much more than this, it conveyed his yearning to be a human being amongst others, able to speak as others do, and free of his autism, which he appeared to experience as a world beneath the water that he could not escape from.

Part of this feeling of imprisonment seemed to derive from a confusion between taking things in and biting my internal occupants out of me:

> I found Daniel in the waiting-room, pressing his forehead against the glass of the fish-tank. Later in the session, he jabbed his fingers into the cushion and said, "Cat! Catfish!" He appeared to be thinking of himself as a cat whose way into the cushion was blocked by its boundary, equated with the fish swimming behind the glass of the tank: eating would eliminate an obstacle as well as providing nourishment.

It is interesting that the cat's impulse to eat the fish leads to a catfish—a hybrid in which the fish presumably becomes imbued with the cat's devouring qualities. Daniel found himself trapped in the underwater world of speechless autism: a water–mother–sorceress whose fish–inhabitants (father or children) had been devoured became filled with devouring holes that in retaliation bit off Daniel's tongue or swallowed him up.

Falling off or falling in

For Daniel, then, the oedipal couple was experienced on a part-object level, so that the physical boundary with the mother implied that she was united with a third object that pushed him out into life-threatening situations.

> For example, he might say, "Walk the plank!" and then "Hook!" (the murderous pirate in Peter Pan). The reference to Hook would be followed by attacks on his own thumb, as though to bite off a threatening male protrusion. This was not a workable solution, as it left Daniel with a mutilated object. He would giggle in terror, staring into the palm of his hand—an autistic ritual he resorted to whenever he was frightened of falling.

In other words, Daniel faced the dilemma of being pushed to his death through falling off the object, or else falling into a hole he had made in it. (In fact, it turned out that part of his difficulties with introjection arose from the equation of his own insides with mine: the phantasy of crashing through the boundary into me transformed my inside—and, by identification, his—into what he called "wells", down which experience could get lost.) This impasse is reminiscent of Sydney Klein's (1973) patient, who felt that he spent his life as though in the doorway of his house, suspended between going out and staying inside (see also Rey, 1986, on the "claustrophobic–agoraphobic dilemma").

Protection from impingement

The oedipal couple was felt to be impervious to Daniel's urgent anxieties. For instance, he often repeated, "Emergency! Break the glass!" when passing the fire alarm. It is as though emotional and physical boundaries were confused, so that an emergency could only be communicated by shattering a physical boundary.

After a cancelled session, he slapped my hand, then jabbed at the drawing paper with a felt-tipped pen. What began as an essential communication of anger quickly led to serious damage: the hole in the paper grew into a tear that cut the sheet in half. Daniel pulled down the window blind, as though re-instating a boundary, and retired to his womb-like retreat on the couch from where he scanned the window, looking terrified whenever there was a noise outside.

In this example, Daniel seemed to feel that communicating his anger damaged the essential structure of the boundary, forcing apart two halves of the paper and making it necessary to re-enforce the boundary presented by the transparent window glass by means of the more opaque blind. Even so, he appeared to feel completely at the mercy of invasion by noises. These seemed to be an amalgam of outside events and his own anger, which had been communicated but not contained.

Sydney Klein (1980) writes of a "hypersensitive part of the personality". Daniel's was acutely vulnerable and exquisitely tuned to outside influences. On one occasion, when unpleasant thoughts were intruding into my mind, it was at first impossible to get through to him, but he responded when I said that perhaps he was keeping safe from the nasty thoughts in my head.

Daniel often tapped on the wall, as though reassured by its solidity. He emphasized to me that this really was a wall: he was obviously worried about something dangerous—whether from past experience or his own impulses—breaking through the division. In contrast to the wall's homogeneity, the tiled splashback over the sink was divided into squares by lines of grout. When Daniel said, "She grouted them: one, two, three!" I realized that this was a punning reference to a well-known children's song about "Goldilocks in the House of the Bears", which has the refrain, "She counted them: one, two, three", and that he was telling me that bears might burst through the lines and, presumably, attack him for being in their house.

In other words, Daniel seemed to be putting up an autistic barrier partly to protect himself from having his mind invaded in the absence of useful normal boundaries. Part of this is probably traceable to his actual experiences, such as his mother's unpredictable violent outbursts and the inevitable projection into him and his brothers of some of her own difficulties. It is likely that he was exposed to her relationships with men, and indeed he would lie on the couch giggling in response to noises outside the window with a mixture of fear and excitement. Partly Daniel also seemed to be identified with someone inside a mother-figure who was insufficiently protected by the enveloping boundary (the Catfish). On one occasion when the neon ceiling light was flickering, he lay on the couch shaking in rhythm to it: it was as though he held himself responsible for the damage and then equated himself with a damaged inside figure.

The difficulty lay in establishing a boundary that was effective without being impervious—one that could filter out undesirable impingements without leading to autism. I believe that this difficulty stemmed partly from Daniel's hypersensitivity, and partly from his identification with a maternal object who was either impervious or overwhelmed. [Bremner and Meltzer (1975) have described an autistic child's increasing sphincter control and sense of mastery over his body that came with the experience of a therapist who could not be intruded into at will.] The sequence in which Daniel angrily tore the sheet of paper and then became frightened of outside noises illustrates the fear that communication destroys the object's boundary. The outside world is then experienced as unable to contain his impulses, so that he too is left open to invasion.

The structure of the boundary
and the male–female link

Again after a cancelled session, I caught snatches of a muttered story about a farm horse who was so angry that he broke through a fence, causing all the animals inside it to fall down in a chain reaction. I talked about needing to find a way of making me understand that he was angry without breaking fences.

The following session, he was frightened by the noise of the fan in the lavatory. He reassured himself by talking about going back to the room: "Room 217; T for TwoOneSeven; Second floor; TwoND floor; Two–EN–DEE floor; T–Wendy-floor" and so on, until the words ran into each other in a meaningless chant. I talked about making everything the same, so that he and I were the same, after a noise had seemed to jump out at him. Perhaps he could not believe that TwoOneSeven was not all one word, and that I had not joined up with someone scary inside me.

At the sink, he said, "White tiles". I talked about needing to be sure that nothing nasty would come through the cracks. He said, "Pull down the blinds"; then, "Cobweb; spider's web; webbbbb". I talked about the difference between solid tiles and a web that was barely visible but contained a spider that might be frightening. Perhaps when he said "webbbbb" so that he could feel his lips pressing together, he was making sure that his mouth and the web were all right.

He said, "Father; Son". I asked, "Do you mean the Father, the Son, and the Holy Ghost?" He said: "Mass." I asked what he understood about these three who were different and yet the same. He went to the couch and said: "Hammock!" Then: "Rockabye Baby." I said that there needed to be a hammock that did not tip him out. After a cancelled session, I needed to understand his anger, but still be strong enough so that I did not break like the fence and so that we did not end up in the mud together.

He said, "Daddy" and went to the sink for a drink of water. Then, with mounting pleasure, he referred to his respite home, which had just moved back to refurbished premises, and exclaimed: "Trampoline! Move the equipment!"

Daniel seemed to be thinking about a continuum of penetrability/opacity, extending from the seamlessness of "T for TwoOneSeven" through the opaque tiles with their pattern of potentially vulnerable grouting to the semi-translucent blind drawn down over the transparent windowpane, and finally the barely visible spider's web. The properties of these different structures seemed to be associated with the nature of the relationship between their constituent components. "T for TwoOneSeven" implies that TwoOneSeven is a single entity, not an association of separate words. Grouted tiles (unlike a homogeneous wall) constitute a solid layer in which the constituent elements can be distinguished. Windowpane and blind form a parallel, easily reversible association of obviously separable parts. The flimsiness of the barely visible spider's web prompted Daniel to stress the final consonant in "webbbbb", as though in search of a solidity attributable to a Father element with which the solidity of his (the Son's) own lips could be equated.

I suspect that for Daniel, the Holy Ghost would have been a ghost associated with holes, and that being a son who was not identical with the father exposed him to being tipped out of a hammock or to falling through holes in a web too weak to support him. A hammock that supports one has ropes of the right strength and holes of the right size: in fact, I discovered that Daniel chose a hammock to play in with a special friend. In contrast, Alvarez' patient Robbie, who spoke of being lost down a well, felt that he slipped through the attention of an object that he described as "a net with a hole in it" (Alvarez, 1992).

A separable father element: introjection and splitting

It was after thinking about a hammock, which for him seemed to represent a good container in which solid elements and gaps had the right relationship to each other, that Daniel said "Daddy", had a drink, and spoke of "moving the equipment". "Daddy" conveys a very different feeling from the Father-and-Son of the Trinity. It is as though the presence of a good father allowed Daniel to introject, literally to "move" experience from one place to another. Once before, much earlier in the treatment, he had said "Daddy" when cutting through some Sellotape that was constricting his fingers. The good father who had then been felt to prevent entanglement was now the source of strength in the hammock.

At the same time, this good father was not seamlessly fused with the mother: communication and nourishment could pass across the boundary without damaging it. Daniel had previously made a point of showing me that he could suck water from a sponge without harming its solid structure. In fact, at the same time as he began to say "T for Two, O for One, S for Seven" instead of "T for TwoOneSeven", he began to mention events that had taken place years previously. It is as though the recognition of the separateness of the words meant that he could take things in—and therefore access memories—without separating elements that needed to be together. Parenthetically, in contrast, another autistic child ate the bits of glue with which he stuck a "plaster" onto a face made of holes in the wall: eating became confused with damaging the object by removing the substance that joined its component parts, rather like Daniel and the Catfish, or Sydney Klein's patient (1980, p. 396), who "attack[ed] the cement which bound her together, namely [the analyst's] interpretations".

Similarly, constituent elements must be freely separable for appropriate splitting to take place without damaging the object's basic structure. For example, Daniel depended on the light in the lavatory to reveal his reflection in the mirror and confirm that he still existed, but he was terrified of the noise of the fan that came on at the same time. For some while, he began every session with the words, "Fanlight: Go and check them", as though good and bad aspects of the object could not be separated without destroying the whole. This may well be related to a confusion between making space for himself, something that should be part of engaging with life, and the destructiveness arising from the experience of being blanked out (see H. S. Klein, 1974, p. 267).

Condensation, rarefaction, and perpendicular distance

The continuum extending from "T for TwoOneSeven" to the spider's web seems like a continuum of the condensation–rarefaction of matter, and can be visualized in terms of the relationship between the "solid" components of the boundary membrane and the permeable "pores". Bion (1963, pp. 40–41) describes the compression of β elements to form an agglomerated ♂. One could imagine that an unreceptive or rigid container might make it seem as if the membrane were laterally compressed, so that the pores would seem to decrease in size and the solid components to protrude. They would take on the qualities of Captain Hook rather than those of a supportive "Daddy". For a long time, Daniel covered his ears if a man came towards him through a door, vividly conveying the concreteness with which he felt invaded. Similarly, he was easily frightened by two rulers held at right angles, and quickly rearranged them parallel to and on top of each other, as though adhesively equated. The fear of being invaded by protrusions, of course, makes it extremely difficult to manage issues of distance, perspective, and emphasis (H. S. Klein, 1973, p. 6)—to be able to concentrate on something while temporarily relegating other factors to the background.

It is worth mentioning à propos of condensation–rarefaction that Daniel passed through a phase of looking at himself in a hand-held mirror, then bringing it closer and closer until it touched the right and left side of his face, the top of his head, and his chin. It was as though, when the distance between himself and his reflection went to nothing, this produced by condensation the physical boundary of his skin. Similarly, he experimented with the distance between himself and the window (looking either through it or at his own reflection) and with finding the right degree of "substance" and opacity that allowed his object to remain itself and still register his impact. Thus, breathing on the window-pane allowed him to trace letters that showed up against a contrasting background, whereas his finger left no mark on the too-solid back of the couch. Again as with the Catfish, he seemed to attribute this imperviousness to the effect of something on the other side of the boundary: he observed that his finger cast two shadows, which looked as though they were opposing his finger from inside the cushion, producing, as it were, an excess of opacity.

The use of an alphabet

Themes concerning the appropriate separation of components were reflected in Daniel's idiosyncratic use of the alphabet. The letter W (Double–You) was important from the beginning of treatment: Daniel made a W out of pencils when a colleague and I, whom he called the "Two Ladies in London", saw him for assessment. Later, in individual sessions, his emphasis on Vs (half–Ws) could be linked to his anxiety about what had become of my colleague, as well as to anxieties about losing half of his own body.

When Daniel first began to write, words were pictorial representations of objects rather than arbitrarily agreed, abstract means of visually encoding auditory information. For example, on a page containing writing he drew a picture of a swing hanging from a beam that was supported at each end by a tripod of metal poles with crossbars. The swing could have been mistaken for the letter H, whereas the poles with crossbars looked exactly like "A"s. At another time, "A"s looked like the side and roof of a house with supporting cross-beams.

For some time, he appeared to conceive of both the alphabet and of individual words as though they were bodies, and the letters "organs" that could not be moved without injury. For example, he left no gaps between words when writing out "TWOEYESTWOLEGSANDABODY": this appeared to be less a symbolic representation than a magic spell intended to ensure bodily integrity.

Working on anxieties about gaps enabled Daniel to separate words appropriately and to realize how meanings could change depending on where the gap was located: NOTRACK, for example, could mean NO TRACK or NOT RACK. LADYBIRD illustrated how much anxiety could be associated with bringing elements together: LADY and BIRD both seemed safe, but LADYBIRD meant the frightening black dots on the insect's back, probably representing the burnt children in the nursery rhyme ("Ladybird, ladybird, fly away home/Your house is on fire, your children all gone"). Rearranging one or two letters, as in anagrams, could lead to a complete change of meaning, as between MEGSCASTLE (Meg's Castle) and MEGSATSEA (Meg's at Sea): the meaning of a word was therefore not just to do with which letters were present but with their specific sequence and structure.

At a time when Daniel was concerned with his reflection in the mirror, he wrote SAWAS and WASSAW. While WASSAW can be separated into WAS and SAW, SAWAS cannot: the W would have to be cut in half. This may reflect Daniel's development from a position of feeling that mouth and breast competed for the nipple and could not be separated without injury (the light-switch material), to a position in which he and I could safely move together and apart by virtue of his having been observed and reflected upon.

Overlapping in space and in time

In an early drawing showing the same structure as SAWAS, an oblong swimming pool was divided by a vertical line into sections for swimmers and non-swimmers. Two intersecting circles, like a Venn diagram, were so positioned that the overlapping section, coloured in black, straddled the dividing line. One of the circles was in the Swimmers' section and the other in the Non-swimmers' (possibly related to the respective worlds of air and water-dwellers in the story of *The Little Mermaid*, which Daniel may have felt he was straddling when sucking his thumb on the couch). The bottom edge of the swimming pool had MEGTASEA written over it; the top edge, MEGSONTHEMOON, where the two Os looked like the halves of the Venn diagram that had managed to separate. However, the words were still run together, just as the circles of the Venn diagram overlapped in space, and could not be separated without damage to one or both.

After the terrifying session in which Daniel had felt that his skin was coming off, he drew letters as spaces enclosed by parallel lines, as though they were bodies completely enclosed by skin and could therefore be moved and rearranged without injury. While talking to him about this, I saw with delight that the letters he had just finished drawing spelt the word TIME. It was as though, at that moment at least, he felt that the two of us had complete bodies, and that being together could mean overlapping in time rather than in space. Moving apart need therefore not mean bodily mutilation, and time could be a dimension within which events could be shared (and subsequently remembered by both of us). This is very different from the experience of alternating between timelessness (fusion) and catastrophe (separation).

As I talked about this, Daniel added an x to TIME, making it into TIMEX (a brand of watch). In the following session, he wrote EGG TIMER and SAND TIMER. As well as being an arbitrary shape that transformed the word TIME into TIMEX, the letter x was also the picture of a time-keeping device—an hourglass filled with sand— as well as two half-Ws delicately balanced point to point in a way that expressed the precariousness of the newly achieved overlap in time rather than in space.

The move towards seeing letters as abstractions rather than pictorial representations in fact parallels the development of non-alphabetic systems of writing such as hieroglyphics, in which pictograms were gradually replaced by signs that represented sounds. The final x of TIMEX resembles determinants—a class of signs that depicted objects visually and were positioned after the phonetic rendering of a word.

Discussion

Daniel's material illustrates his tentative progress towards the experience of a psychic skin made up of male and female components so related as to constitute a supportive "hammock", with the proper balance between strength and receptivity. At such moments, the male and female components were not experienced as presenting a barrier to his communications through being fused, but as coming together in a way that supported his sense of existence and identity. This was true in the earliest weeks for the baby that Sydney Klein's patient described (H. S. Klein, 1980, p. 399). Indeed, I think that in Klein's work the capacity for explanatory understanding comes together with the capacity to see beyond it, to a knowledge of the essence of a patient's humanity. This union, I believe, encourages the patient to grow into that humanity.

Daniel needed to establish the experience of a good father-element that did not block his communications, and to clarify something of his confusion between being emotionally obliterated and being presented with a physical boundary ("Emergency! Break the glass!"). Bion (1962a) has proposed that an absence of receptivity to the baby's communications may lead to an excessive emphasis on corporeality, while Britton (1998) has suggested that the baby may maintain his attachment to an unreceptive mother by attributing her imperviousness to the third party in the oedipal triangle, the "closure" of which may then be felt as a catastrophe.

Daniel's material implies that he experienced the father's supposed blocking function as a physical obstacle, not just as a mental one (see Wittenberg, 1975); and that he confused both getting through emotionally and taking things in with separating aspects of a primitive parental couple that belonged together. The experience of a "supportive third object" was undermined, and with it the later development of the capacity for appropriate splitting. His inability to separate the terrifying "fan" from the vitally sustaining "light" in "fanlight" may be relevant to synaesthesia, with its incomplete separation of sensory modes. Similarly, the difficulty in bringing together the two senses of hearing and vision without feeling obliterated as though by an impervious couple might partly account for the fact that pictograms preceded phonic signs when he learned to write.

Meltzer (1975) has suggested that the "gentle" device of dismantling, by which the autistic child's identity passively falls apart along lines of demarcation associated with the various sensory modes, may be related to separating the parental couple by means of the device of equating mother and father with different senses so that they are felt to inhabit different universes (what he calls the Mummy with the uniform and the Daddy with the bell who pass

each other in the night of the child's mind). Daniel's habit of covering his ears when a man came towards him through a door is a
striking illustration of the specific association of a man with the
specific sense of hearing (the same sense associated with the father
in Sydney Klein's example of the baby). It also conveyed powerfully the concreteness with which he could feel invaded and the
way in which the experience of being invaded or projected into
is mediated by the masculine element of the primitive combined
parents. I have already suggested that an unreceptive or rigid
container could be felt to compress experience in the way Bion
(1963, pp. 40–41) described with regard to β elements; and that this
may shed light on Daniel's continuum of condensation–rarefaction
as well as on the transformation of a good father who prevents
entanglement into a bad father who pushes the child off into space
and invades him.

The internalization of such experiences of relating to the
boundary has implications for personality structure. For example,
Melanie Klein (1952) proposed that the degree of communication
that was possible between different parts of the self—the degree of
permeability of internal boundaries—depended fundamentally on
the "width" of the primal split. If one thinks of the permeability of
internal boundaries as deriving by introjection from the relationship to the boundary with the mother, then Daniel's fear that the
maternal object—and in turn his own mind—constantly risked
being invaded and overwhelmed is relevant to the borderline
child's fear of being invaded by his own impulses or by a part of
himself. It is interesting to speculate about similarities and differences between such a situation and that of Sydney Klein's adult
patient (1980), whose autistic part was encapsulated within the
personality.

Similarly, fears about damaging the boundary, which held
Daniel back from accessing the content of the breast (the "Catfish"
material), might be expected to hold him back from accessing the
internalized breast and, indeed, anything internal, such as his own
capacities. (For example, he could only show that he remembered
past events when the seamless boundary of "T for TwoOneSeven"
had yielded to the separability of "T for Two, O for One, S for
Seven", which allowed him to get through and to take things in
without tearing apart components that belonged together.) This

could be seen as an extreme case of the stance of some children with learning difficulties, whose play points to something precious that must be so carefully protected that it cannot be used.

Daniel's material suggests that the capacity to split appropriately, in a way that does not damage the primitive mother–father link, underlies the capacity to make fully symbolic, abstract use of an alphabet and to separate and recombine letters freely. This *capacity* may serve as an approximate metaphor (Bion, 1963, p. 2) for the kaleidoscopic thought process (Bion, 1967, p. 127), which allows new patterns to emerge. If the boundary membrane is felt to have sufficient "give" and elasticity, this may make it more possible to tolerate Bion's Ps ↔ D, so that different components of a pattern may come to occupy the foreground and NO TRACK for instance, can appear as NOT RACK. Autistic children can feel extremely threatened by such changes in emphasis, perspective, and perceived distance: they may feel terrified by something "coming at them" and experience a corresponding difficulty in relegating anything to the background, or they may feel that movement means the irreparable disintegration of basic structure. In contrast, confidence in the elasticity of the boundary permits the use of devices such as deliberately viewing all the parts of a familiar pattern from an equal distance, which in turn makes possible the experimentation with different perspectives and the recognition of alternative patterns. Perhaps such flexibility of thought processes depends on how far at any time the Little Mermaid's response to something foreign outweighs Goldilocks's—on how far intimations of something from another domain are experienced as a potential revelation rather than *a threat*.

CHAPTER SEVEN

Some reflections on comparing obsessional neurosis and autism

Mauro Morra

Mauro Morra compares obsessional neurosis with autism, which always has obsessional features. He finds that omnipotent control is the underlying structural element shared by both, and he comments that Meltzer sees them as the same—both involving an attack on certain mental capacities. An autistic nucleus is illustrated in four clinical cases ranging from childhood to adulthood. The chapter includes comments by Frances Tustin, who suggests that the over-closeness between mother and infant is sensual, not emotional.

I have always been struck by the fact that there are certain similarities in the symptoms of adult obsessional neurosis and child autism, which undoubtedly are two separate disorders. The main common features that we can find both in the literature and in our practice are the withdrawal of affects and the presence of obsessional tendencies.

On the question of whether the presence of common symptoms in the two illnesses is fortuitous or whether there is, on the contrary, some underlying similarity in personality structure, I do not have a definitive answer, but I am inclined to think that there are some important common features in both those organizations of the mind.

Freud never mentioned what we today call "childhood autism", but anticipated its existence in intuitive way, saying: "A neat example of a physical system shut off from the stimuli of the external world, and able to satisfy even its nutritional requirements autistically (to use Bleuler's term) is afforded by a bird's egg with its food supply enclosed in its shell" (Freud, 1911b, p. 219).

We could comment today that the obsessional patient, too, gives the impression of nourishing himself with his ruminations. Freud described in a vivid way—which at that time appeared to be exhaustive—what happens to the obsessional patient: "The trauma, instead of being forgotten, is deprived of its affective cathexis; so what remains in consciousness is nothing but its ideational content, which is perfectly colourless and is judged to be unimportant" (Freud, 1909d, pp. 196–197).

Later on in the same quotation, touching on obsessional actions as well as obsessional ideas, Freud gives the example of a government officer who was troubled by innumerable scruples, such as taking a fallen branch off the path in a park and later putting it into its previous position, the reason for both actions being his worry that people could get hurt. Furthermore, when paying his analyst, he used to give him bank notes that had previously been ironed. The same man described, without any affect, how he sexually abused some young girls who were in his care.

Freud's comment is: "In this disorder, repression is effected not by means of amnesia, but by a severance of casual connections brought about by a withdrawal of affects. These repressed connections appear to persist in some hind of shadowy form (which I have elsewhere compared to an endopsychic perception)" (Freud, 1909d, p. 231).

In considering what happens to the affects in autism, Tustin (1986), talking about psychogenic autistic children, says: "Overall there is a gross early arrest of cognitive and affective development." She continues: "These children also sometimes play in a restricted obsessional way." Clearly, Tustin reserves the term "autism" for certain specific pathological conditions in which there is an absence of human relationships and a gross impoverishment of mental and emotional life (Tustin, 1991, p. 585).

Certainly, although there are similarities between the two disorders, differences also seem evident.

First, withdrawal of affects and arrest of affective development are not the same: indeed, in the obsessional neurosis the affect is supposed to have existed previously and to have been displaced elsewhere (as in Freud's patient already quoted), whereas in autism the affective organization is believed never to have reached its proper development. Furthermore, in autism it is not only affective development that is stopped, but the cognitive side as well, and generally we do not find such cognitive arrest in obsessional neurosis.

But some authors take a less definite approach. In her last paper, Tustin (1991) considers autism from a different point of view. Reviewing her previous opinion that autism could be a normal phase of development to which the child could regress, she says that autism is an early developmental deviation, not a halt to, or a regression to, a normal early infantile stage of autistic unawareness (p. 585). Later on: "[It is] an abnormal state in which both mother and child had colluded" (p. 586) and "Autism is a system of perverse reactions [with] protective and preservative functions" (p. 587). She adds that *idiots savants* are autistic, but have an isolated talent, which they express in an obsessive way (p. 587). It is surprising how often the adjective "obsessive" or "obsessional" appears in the writings of all those who talk about childhood autism. According to Tustin (1990), some cured autistic children remain slightly obsessional (p. 28). She says: "There are a few autistic children whose cognitive development may go along a restricted narrow line with an obsessional interest in one thing" (p. 19).

Tustin points out how intense the need for omnipotent control is in autistic children and how successful it sometimes is. For instance, "Rituals have the functions of maintaining self-control and keeping the environment from changing" (1990, p. 4), and later, "So he [the autistic child] defends against feelings of non-existence by using all his strength and ability to try to build a shell of indestructible power" (p. 5). More conclusive appears her statement: "Although autistic children look so ethereal, they are in fact extremely dominating and powerful. They have developed an adaptation that is extremely effective for shutting out the outside world and for being in control over what happens to them. Unfortunately, this has prevented other adaptations from developing" (p. 19).

Again, one's mind goes to obsessional neurosis, with its controlling power. This is particularly evident in the way autistic children rock, spin, and override awareness of the objective functions of objects by the tactile, subjective use of such objects in a stereotyped and repetitive way (Tustin, 1990).

On the other hand, Elizabeth Bott Spillius reminds us that Melanie Klein developed "a new conception of obsessional neurosis as a defence against early psychotic anxiety instead of regarding it as a regression to a fixation point in the anal phase of libidinal development" (Bott Spillius, 1993, p. 3).

All together, I think that perhaps the underlying structural element belonging to both disorders might be the omnipotent control. Are there any other symptomatologies in which omnipotent control is so central? Certainly there are other illnesses where the need of controlling is evident, but it is neither so aimed at omnipotence nor so destructive. For example, the hysterical patient tries to control the surrounding people through his or her symptoms, but this happens more in order to get attention, to be considered "the special one", to be loved.

Meltzer does not seem to consider autism and obsessional neurosis as distinct structures, even if he sees the pathology of autism as more severe than in the other disorder, and it is more primitive in its appearance. "The workings of obsessional mechanism are employed in this surely most primitive of all obsessional disorders", he says, talking about autism, "where the obsessional mechanism could be seen in pure culture"; he goes on: "The fundamental mechanism consists of the separation and omnipotent control over objects, internal or external." Meltzer seems to summarize what he thinks about this subject in the following way:

My thesis regarding autistic mechanisms in particular, and obsessional mechanisms in general, is that their mode of functioning involves an attack on the capacity to perform mental acts. . . . While the autistic child accomplishes this by dismantling his common sense... the less primitive forms of obsessional mechanisms attack more specific constellations of mental activity, rather than seeking a suspension of mental activity in general. [Meltzer, 1975, pp. 209–222]

What Meltzer describes as "dismantling the common sense" seems evident in the case of a child aged 3½, whom T saw for assessment. Both the withdrawal of affects and the obsessive repetition were present.

Clinical vignette: "A"

Although "A" was not a typical case of childhood autism (these cases are luckily not very frequent) he undoubtedly presented some important autistic features (which is much more frequent).

He came with me to the consulting-room without difficulty, leaving his parents in the waiting-room (which is unusual for such a young child, but not for an autistic one). But when the waiting-room door was shut and he remained with me in the corridor, he hesitated a while before following me, looking at the closed door with intensity.

When we were in the consulting-room, he spent most of the time (almost one hour) doing the following: he covered the writing that was on the lid of the colouring-box using the black crayon, and immediately afterwards he scratched the black off, using one of his nails, so that the writing appeared again. He repeated this action many times. I understood this as the child trying to master the separation from his parents (the closed door) making them disappear and appear again.

It is indeed reminiscent of a very young child's game described by Freud. This toddler tried to master the separation from his mother by making a reel of cotton disappear and appear again (Freud, 1920g, p. 15). But the difference is the affective cathexis: in Freud's case we see a lively child, interested in an exciting game, whereas in my Case A one could not avoid thinking that in his obsessional and stereotyped activity (it was too cold to be called play) the child was not able to use his mind in a profitable way, as if his mind were partially dismantled, in the fashion described by Meltzer.

When we talk of autism, we cannot avoid thinking of narcissism, even if it seems hard to define what the relationship is between the former (which is a clinical entity) and the latter (which is more a particular organization of the mind). I do not want, now, to embark on the complexity of the problems of narcissism, but I would like to pick up some points that could be relevant to the topic of this chapter.

In his approach to narcissism, Freud writes:

> Thus we form the idea of there being an original libidinal cathexis of the Ego, from which some is later given off to objects. [Freud, 1914c, p. 75]

Later:

> We have discovered, especially clearly in people whose libidinal development has suffered some disturbance, such as perverts and homosexuals, that in their later choice of love-objects, they have taken as a model not their mother but their own selves. . . . In this way, large amounts of libido of an essentially homosexual kind are drawn into the formation of the narcissistic ego-ideal and find outlet and satisfaction in maintaining it.

Freud goes on:

> Everything a person possesses or achieves, every remnant of the primitive feeling of omnipotence which his experience has confirmed, helps to increase his self-regard.

When discussing the pleasure principle and the reality principle, Freud says:

> Our dreams at night and our waking tendency to tear ourselves away from distressing impressions are remnants of the dominance of this principle and proofs of its power (pleasure principle). [Freud, 1911b, p. 219]

So Freud did not lay down the problem of success or failure in moving from pleasure principle to reality principle in a rigid way, but maintained that up to some point, the two could coexist. Indeed, talking about repression, he says:

> It can be employed to bring back under the dominance of the pleasure principle thought-processes which had already become rational. [Freud, 1911b, p. 223]

The impression we get from the observation of autistic children is that they are under the sway of the immediate and sensuous response, and so of the pleasure principle, but what can we say about obsessional neurosis? Is not the tendency to tear oneself away from the disturbing feelings and fantasies present as well, both by obsessional thinking and also mainly through tactile action?

In his review of Freud's "On Narcissism" (1914c), Brenman (1993) writes:

> It is a big step forward from narcissism = auto-eroticism, and Freud spells out that narcissism is both a perversion and also a part of the egoism of self-preservation . . . in which he emphasized two main features, megalomania and the corresponding withdrawal of interest from the outside world. . . . Narcissism is no innocent indulgence.

Case study: "B"

The case I want to present now illustrates withdrawal of affects of obsessional nature in the early stages of analysis, followed by the revelation of a core of psychotic thinking. We can also see the presence of important homosexual drives towards the patient's own brother and the analyst. I wonder if this patient's efforts to reject any kind of emotions and affects, expressed with pride and arrogance, were not aimed at keeping the perfection of a narcissistic ideal ego, to quote Freud's definition.

"B" is a late adolescent I had in analysis for three years. Aged 18, he came into analysis because of some occasional moments of diminution of sight, together with the vague and painful feeling of getting lost (depersonalization?). In addition, he suffered from agoraphobia and also from difficulty in concentrating on his University work (the latter had, nevertheless, not prevented him from taking the equivalent of his A levels at 18 and from going on to University immediately).

In his first interview, B mentioned that he was rather isolated from his friends, but he tended to minimize this problem.

Some salient facts of his history are as follows: he was aware that his mother had got pregnant with him when she was un- married, and for this reason his father had married her when they were both in their early twenties. Just a few months after the patient's birth, his mother became pregnant for the second time, and when another boy was born, she realized that she was not able to cope with two young children. So B was taken by his paternal grandparents, and he lived with them, appar- ently happy; as he explained, he was happy partly because they lived out of town in a nice cottage with a garden. He kept some contact with his parents and brother, and also with a little sister who was born four years after him.

The relationship between the two families was rather cold, and the grandmother used to criticize her daughter-in-law openly in the presence of B.

Suddenly, when he was 8 or 9 years old, his grandparents moved, and they told him that there was no room for him with them any longer. So B was given back to his parents. He did not know whether behind such a decision there was an open re- quest from his parents to have him back. This dramatic account was given calmly, without any sign of emotion. My impression was of a mixed and complicated pathology, as we often find in young people, but I was struck by the lack of affective reac- tions, which became more and more evident when we started the analysis.

B used to talk a great deal, telling me long dreams that he tended to interpret himself rather than trying to free-associate to. Often he discussed my interpretations, asking me where in the material I could find evidence of what I was saying. Some- times he was able to criticize in an acute way, but often he took refuge into a world of abstract theories or even bad generalizations. His obsessional withdrawal was brought to analysis consciously, as when he said he felt compelled to pay attention to paying attention, more than to what was being said. He acknowledged being tormented by that compulsion. Once he said that his words were not a means of communication but, rather, a way of expressing his discomfort.

Often B started his session saying that, when passing near me on his journey from the door of the room to the couch, he had the sudden idea that I could take advantage of his turning his back to me and attack him sexually. But this idea was communicated to me as a cold statement, without any emotional involvement. His transferential attachment to me was almost like a nearly psychotic transference (not unusual in the case of adolescents' transference)—extremely intense but never expressed verbally in an explicit way.

After some symptomatic improvement in the initial phase, his parents considered the possibility of stopping the analysis, thinking that B was cured. At this point, the patient brought the following dream: *"I was in a car with my father when I realized that I was losing my hair. I felt desperate and said I was going to die. Later my brother was trying to convince me that it was not important, that it was a small thing. Later on, I was having sex with my sister."* All his associations were related to the risk of a premature end of his treatment. My interpretation was that his brother represented the part of him that tended to deny what he really felt— namely, that losing me would have meant for him losing his head, the hair representing his hope of having thoughts and emotions. This consequently meant his emotional death. I think that the final section of the dream expressed B's attempt to overcome the death feeling through sexual excitement. Perhaps one could have interpreted following a more classical model (incest and castration), but B's associations were not in this direction.

A couple of sessions later he came in a very gloomy state of mind and said that the analysis was over, that a continuation would not make any sense. He felt dead, and that there was only death between us. I told him that he felt the need to control the feared end of the analysis by anticipating it, either literally or emotionally, as he was not able to stand the agony. I also interpreted that his despair and anger had killed him emotionally as well as the relationship between us. I was really worried that he would commit suicide. His reaction to what I said was to burst into tears, and he went on crying till the end of the session.

It is difficult to describe the emotional impact on me, and the pain that I felt. I thought of the speculations many authors have made about what lies beyond the protective shell in autistic children. I mentally visualized the child who had lost his family twice, and who previously did not allow himself a feeling of such despair, being compelled to adapt himself in order to survive. I tried to convey that in an interpretation, putting myself in his mother's role; B's answer was that he never felt his mother's loss but, rather, his grandparents' loss (which, in a sense, could have been true, at least at a conscious level).

The following week the patient brought a dream in which *his grandmother asked him to switch the stereo off, because one could hear it in the next room.* I interpreted that he was showing me that his emotions were felt to be too strong, and so an internal grandmother had told him to switch off the music (feelings, emotion, affection towards me, despair) in order to avoid it being heard in another room (his consciousness).

In one of the following sessions I had the opportunity to tell him that he did not want to lose his grandfather's affection (myself in the transference)—the unique precious thing of his existence. But this unleashed a situation of obsessional doubt: B was not sure he could remember his affection for his grandfather.

Another obsessional doubt was: could his parents understand that he wanted to come to me? There was a revival of the homosexual transference, but no longer abstract and cold as at the beginning of the treatment. Now, instead, these fantasies were quite painful and worried him; they were accompanied by disturbing physical sensations in his bottom and his testicles.

B brought a dream in which *he was on a boat with a friend. He was also in the sea as a drowned man, and even reduced to a skeleton. Both of them were trying to rescue the skeleton.* After this dream he said that the following day would be his birthday. I interpreted that he was showing me the feeling of having had a dead part of him since his birth (mentioning his birthday seemed to me an allusion to his birth). But he interrupted me, affirming that he had always felt his mother as a dead person. I (represented by his friend on the boat) and he were trying to rescue that part of him.

After the summer holidays, he showed a tendency to cut himself off from me more clearly. He mentioned masturbation without sexual excitement, as if it were something mechanical. He communicated his fantasy of a nice breakfast with me (the session is at 8 a.m.) and associated an excursion with his grandfather and a good breakfast in a luxurious hotel. But he remembered that suddenly his pleasure was spoilt by thinking of a homosexual contact he had had with his brother previously. He brought another association about the house of an enuretic child, which smelt of urine. This shows, in my opinion, a continuous alternation between a contact with me (the nice breakfast with his grandfather) and an encapsulation away from me represented by the homosexual relationship with his brother (which seems almost a relationship with himself), by the cold masturbation, and by the enuresis, both being ways of finding strong bodily sensations in himself, as autistic children are thought to do.

Eventually B dreamt of *a tunnel,* which he associated with the inside of the maternal body, and he added that many people imagined they were being sheltered by it, but he did not. He commented on his feeling of having been rejected since that time, and that monsters and witches are inside the maternal body.

At this point some fascination about destruction and death started appearing in the analysis, giving me the feeling of meeting with a kind of madness, a nucleus of his personality that was not far from psychosis. The association between death and madness seemed confirmed by a Monday session, when he started with the following dream: *"My grandfather is dead, I can see a lift which carries my grandfather's clothes. I think that it cannot be my grandfather because he is dead, it can only be his clothes."* He added more dream material, rather confused. After that, he took notice of some shelves that had been installed during the weekend; the struts supporting the shelves were touching both the floor and the ceiling. B commented that maybe the ceiling was fragile and could not stand the push of the shelves against it. I think he realized that I had difficulty in being able to stand the pressure of his psychotic part, but, on the other hand, he certainly had the feeling of being too fragile himself. So he and I were equalized through projective identification. The general impression was that something ill-defined was going on, and in the countertransference I felt myself fragmented. I tried to interpret, saying that B felt me only as clothes and pure appearance, so that the analysis itself could become only a formality.

In another session he stated that masturbation attracted him more than having a woman. Masturbation had the advantage that he could do it when he wanted, he didn't have to convince a woman to agree. In my opinion the patient had some knowledge of the existence of a psychotic island inside him, full of an almost delusional omnipotence. But he could be defiant in his perverse attachment to his illness.

Such defence seems confirmed by a session in which B started telling me that he did not want to talk about what he had done the previous night and the day before. But he told me the following dream: *"From a window of a palace overlooking the sea, I can see a storm. A dog is in the rough sea: maybe it is dead, maybe it is playing, but instead, it is drowning. I do not want to rescue it. I go back inside the house, and I see an old lady who lives in a flat furnished in an English style. She disgusts me, and I go away."*

There was silence, and I felt a very strong emotion. There was no proper association, and so I said that the dog represented him, who maybe was playing (he did not want to tell me what he had done) but maybe was really drowning. I meant that he realized that there was no space for jokes, and that he risked been drowned if he did not cooperate with me in his analysis. He wanted to let the dog drown, and he rejected the lady who invited him into her flat with the English furniture, representing me (B was aware that I had spent several years in London). After my interpretation he talked about the previous night. He had not been able to detach himself from the television set, he could only change the programmes. When he found a suitable programme, he masturbated. He went to bed at almost 3 a.m. and read until 4 a.m. He stayed in bed until 1 p.m. and masturbated again. (I was aware that he would have an important and difficult examination in two days' time.) His comment was that he was attached to the television by a kind of passion. Later in the session he added that at the beginning of the same night he had seen a programme about a singer who committed suicide.

Now I would like to make a few comments about this case. One can see that his more superficial defences—those that appeared at the beginning of the analysis—were mainly obsessional. But later on in the analysis B's withdrawal of affects became more dramatic, even more pathological. This reached its highest point when he mentioned his compulsive masturbation and his cold isolation from me, from people, from work. His isolation was sought or at least reinforced by a perverse attachment to himself. In this way, B was expressing a very ill part of his personality, something that he had kept isolated in order to survive. We can presume that that part, a kind of emotional death, was what some authors describe as the persistence of an autistic nucleus from childhood in the neurotic adult.

As far as I know, the first person who mentioned such nuclei was H. Sydney Klein (1980), who demonstrated, with some clinical examples, that often people who suffered from such autistic nuclei were successful professionals. In spite of his youth, we could say that this was the case with B.

Tustin (1986) elaborated extensively on the way people can grow up coping with autistic features in a precarious equilibrium. But there are other authors, after Klein and Tustin, who have discussed this problem. Innes-Smith mentions pockets of autistic functioning that can characterize an interminable analysis marked by implacable and repetitive resistances. These pockets of autistic functioning could have their origin in relation to a mother as a "sensation object" and would entail a relatively undifferentiated autosensuality (Innes-Smith, 1987).

Gomberoff and others affirm that the fusion of the autistic object with the self implies that separation produces laceration, a kind of mutilation (Gomberoff, 1990).

Mitrani (1992) says that further discrimination is necessary, in our work, in order to distinguish between the analysis of these autistic mental states, which are related to the threat of unintegration, and those still primitive yet more organized states of mind that involve anxieties of a paranoid–schizoid or depressive nature. The mothers of patients who suffer from such autistic states are felt to be both too close and too far away (too much closeness on a physical level, compensating for a frailty of emotional contact). This author quotes the case of "Bill", who used to speak of masturbation as a means of stopping some physical reactions clearly equivalent to anxiety. Quickly and controllably, by his own hand, he would have his "little death". This is reminiscent of the obsessional masturbation of my patient B.

Clinical vignette: "Miss C"

The existence of a real autistic nucleus seems more evident in another patient, a young woman in her late twenties.

"Miss C" came for treatment because of depression, loneliness, and episodes of self-aggression. She used to cut or burn her arms in a compulsive way. She was attractive and highly intelligent, and her professional achievement was considerable. I cannot remember any obviously obsessional rituals, but I am sure she had an obsessional structure. C was able to spend many sessions in endless ruminations about her not wanting to think, not wanting to feel, not wanting to talk to me.

Apparently she was emotionally isolated from me, but once, when I mentioned holidays as a separation from me, she surprised me by saying: "And what about the separation from one session to the next?"

She was considerably absorbed by rumination in one session in which she expressed her concern about the possibility of getting any good results from the analysis. She was convinced that there was no point in coming without talking (actually, she was not more silent than most of my other patients), so perhaps it would be more sensible to stop the analysis. She could commit suicide. But at the same time she had a fantasy of the analysis lasting for ever.

The following session she started by saying: "I thought a lot about you in the last 24 hours (this was highly unusual—generally she tended to avoid expressing feelings about me), and I have realized that you exist even when I do not come to the session. Last night I went to visit my parents, and at 11 p.m., coming back home, I had the temptation to pass in front of your house in order to see if you really existed. Of course I did not." My interpretation was that she seemed surprised that I existed as a separate entity, that I was not just an extension of her body and her mind, as would be the case if I existed only when I was with her. She accepted the interpretation and added that her mother forced her to stay in that state of detachment.

The following day she said she was not able to do any work. She did not answer the phone either in her office or at home. It was clearly the expression in the transference, of cutting any link with me. In addition to that, from the point of view of the countertransference, I felt quite somnolent and isolated, as if responding to a charming invitation not expressed verbally: let us drop any unpleasant feeling. It was the first time that I thought of autistic children, who often seem unable to receive communications.

A few sessions later, she was panicky. She said she was frightened of finding just herself and nothing. I interpreted that she felt the nothingness as a quality of mine. This also reminded me of autistic children.

Finally I want to quote something peculiar, which occurred near a Christmas break. C was worried about a possible cut in the number of her sessions (her private insurance had decided not to pay any more, and she was adamant that she could not afford to pay for five sessions a week). As in the case of B, a desperate reaction was aroused by an external danger threatening the treatment. But C was worried about the Christmas break as well (which coincided with the first anniversary of her brother's death). In a Monday session, she talked about being in a dark corner and at the dead end, and I made a general comment about her being in despair (dark), with the feeling that at the depth there was some kind of death. She reacted angrily, saying that it was I who put her into an impossible situation, into a hopeless corner.

In the following session she was almost paralysed, and she kept mainly silent, only stressing that her version of the dark corner and mine were very different from each other. I said something to do with my not being able to see the difference, but now I think I was wrong. Not only had I rejected the patient's projection, but I had also shown her that the problem was hers and not mine.

John Steiner (1993) has differentiated "patient-centred" interpretations from "analyst-centred" interpretations, the latter showing the patient how the patient feels the analyst's attitude towards him to be. This kind of interpretation should be privileged at the beginning of the treatment and when the patient's pathology is quite severe, as in this case.

On Wednesday C said that she had thought a lot about the two different versions of the dark corner, and she decided to draw them. After some hesitation she handed her drawing to me. Clearly this "acting in" was due to her distress and to the feeling that verbal communication between us was either impossible or useless. At that time, I felt as if I had a child in analysis, and instinctively I took the drawing and looked at it. I will try to describe it now, as well as I can. On the left (her version of the dark corner): a lot of black, like a black wall or Imam, and a black-dressed lady seen from her back, facing towards the vertex of the corner (where there was some brilliant yellow). On the right (my version): a clown, sitting in a restricted space inside a geometric shape, and some lines, which were converging towards a comer. No colour, except the clown's hat, which was red. The only association she brought was that the yellow was the light. My tentative interpretation was that, from her point of view, she could have been hopeful: there was light (brilliant yellow) at the vertex, at some distance, as in fairy-tales when children get lost in the forest at night. Instead, she felt I had put her into a sterilized setting, lifeless, without living space, without colour, only geometry (clearly I had in mind what all authors imagine should be the autistic child's internal world). But, I went on, the only exception to the colourless atmosphere was the red cap, and I suggested that this stood for blood and fire, and so violence—the only feeling she felt I had left to her (of course I had in my mind her burning and cutting her arms). At the end of the session, she collected the drawing.

The following day C started wondering to what extent her impression of the way I was treating her was a projection of her own.

So it seems that in this case the autistic imprisonment was felt by the patient as the consequence of my persecution. Only later did the acknowledgement of my contribution to this (even if not expressed verbally to her) modify our dialogue and the atmosphere of the sessions. The patient was then able to have better and more complete insight.

In other cases, instead, the attraction towards the closed-in space and towards the isolation, which we could call "claustrophilia" is immediately recognized by the patient as coming from inside himself or herself.

Clinical vignette: "D"

A 15-year-old girl, "D", for example, communicated her habit of reading in order to avoid seeing anybody, for instance when she was waiting for the bus. She went on to say that sometimes at school she felt as if she was in a glass box, of the same kind as the ones used for television games, and she wished her school-mates were in the same situation. She would have been happy to have everybody communicating through headphones.

D remembered a science-fiction tale in which the pupils of the twenty-first century were working each on his own in front of a computer. These children read a story that described the schools of the twentieth century, where the pupils talked to each other, made noise, and had the physical presence of the teachers. The children of the twenty-first century were amazed and said that maybe the previous century's schools were better, and their pupils lucky. "How could these young people think that it was better before, how could they not realize that they themselves were the lucky ones", was D's comment.

In this girl the autistic nucleus is more evident than in other cases, where it can be reached only through some psychoanalytic work. But again we know that D can function in her life, even if in restricted way.

We can see from the literature that other serious pathological cores, in addition to autistic nuclei, can persist in individuals who function in a more or less satisfactory way.

As long ago as in 1957, Hanna Segal wrote:

> Some integration and whole object relations can be achieved in the depressive position, accompanied by the splitting off of the earlier ego experiences. In this situation, something like a pocket of schizophrenia exists isolated in the ego and is a constant threat to stability. At worst, a mental breakdown occurs and earlier anxieties and split-off symbolic equations invade the ego. At best, a relatively mature but restricted ego can develop and function. [pp. 59–60]

Later Herbert Rosenfeld in his paper "The Relationship between Psychosomatic Symptoms and Latent Psychotic States", affirmed: "In this paper I have tried to illustrate the existence of encapsulated psychotic parts of the self which I call psychotic islands, which exist in many people who suffer from neurotic symptoms but generally appear to be not seriously ill" (Rosenfeld, 1978, p. 27).

Probably the obsessional structure is particularly apt to cope with the walled-off parts of the personality. For instance, in their comment on "On Narcissism: An Introduction" by Freud (1914c)

Segal, and Bell quote the case of a patient who had a psychotic breakdown in the past, but at present she showed marked obsessional behaviour. This woman often had to engage in obsessive counting rituals at various points in the session to ward off "catastrophe" which usually meant her death, the analyst's death, or her parents' death (Segal & Bell, 1991, p. 171).

As a conclusion, we must assume that the passage from the paranoid–schizoid position to the depressive position is not a linear process, in which the maturation involves the whole of the personality, but rather an irregular process in which some parts develop more than others, and the latter ones can remain as split-off or walled-off nuclei.

Thus, on the one hand, we could suggest a quantitative hypothesis in that if omnipotent destructive control is the main feature of such nuclei, either an obsessional neurosis or an autistic structure develops, depending on whether more or fewer parts of the personality have been invaded. On the other hand, we also know that there is a different structural quality as well. Through obsessions, a person expresses the tendency to deny damage done in fantasy or reality, or to repair such wounds in an inefficient and grotesque way. By contrast, in autism, the desultory repetition has more the aim of giving safety and protection, like an external skeleton or a magic food.

Frances Tustin said of patient B that when he was threatened with a premature ending of the analysis, this revived the time when he had been taken away from his grandparents at the age of 8 or 9 years, and also when he was taken away from his mother, with whom he had scarcely lived. During the time in analysis when he was talking about being taken away from his grandparents, he had a dream in which he felt that *he was losing his hair and was going to die.* This reminded her of her recent realization that many autistic children have experienced a sudden break from the caring person to whom they have been unduly close, but this closeness is not an emotional one but is based on bodily sensations. The topography of this experience is very important—that is, where the sensations are located in the body. Meltzer has drawn attention to this. Since this experience is a sensation-dominated one, emotions do not enter into it. The trauma of suddenly finding that their body is separate from the body of the mother is a catastrophe that causes them to freeze up, to be paralysed, and to cease all activity. In B, the loss of his mother's body was symbolized by the fear that he was losing his hair, because his mother had been felt to be an integral part of his body. In the dream he worked over this trauma again: he was paralysed by his sensations, and his emotions were in abeyance. So here was the starting point for his obsessional neurosis, which had much in common with the experiences of autistic children. For some reason, however, a limited amount of emotional life has been left with these obsessional children. Why had they not been so grossly affected as the autistic children? Perhaps it is an inherent difference in constitutional predisposition, or perhaps there was a difference in the way the mother reacted to the situation or a combination of the two. Perhaps obsessional neurosis is associated with mothers who are predominantly too far away, whereas autism is associated with mothers who are predominantly too close.

NOTE

I am very grateful to Mrs Elizabeth Spillius for her invaluable comments and suggestions.

CHAPTER EIGHT

The anal organization of the instincts: a note on theories past and present

Edna O'Shaughnessy

This chapter explores the changes in Freud's theory of successive libidinal stages during the subsequent evolution of psychoanalytic thinking, looking especially at the anal stage. Melanie Klein saw all zones as operating simultaneously. Edna O'Shaughnessy describes various body splits, front and back or upper and lower parts, and illustrates this in a patient with obsessional neurosis who withdrew from relating to a dead breast and slipped down into an idealized anal psychic retreat. His despair about reparation, his imprisoned pain, was defended against by a controlling, perverse, and sadistic transference. She believes that if anal sadism dominates the child's object relations, it is an abnormal development.

In the field of psychoanalysis, when a new theory wins acceptance, the old often lingers and co-exists with the new, without the two being placed in formal juxtaposition. I should like to return to Freud's concept of an anal organization of the instincts and discuss it in the light of later psychoanalytic findings. I suggest that, like a trunk in the attic stuffed with all kinds of things from the past, we keep it because we know there are things of much value there, even though we never sort them out. On reading again Freud's *Three Essays on Sexuality* (1905d), one is struck with awe. Freud was the pioneer in a vast terrain of sexuality, development, and pathology. I discuss the evolution, as psychoanalysis has progressed, of one strand of his thinking about sexuality—namely, his theory of successive libidinal phases—oral, anal, phallic, genital. The psychic importance of all the erotogenic zones is accepted by analysts, but for a long time there have been new hypotheses about their interaction—that is, that they interact not consecutively in a linear course of development, but simultaneously. Yet, as Kernberg (1969) has remarked, the idea of a consecutive sequence of libidinal phases still exerts a powerful hold on the psychoanalytic imagination.

Many analysts have questioned Freud's conception of successive pre-genital organizations of the libido. I offer a Kleinian approach, which could be put this way: there is not a stage of *normal* development that can properly be called an anal stage; rather, from the beginning, the anal zone enters into the infant's awareness in an important though subsidiary way to orality, and it continues to play a changing and complex but normally always subsidiary role as development proceeds to genitality and the Oedipus complex. Moreover, I would add, where there is an organization of the instincts such as to merit the description of "anal", this is a pathological organization, most probably defensive in origin.

Freud revised *The Three Essays* (1905d) many times, but he did not incorporate into them two major new conceptions from his late thinking: his changed view of anxiety as a primary emotion in its own right, and his final theory of the instincts as a duality of life and death instincts. However, in *Beyond the Pleasure Principle* (1920g) he made a brief attempt to connect the life and death instincts with instinctual development, and straight away he met the dilemma that the instinct of aggression destroyed the object that should remain in existence to be loved. As he put it, "during the oral stage of organisation of the libido, the act of obtaining erotic mastery over an object coincides with that object's destruction" (p. 54). This dilemma of how two instincts—one of destruction and the other of life—can operate conjointly and yet preserve the object was resolved by Melanie Klein's concept of splitting. She postulated that in earliest development self and object are split: a persecuting object receives and threatens destruction, and an ideal object receives and provides love and gratification. This theory makes use of Freud's changed view of anxiety as autonomous, developing it further by differentiating anxiety into persecutory and depressive. And, as is well known, Melanie Klein formulated a new theory of development in which the instincts were no longer conceived as developing in a sequence of psychosexual phases— oral, anal, phallic, genital—but instead were seen as simultaneously operative in internal and external object relations, body parts and zones, anxieties, and unconscious phantasies. Initially, in her view, in what she called the paranoid–schizoid position while the oral libido is still in the lead, anxieties about persecutors are the source of anal phantasies of expelling dangerous inner contents from the self into the object to relieve the self, and to penetrate, control, and possess the object. Not only does the infant gradually split his love from his hate and his objects into gratifying and persecuting, he also makes a split in his body: the upper part of the body and head—through the introjection of, and identification with, objects felt to have space for him—become the infant's good places for introjected objects, in contradistinction to his bottom, which in phantasy is felt as a bad chamber, where bad objects are kept and from where they can also be evacuated. Sometimes such a split is between the front of the body and the back. Periodically the normal infant loses the splits he has achieved and becomes confused about his impulses, his objects, and his bodily zones; and periodically he also feels that he does not retain his good objects, and that, for example, they slip down into his bottom, becoming urine and faeces, so leaving him with only internal persecutors. In the main, however, his relations with ideally gratifying objects will predominate over his struggles with bad objects, and his growth through the building-up of his inner world as well as his relation to external good objects will be oral and invested with oral meanings.

If, however, normal development does not take place, either because of deficiencies in the object or because of physical or emotional difficulties in the infant or both, one form of abnormal development is a psychic retreat from primary oral object relations, and a turning instead to anality, so that the anal zone, instead of being subsidiary, becomes the centre of the infant's and young child's experience.

Clinical vignette: "Mr G"

By way of illustration, here is the infantile history, as I reconstructed it from his analysis, of a patient, "Mr G", who was assessed in consultation as suffering from an obsessional neurosis.

As an infant, Mr G had retreated from oral relations with a breast that he had experienced as unresponsive, or even dead. A heavy, deadening contact in which he was at a distance occurred over and over again between him and me in the analysis, and seemed to be primary. Mr G pictured this situation in various dreams; for example, one dream was about *an animal that had a distorted jaw with a long shape because it had been trampled on*—an accurate picture of both his long and expressionless face and also of the heavy "trampling" effect of the words he spoke, as if from far away without awareness of meaning, which crushed vitality in me, in the manner I think in which vitality had been crushed in him. It emerged that in unconscious phantasy he felt he had withdrawn into himself and slipped down into his bottom, which he idealized as his home and which became a zone of intense experience containing the emotional parts of himself. His mouth and body surface were felt to lose their living qualities and be only a husk that encased him, a husk from within which he spoke. This abnormal splitting of his self into an outer dead shell—later we saw that he also idealized it as a high penis superior for its very unresponsiveness: a phallus in the sense given to it by Birksted-Breen (1996)—and a lower living kernel meant that the fundamental normal splits were not made, and in the manner described by Rosenfeld (1950), whose patient was also preoccupied with faeces, many confusions set in. My patient felt his head was like a bottom and functioned like a rectum or bladder: it filled with stuff—impulses, words, images, notions that entered and left it outside his voluntary control or interest. His bottom was exalted and confused with a breast, and his omnipotent phantasies were confused with reality. His withdrawal of himself was felt to destroy further the living links between him and his objects, as it did between him and me, and made him feel more deprived and anxious, which in turn increased both his evacuation of the confused and persecuting contents of his internal world and his anal sadistic control of everyone. This underlying unconscious situation was gradually revealed only after considerable analytic work, during which Mr G controlled me to the point of torture and expelled into me words he took no interest in and about which he was unsure whether they had meaning or were worthless.

In an anal organization such as Mr G's, we see a particular balance of the instincts. There is a marked emergence of a death instinct, which is opposed to his life instinct's impulses to connect, preserve, and love. Freud gives this description of the two instincts in *Civilization and its Discontents* (1930a): "Besides the instinct to preserve living substance and to join it into ever larger units, there . . . exist[s] another, contrary instinct seeking to dissolve those units. . . ." And in particular, Freud's clinical finding was that in the anal character the balance of the instincts is such that love and hate are of equal intensity.

I could put it this way. When there is an anal organization of the instincts, neither plain love nor plain aggression is possible. In place of open love—or, better said, love in the open—a desired object must be seduced into and kept trapped in the bottom, which degrades and harms it, and in place of frank aggression that could lead to a hostile object, the object is controlled into complying with sadistic treatment. As Mr G's analysis proceeded, exactly such a confused, sadistic, and perverse relationship—at root a defence against his despair about the repair of himself or his objects— emerged in the transference. His anal organization of his instincts was clearly defensive in origin and of far-reaching pathology. In this regard, it is interesting to note that Abraham connected the anal character not only with obsessional neurosis but also with melancholia.

My general contention is that an anal organization, in the sense of *erotized anal primacy*, is a defence against some unbearable psychic situation. Like other forms of narcissistic withdrawal, it may be temporarily needed and used in the course of development when object relations, for one reason or another, become too persecuting or too damaged (often felt in a confused way as self and object being reduced to faeces), but if it persists and predominates, it has become pathology. In working with Mr G, it was the understanding of his underlying state of despair and his feelings of confusion about his impulses and his objects—were they good or bad? dead or alive?—which, more than anything else, helped towards a relinquishing of his anal organization.

Abraham (1924) illustrates the predicament that arises where there is a failure of splitting (as we could now conceive of it) between good and bad objects. He gives an account of a melancholic patient who remembered how

> A road was being constructed in his native town and the workmen had dug up some shells. One side of them was covered with earth and looked dirty, but the other side glistened like mother of pearl. . . . The idea of mother-of-pearl shells, moreover, proved in analysis to be a means of representing his ambivalent attitude towards his mother. The word "mother-of-pearl" expressed his high esteem for his mother as a "pearl". But the smooth shining surface was deceptive—the other side was not so beautiful. In likening this other side which was covered with dirt (excrement) to his "wicked" mother, from whom he had to withdraw his libido, he was abusing her and holding her up to scorn. [pp. 446–447]

Melanie Klein's (1952) huge shift of psychoanalytic theory away from a linear libidinal progression through oral, anal, phallic, and genital phases to a new conception of development as the vicissitudes of self, object, and instincts through two constellations, the paranoid–schizoid and the depressive positions, and her clinical analytic finding that, rather than a succession, there was an interaction, of oral, anal, and genital sensations and impulses, plus her discovery of the mechanism of projective identification, opened the way to research on a new basis. A key contribution in this area was made by Meltzer (1966) in his paper on "The Relation of Anal

Masturbation to Projective Identification". He shows how by the mechanism of projective identification the contents of the rectum are confused with desired objects and become idealized, and he examines the pseudo-maturity that results in a personality based on such anal confusions.

H. Sydney Klein, in an important paper "Notes on a Case of Ulcerative Colitis" (1965), describes a patient whose anal zone had become the leading zone, both in being afflicted with a serious physical illness, ulcerative colitis, and also in being the central carrier of the confusions and psychic meanings of a serious psychological illness. Sydney Klein writes (p. 342):

> My hypothesis is that we are dealing with a fixation at an early stage of development when the infant is unable to differentiate between physical pain or discomfort and its emotional counterpart. Because of the experience that defecation gets rid of painful or unpleasant intestinal feelings, the infant believes he can get rid of emotional feelings in the same way. . . . These feelings may be of anxiety, persecution, guilt, jealousy, envy, confusion, uncertainty, concern or loss. As parts of the ego are also expelled the result is weakening and impoverishment of the personality. [p. 342]

Sydney Klein's next reference is to Bion. And it is of course pre-eminently Bion who, in highly original work on disorders of thought, showed how the mind, instead of thinking, under certain stressful internal and external conditions functions like a rectum, evacuating intolerable contents. Sydney Klein's patient told him that "as a child he always thought the trains entered and left the tube by the same exits", which seems to be (he was getting better by then) his verbal expression of all ins and outs, being for him into or out of an anal "tube". It is of interest to note Sydney Klein's use of language in his paper. He does not speak of "anal organizations" or "the anal character": instead, he speaks of his patient's thinking or being unable to think, his terrible anxieties, doubts, and confusions about impulses, self, and objects and, above all— their multifarious *anal meanings* to him. All of this was there in Freud and Abraham, but not with so central an emphasis, because their overall theory was then so different.

How should we now conceive of what was formerly termed the anal–sadistic stage of development, Freud's second stage of libidinal development, occurring approximately between the ages of two and four? What about that mastery of the anal sphincter? As described, for instance, by Laplanche and Pontalis (1973):

> The stage is characterised by an organisation of the libido under the primacy of the anal erotogenic zone. The object relationship at this time being invested with meanings having to do with the function of defecation (expulsion/retention) and with the symbolic value of faeces. The anal–sadistic stage sees the strengthening of sado-masochism in correlation with the development of muscular control. [p. 35]

Surely this describes not a normal child but a seriously disturbed child, like Sydney Klein's patient or Mr G, who withdraws from open and direct contact with his objects into an alternative world, a claustrum in his bottom?

What used to be seen as behavioural indications of the anal phase—that is, the child's tendencies to cling, to control, to possess—will most probably have been there all along, though previously expressed differently, perhaps more minutely, as part of his response to objects whose separateness causes him anxiety, but now, at this age, his increased muscularity and above all mobility to run after and clutch make such impulses more grossly visible. And what used to be referred to as the "toilet-training struggle" between a child clinging to anal pleasures and an adult frustrating these and instilling him with shame and disgust about his excreta would now be seen differently as a time of further working through, or not, of the infantile neurosis in the particular constellation that it is for an individual child. The child may have to overcome anxieties that his faeces are persecutors; for instance, one small child was frightened to use the pot or the lavatory because he dared not let his faeces out from the secure prison of his bottom into an open space, where they would no longer be under his control and could fly back at him. Faeces may also have an opposite meaning, be felt not as too bad, but as too good for the lavatory, and a child may experience the demands of the parents and the culture for toilet training as a confrontation with his unconscious delusions. Unconsciously, he may have concrete equations in Hanna Segal's (1957) sense that his faeces are food, a penis, or babies, or he may believe they have magic and power, and resist their de-exaltation and the seeing of them for what they are—excreta, not to be preserved.

In addition, the ongoing oedipal situation may arouse further anxieties and confusions at this time: a small boy may fear, for example, that the adult who is trying to toilet-train him is trying to castrate him, or conversely, a child may misinterpret the adult's interest in his excretory functions as a consummation of his oedipal strivings. Anal theories of birth and sexual intercourse, while they may be a child's first attempt to comprehend the parent's sexuality, are also a denial of painful differences between himself and his parents and his exclusion from their relationship and express his hatred by bringing them down to a "lower" and "dirty" level. Meanwhile, in this complex and individually very variable picture, there will be quite opposite tendencies. Through his love for and identification with his objects and his wish to make reparation to them for his earlier phantasied excremental attacks, the child will himself aspire to a proper use of the toilet and will also be trying to relinquish some of his possessiveness. Failure to allow any freedom, or a long continuation of soiling and wetting, suggests that there are underlying disturbances that, for whatever reason, are not being worked through.

At this time, it has also to be remembered, there are significant new horizons for the child. The growth in his comprehension and use of language plays at least as significant a role as his mastery of the anal sphincter. Words offer him symbols to counteract and supplant his infantile concrete equations and the opportunity to express himself and gratify his curiosity in new ways. Language will be part of his working through, with an increased scope, unconscious conflicts in his play. All this is to emphasize that normally a small person, notwithstanding his conflicts, keeps a predominantly loving relation to his objects, and that if anal sadism is the prototype of his object relations, it is an abnormal development. I think few analysts, though many may differ on specific formulations, would disagree with the general tenor of my argument—namely, that oral, anal, and genital trends interact during development rather than, as the early theory had it, being in sequence with an organization that is a stage for each.

Why, then, is it that our psychoanalytic imagination is powerfully held by the idea of a consecutive sequence of libidinal phases, as Kernberg says? Very briefly, I think it is because we do not want to—and we should not—lose the great insights that are tied up with this idea in Freud's and Abraham's writings, even though we tend not to do the laborious work of sorting out what we want to keep and what we want to throw away—not even in the rough-and-ready way I have tried to do here. Freud's (1909d) "Notes upon a Case of Obsessional Neurosis", for instance, is a great domain of psychoanalytic understanding about anal erotism and the existence, in parallel with the ordinary world and ordinary thinking, of a weird universe of compelling, concrete phantasy. We, with our different theories, understand and learn from the Rat Man because the conceptions and clinical descriptions are from the hand of a master, and because our own current theories are, in any case, new developments of Freud's theories, which, like all great creative new thought, opens the way to further advances.

CHAPTER NINE

When the bough breaks:
working with parents and infants

Ruth Safier

This chapter returns again to the theme elaborated in chapter 5: the intrusion into the child of the caregiver's own traumatic experience. Ruth Safier discusses parent–infant therapy with a particular focus on those mothers who are at the extreme end of the containment spectrum—that is, those who project their own anxieties into their babies. She illustrates how these infants are swamped with the mother's problems while their own primary anxieties are not touched. She also relates some of the very painful insights arising from this work to psychoanalytic technique.

W orking directly with parents and infants offers the psychoanalyst another vantage point from which to observe primitive mental mechanisms, and a ringside seat to the tragedy of psychopathology in the making. The challenge for the analyst lies in intervening before the patterns of failure become entrenched. There may also be implications for work with the adult patient in analysis.

This is painful and disturbing work, and the impact on the therapist is very direct. Dilys Daws (1993) says that the acute emotionality that is a feature of the work with parents and infants is both the reason for them presenting and also the vehicle for change.

After an examination of how the presence of the baby in the room affects the process, the main focus of this chapter is on containment and failures of containment, considering the continuum from reverie and normal projective identification through varying degrees of failures of the container, and concentrating specifically on the extreme end of that continuum, where the mother uses the baby as a receptacle for her own anxieties.

How this affects the infant's mind and its development, how this is defended against, and what the implications are for growth, self–object differentiation, and the possibility of concern, reparation, and, therefore, hope are important questions. It is also important to think about what factors might mitigate the baby's experience.

The influence of infant observation

One of the lessons learned from baby observation is that when one is released from the need to make sense and to interpret, then it is possible to observe much more accurately whole sequences of behaviour. It is also striking to see how many unspoken hypotheses are wrong. Unlike the frequent difficulty in recording a session of analytic work, it is often possible to record an observation session in accurate detail—almost like turning on a video-recorder and recording verbatim. This suggests that often interpretations are premature and closing off, frequently derailing the sequence and the sense of what is being communicated. Might a premature interpretation be evidence of the analyst's anxiety projected into the patient?

Another lesson from baby observation is the question of deciding to *whom* the central experience or feeling belongs—is it baby's, mother's, sibling's, or observer's? I came to understand that this was really a question that came further down the track, that the first issue is *what* the feeling is, and only later does *whose* feeling it is become relevant. Alvarez (1992) adds that the last question to ask is *why*? I think we often ask *why* in order to avoid *what* is going on in the session. This is probably true with all patients. In working with parents and infants, identification of the dominant emotion can be reliably hypothesized as the feeling that is directed towards the infant and that needs to be put into words.

The impact of having the baby in the room

Selma Fraiberg (1980), one of the pioneers in infant mental health, said that having a baby in the room is a bit like having God on your side.

The perinatal period presents a developmental crisis for all involved. It is a time of marked vulnerability, when defences are down, and there is a great openness to the possibility of change. However disturbed the relationship, parents universally want their babies to have a better experience than their own, so their motivation is high.

The baby usually helps by demonstrating the issues at stake very clearly, often dramatizing the conflict in ways that allow the analyst to speak with clarity and authority. And because both analyst and parent watch the same piece of behaviour, it carries much more force and is less easy to dismiss, deny, or ignore. For instance, after we have watched her 15-month-old son freeze with fear, a young mother says: "I would hate him to be scared of me." But she can hear me say that it is very important that we don't pretend not to have seen what was in front of our eyes, so that he does not have to have the same experience as she has had.

Another example is a very obsessional woman, who has a 4-week-old son. She is struggling to hold herself together with frantic overactivity and cannot recognize the precarious state she is in. In the session the baby repeatedly falls apart and struggles to reestablish himself around the nipple or dummy. It is possible to help her to see how fragile he is and how as yet he has only a limited capacity to organize himself, and that this is very frightening for her because it reflects how she is feeling at the moment.

The presence of the baby affects how one *is* as a therapist. I say *is* rather than what one *does* because I consider what I do to be analytic in the sense that I use a firm frame, depend absolutely on the transference and, more particularly, the countertransference to inform me, and only offer observation, thought, and interpretation. There is, of, course a clear therapeutic aim, and in this sense it cannot be said to be analytic. Being face to face with the patient in the presence of a baby does not allow the neutrality or impassivity of the more usual stance.

An additional reinforcement comes from the fact that the baby is almost always aware of the analyst as someone who holds the hope of help and understanding. It is noticeable in infant observation, in parent–infant therapy, and in analysis when the patient brings her baby to the session that when the relationship between mother and baby is going well, the baby has little need for the analyst, and the main thrust of the relating is between mother and baby—as it should be, particularly at the start. But when there are difficulties, the infant actively seeks and recognizes an ally. Infants of only a few weeks are able to make sustained eye contact throughout a session. The infant seems to have an innate understanding that there is an object with particular qualities that is needed. I have never seen a baby so afraid or persecuted that it will not make contact. "Oh", says a young mother, within minutes of sitting down, "You're a hit. I've never seen her do that before." Parents say "He likes being here", or "she seems to feel comfortable with you". For very narcissistic and defended parents who could never allow themselves to say or to feel this on their own behalf, this is useful in itself.

However regressed and disturbed the mother, and whatever her transference to a parental figure in the analyst, she is, nevertheless, also in the room as the mother to her infant, with all the responsibilities this involves. It is she who carries the baby, feeds it, changes it. Moreover, her role as mother is valued, and the difficulties and importance of it are addressed usually quite explicitly. So there is an alliance and a pact with the adult, mothering, sane, verbal part of the person of the parent, to look at and think about a baby, real and external but also internal. (Adults in analysis are often terrified that allowing access to a baby part means jettisoning the adult, sane, coping aspects of the personality.)

The aim of the therapeutic endeavour is to improve the relationship between mother and child, so the transference and identifications addressed are more focused between mother and baby, and less between analyst and patient. Of course, the information about that relationship comes from and through the transference and countertransference but is directed towards this other relationship. In a way this defuses the transference and also makes it possible for the analyst to articulate, and for the mother to accept, interventions that would be threatening and unacceptable in one-to-one work at the beginning. For instance, when the baby starts to cry bitterly at the end of the session, as often happens, it is natural to address the baby directly and say that it is so hard to be put out and sent away before you are ready or that it is awful to be interrupted in the middle of a feed or a game. Or when a toddler becomes inconsolable and wants to take a toy away as something to hold on to, or is angry at being sent off, the child is addressed directly, but the parent implicitly. It is a good working reminder of the impact on our analytic patients when we say to them, "our time is up".

The parent—and it is usually the mother—*sees* how I respond to the baby. For it is impossible not to respond to a baby. The reality of that response goes some way towards contradicting the phantasies she may have about how the baby part of her is seen, liked, disliked, criticized, and so on. There is a frank and direct reality testing, which means that, from the start, the mother is more able to be an ally in the work.

The mother sees the analyst's attitude towards the baby as being one of warmth, interest, respect for the baby's capacities, as well as the assumption that what the baby does has meaning. This is likely to have a very big impact on the mother, on her view of the baby, and also on her view of herself. All this is unspoken, enacted, and visible. It is like an interpretation in action or a non-verbal interpretation (Paul & Thompson-Salo, 1997). And it seems to speak to infantile and adult parts of mother simultaneously in a way that is often hard to get right.

Asking mother to observe, think about, and make links immediately makes the mother more separate from the baby and more
able and more supported in the task of thinking about the baby. In
asking "Why do you think he started crying just then, or spitting
up, etc.?" one allows the parent to see the analyst as an observing
scientist rather than a God-like figure (N. Symington, 1996) who
has all the answers.

But of course there is another side—those times when the actual danger to the child makes it hard to think and therefore acts as
a restraint. Danger to the child is impossible to ignore. At times, as
Frances Thompson-Salo says (Paul & Thompson-Salo, 1997), there
is a moral imperative and a developmental imperative to inter-
vene—for instance, to notify where there is clear danger to the
child, or in the case of the child of a deeply depressed and unresponsive mother, to give the infant another experience. Recent
research on the different attachment models developing in the
same individual bears this out. Even brief exposure to others may
provide a mitigating alternate attachment model.

Containment and the failures of containment

The need and the request for containment is the most strikingly
evident issue with the parent and infant who come for help, and
the first task of the analyst is to demonstrate that chaos and anxiety
can be tolerated, and that it is possible to think about mental pain
without becoming overwhelmed. While the cause of the anxiety
may not be understood immediately, nevertheless it can be borne.

In order to get development going at all, the infant's first need
is for a containing object, and this is also the first need of the
patient. This first need is described in slightly different ways by
different writers. For Bick (1964), it is the mother's attention that
binds the parts of the personality together. For Winnicott (1965),
the mother's role is to become preoccupied with the baby and also
to hold the baby. Bion (1962a) presents us with the notion of the
need for the mother to hold the baby in the mind, to think about
the baby and its father with love. When this happens, the baby can

internalize both the container and its function (alpha function). Perhaps this is best summarized as the need for overwhelming anxiety to be transformed into thought. This means that reality can be faced. So it is not, then, a surprise that containment is at the centre of the work and especially at the start. Moreover, this request is urgent, raw, and graphic and often concretely expressed.

Patients arrive overwhelmed by chaos and require of the analyst an ability to tolerate this chaos. They arrive early or late, with baby buggies, and all sorts of paraphernalia in tow. There is noise, crying, running up and down steps and in and out of rooms, going to toilets, and getting drinks. It is the analyst's capacity to contain this real and psychic mess that attaches the family to the therapy. After this, it becomes possible to go on and explore the projections and to try and link past, present, and future and to understand patterns of behaviour. It is probably true to say that presentation at this early time of life is always a statement about some degree of failure of the container.

It seems reasonable to think about containment as existing along a continuum. This continuum runs from the mother's capacity to receive and process the baby's persecutory feelings, and to return them in a detoxified form to the baby in what Bion (1967) called "normal reverie". It continues through to that state of the mother where there is a degree of imperviousness to infantile terrors (the mother may repudiate something in herself and therefore cannot hold it for her baby). The next step is to a situation where the mother is so disturbed and stirred up by the infant's demands that she not only cannot modify them, but she adds a quantum of her own fears to what she "sends" back to the baby. Bion suggested that when the baby's normal projective identification is rejected, then the baby is filled with nameless dread, is left to manage unmanageable feelings alone, and, in addition, is asked to carry some of the mother's projections. Finally, at the extreme end of the continuum, the mother uses the baby as a receptacle for anxieties that are entirely her own (whether or not they are stimulated by the infant is moot). It is on this end of the spectrum that I want particularly to concentrate.

It is probably a fact that all mothers project into their babies at times, and we analysts also probably project into our patients. For example, when we prematurely interpret, we perhaps make the patient bear our anxiety about the unfolding unknown.

It also needs to be said that while mothers use their babies as containers of and communicators of catastrophic anxiety and pain relating to their own earliest and unarticulated feelings, they also use their babies and their situations as constructive lifelines to help. These mothers are those who have come for help, in spite of all the tragic failures. The fate of all those other babies and children where there is no recognition that there is a problem at all is really unthinkable.

Clinical vignettes

My first experience of seeing a mother and child together took place when I was training in child psychiatry, long before I had heard the word *container*.

A 20-month-toddler was referred for assessment after his third admission for accidental poisoning and accident-proneness. In the waiting-room this child came close to demolishing anything not fixed, and a colleague who was researching attention deficit and hyperactivity disorder said to me that this was a classical hyperactive child who would probably need Melleril as well as Ritalin.

Mother was a disturbed, borderline woman, and father was an army man who was often away. In the consulting-room the child began to fling trucks and blocks around in such a violent way that I thought someone would be injured. Mother seemed ineffectual in putting a stop to this behaviour. She was more interested in letting me know about her rage with the child, the hospital, and her husband. As she talked and I listened, she settled, and the child crept onto her lap, falling into a peaceful sleep. I had made no contact with or links to the child's behaviour. This pattern was repeated every week for five weeks, and the situation at home settled down between visits. Selma Fraiberg (1980) said that when the analyst listens to the cries of the mother, then the mother is able to listen to the child. But when I went on a three-week holiday, mother returned and told me she had had a reduction mammoplasty in the interim. Shortly after this, the family moved away.

I include this example because there are many common themes here: an absent father, a borderline mother, aggressive expulsion into the child, violent responses to separations, and graphic and explicit acting out.

The second example comes from a borderline patient in analysis, who has a 4-month-old son whom she brings to the sessions.

After I had charged her for a missed session, she said little, but suddenly she decided to introduce solids into the breast-fed baby's diet. During the next two sessions the baby screamed continuously, and mother adamantly refused to accept the possibility of there being any link between the indigestible feed I had given her and the baby's distress. Here the baby had to experience something that she could not tolerate and would not allow herself to feel. A year later, in the run-up to a holiday break, the baby became ill with something indefinable. She went from one general practitioner to another and then finally had the thought that perhaps her son was suffering from an anxiety attack. This time she herself made the suggestion that it might have something to do with my pending holiday, and when she did, the child's symptoms disappeared.

The next two examples come from parent–infant therapies and are described in more detail.

Case study: "R"—a depressed woman with a personality disorder, and her boys, "E" and "K"

"R" was 38 and newly pregnant with her second child when she and 21-month-old "E" were referred to me. The presenting problem was E's sleeping difficulty, which had been present from birth. Mother had been quite severely depressed. She had sought help from a number of specialist mother–baby clinics since E was 6 weeks old, and the family was visited weekly in the home for about a year. They were referred for more intensive parent–infant therapy, because the individual therapist felt that the levels of anxiety were *devastating* and because there was a question of abuse. There was also the problem of an extraordinary mess at home, for which mother initially blamed E. It became apparent that she had always lived in state of disastrous mess and chaos and that this was a major issue in the relationship with her partner. Father was, however, largely absent, as he worked off-shore on an oil rigger for ten months a year.

In the first four assessment sessions, E's temper tantrums and mother's inability to set limits were addressed with my help. It was possible for me to show her that he was enormously relieved when she could say *no* to him, and that the annihilating anxiety she feared he'd be exposed to was really her own and not his. After this, E slept through the night.

Over the next few weeks, she became able to understand that E was in her bed because of her own need to have someone to hold on to, rather than his need. "E" then moved to a bed of his own. His language developed in a spurt, and he started to refer to himself as *myself*. Of course it did not end there, though this symptom has not returned.

Mother's history is that she was put into paid foster care from the age of 3 months, and that she and a twin sister, who was separately fostered, would spend weekends with the biological mother, returning into care for the week. This continued until she was 18 years old. Her understanding of this was that she was lucky to have two families and that she lived an exotic and unconventional life. Both she and her twin are in relationships with men who are only available very part-time and, again, this was felt to be an unconventional and fortunate style of life.

Over the five years we have worked together, R has suffered some serious depressions, and during these times, when the reality of her life and her current situation are too painful to bear, she uses both children in ways I will describe. At these times the children are in situations of high risk. On one occasion she managed to stop herself attacking the baby with a carving-knife.

I have learned a great deal from working with this family, but here I want to focus particularly on the impact of projection into the children. Initially, R was unable to come to either the last session before a break or to the first one of the new term. She told me it was a great relief not to have to come and genuinely seemed bewildered by my suggestions that she and the children might be affected or might miss me. When the younger boy, "K", was 11 months old, she arrived at the session just before the Christmas break full of anger and contempt for a young cousin, who had become very upset by not being invited to a family function. She spoke about this cousin in an unusually rough and dismissive way, saying that she had no right to be upset by being excluded, because she was not really part of the family.

R dismissed any suggestion that she was projecting her own pain about exclusion and separation into a number of external figures. But as the session continued—and, I suppose, as the projections were interpreted and she became more backed into a corner—K, the 11-month-old child who had been comfortably playing, was suddenly possessed with a catastrophic state in which he threw himself about and screamed uncontrollably. He remained inconsolable until I was able to say to her that unless she could recognize her own painful feelings, her child would be forced to feel them in her place. At this point the little boy stopped as suddenly as he had begun, as if he had been released from something alien to him, and the mother wept bitterly. Then she remembered how she had never been included in her foster family's Christmas and holidays. The question is, what does the child make of this sort of experience? It seems to me that it might be experienced as being possessed by alien feelings or of having a foreign body thrust into him.

At another time, again under the influence of the distress of a separation of the pending holiday break, mother somehow would *allow* the children to have accidents of a most distressing nature—for instance, catching E's foot in a car door when the child tried to get in to the car and she wanted him to stay at home. The feelings of being locked out are agonizingly communicated and painfully wreaked on the child. The anguish of being shut out, and the intense quality of this pain, is communicated to the analyst in a wincingly vivid way.

In this instance, the mother started off the session by telling me about the accident and about the treatment at hospital, which involved a painful needling of the nail to release blood. She told me how E had screamed for an hour. When I saw him several days later, he was sad and withdrawn and still limping. At first, R was angry that her sister had said she must feel guilty. *It was just an accident*, she said. Later, she began to think about how this was the third time that this child had had an accident just before I was due to go away. At this point she became deeply distressed and remorseful, and her complaints about E's naughtiness were replaced with concern and apology to the child. She was then flooded with memories of leaving home at the end of the weekend, of her mother never coming with her for the drive, of her father seeming angry and her foster mother getting upset if R complained or cried.

Experiences like these are shocking to hear about and painful to watch. The impression is of a child possessed by feelings that do not belong to the child, and being made to suffer pain that is unprovoked. Such children certainly make one know about the reality of projection and about the difficulty the child—and later the adult—might have in knowing what belongs to the individual and what is outside.

One technical factor stands out: when the mother is cut off from her own experience, any attempt to make her empathize with the child's predicament makes her more furious with the child and more persecuted. I have found that I need to attend to her feelings first, using the information from the child's behaviour but putting the child aside from my attention. This is not easy to do when the situation feels abusive.

This need to empathize with the mother/adult predicament first has implications for which part of the patient one addresses when one is with the adult on the couch. It has certainly made me think a great deal about which part of the patient is hearing me, and I realize that asking an adult to understand a baby part of themselves may leave them feeling very persecuted and criticized.

> Five years of work have made a difference, of course, but when R is depressed or in a rage, she can still be cruel to the children, both physically and verbally. I feel less concerned about these episodes now than I did at the beginning. After she had hurt K, the younger one, who is now 4, he said to her "*But I didn't do anything. Why did you hit me?*" and after she had lost her temper and told E that he was stupid, E could say "*I'm not stupid, Mum, I just lost my tie. You are cross.*" She was then instantly remorseful and also admiring, because she recognized that she could never have said things like this herself as a child. Although the situation is not a good one, there is enough evidence to show that as a small family unit they can talk things through in quite a significant way, and that this protects the children from much of the impact of the abuse.

Peter Fonagy's (Fonagy et al. 1991) findings are relevant here. He says that the mental health of the child, as measured by the attachment status, depends on the parents' capacity to have an articulate account of their own, even very adverse, childhood. This means that even traumatic events, if they are known, acknowledged, and named, can be encompassed, therefore the past does not have to be repeated.

The last example comes from the extreme end of the spectrum, where there is no, or minimal, or erratic awareness of the baby's experience and, instead, a use of the baby as receptacle for the mother's psychopathology.

Case study: "F" and her baby, "M"

> "F", a 22-year-old Indian woman, has a severe borderline personality disorder, at the psychotic end of the spectrum, where there is little self–object differentiation, minimal ability to feel concern and empathy, and where guilt rapidly becomes persecutory. She is the child of a frankly psychotic mother, and

her intrusions into her son, "M", made a diagnosis of Munch-hausen by proxy inescapable. This diagnosis has become more certain over time. Mother and child were referred for parent–infant psychotherapy when M was 5 months old, and a number of other agencies, including the protective office, are involved.

F is an only child. Her parents were divorced when she was four, and she has not seen her father since. F's mother has schizophrenia, and she was overtly psychotic for significant periods during F's first 16 years, and seems to have incorpo-rated her into some of her delusions. She was scheduled and hospitalized for the first time when F was 13, and this was when F first came to the attention of the authorities. The school had reported her frequent and long absences to the welfare authorities before this, but either the situation was not recog-nized or they were not able to act. This was corroborated by mental hospital records.

At 16, F left home and has since wanted no further contact with her mother because she is afraid of getting caught up again in her delusions. F is very bitter about the fact that she was left in an unmanageable situation by the authorities. M was conceived when she briefly became a sex worker in order to *explore her sexuality*. She was in a sexual relationship with another young man during the pregnancy. This ended some weeks before M's birth, but she speaks of this man as M's father and has come to believe that this is so. She decompensated during labour and spent 6 out of the first 17 weeks either in an in-patient mother–baby unit or the Children's Hospital for various feeding diffi-culties.

Before M's birth, F had had a number of therapies, including a three-month stint of psychoanalysis, which she broke off at the first break. Her analyst said that she was offended by any sort of emotional contact and that she could not tolerate him saying anything that she had not thought of first. He also felt that her whole life and personality were structured around repudiating any connection with her mother.

None of this makes her sound like a promising candidate for an insight therapy, but in her work with the psychiatrist after M's birth F was shocked to come to understand that her treatment of M was much like the treatment she had been exposed to herself as a child. She would leave him to cry for hours at a time, believing that her need for sleep was the priority. She was shocked to remember herself as a very small child, crying and waiting for her mother to wake up. It was this link and understanding that made her accept referral to an analyst.

It seems that the first contact with a mother–infant pair is absolutely crucial. Both F and R had very clear understandings about the link with their own infantile feelings and history, which produced significant motivation.

When I first met them, I found myself looking at a sick baby and a small, neglected girl, who told me she was *hopelessly lost*. By this she meant that she had been a student all her life, and that without this identity she felt lost. I thought this was an accurate description of her defences and of her current state. M was a limp, flat baby who would make beseeching eye contact with me. He seemed absolutely exhausted. He was very underweight and neglected, often dirty and smelling, and mostly inadequately dressed. She said at the start of the first session that she was afraid to get too attached and connected to him, in case something happened. This *something* was that she might abuse him or be bad for him. She had made a pact with herself that if she became abusive to him, she would have to give him up immediately. But if she had to do this, she felt that she would not survive.

The stakes here are explicit and high. She has been and is abusive, but to allow herself to see and to know what she does is unbearable. This is really what the work revolves around. Apart from supporting her, helping her to understand and to think about M's needs, and helping her to differentiate her experience from his, there is a need to help her confront the excruciating reality of what she does to him in the periods when she is depressed, cut off, dissociated, enraged, or projecting into him in a dangerous way. The corollary of this is to really know what was done to her.

There is a great deal to say about this mother–infant pair. I have learned a great deal about the genesis of borderline pathology from them, but for current purposes I want to narrow the focus and concentrate on three areas:

1. F's intrusions into the child;
2. the impact on the child of F's extreme changeability and erratic-ness;
3. F's inability to differentiate herself from the baby.

In terms of borderline pathology these all go together and also include use of splitting and projective identification, extreme lability of mood, and an inability to contain anxiety.

I want further to focus on the extreme nature of the intrusions into the baby, F's use of the child not only to contain her own unprocessed distress in all sorts of ways, but also most extremely and ominously, in creating actual physical symptoms in him. Over time I have become aware of how, in states of distress, she cuts off or dissociates and evacuates her own anxiety and pain into the child, who is then presented for investigation and treatment.

Projections occurred all the time, but much of the extreme act-ing out was related to breaks in the treatment. This raises technical and ethical issues. The response to the first break was not quite of this order, though it was difficult to deal with.

F spoke of suicide by hanging and of killing the baby. It was possible to avoid a hospitalization by increasing other support for the time I was away. But on my return from my holiday, M was admitted with suspected meningitis and needed a lumbar puncture and other investigations. Mother left M in hospital on his own. At the next visit, M vividly played out for me the experience of being stabbed in the back and abandoned. He was very shaky on his feet and inched around the room with his back to the wall, covering and shielding his back, trembling and falling.

The next episode occurred in the lead-up to the Christmas break. At this time M was admitted to hospital, collapsed with hypothermia and hypoglycaemia. When this was teased out and the sense of mother being left out in the cold and starving was worked with, she was briefly and momentarily able to face how she had not fed him for many hours and had left him with the fan turned onto his cot for several hours, unaware of how long it had been.

On the next visit, M's state was lamentable. He was in absolute despair. When mother put him down after coming into my room, he looked at me, then fell straight back, hitting his head on the desk. He made no sound, uttered no cry. When he got up again, he looked at me and then collapsed face down onto the floor, lying in a crumpled heap. When mother picked him up, he lay limply on her lap, gaze averted, and so shockingly unresponsive that she quickly put him down again. He could not turn to her or look at her, and she was lost in shame, distress, and humiliation, which made it harder.

Finally, at Easter, there was another admission, this time for sleep apnoea, hypoglycaemia, and hypothermia. Mother followed up by treating her own overwhelmedness in a medical, detached way, by finger-pricking him hourly to get a blood sugar reading, by taking his temperature repeatedly, and by learning cardio-pulmonary resuscitation. On this occasion she absolutely could not tolerate any suggestion that she was dealing with a collapsed state in herself, related to being left, and that she was projecting this into M and becoming a nurse/doctor to her child. It took some weeks and re-notification to get her to stop treating M in this way.

In the sessions following this period, M was aggressive, coercive, and phobic about the bucket of toys he usually loved to play with. He darted to the bucket, upended it, and then stood on it in triumph. For the next two sessions he would not touch the toys.

This child is showing the clear development of D attachment patterns—namely, freezing, collapsing stereotypes, and also becoming quite coercive at times with the mother (Main & Solomon, 1986). I would have to say that the child's dominant experience is of uncertainty about the state of mind of his object, as well as the need to protect himself from malignant projective processes. This young woman is devoted to her child, but at times when her own distress and needs mount to a certain level, she becomes frighteningly and abruptly enraged, or she withdraws into complete unresponsiveness, becoming deaf to his crying and blind to his most basic needs. I have seen her change visibly into a persecuting and terrifying figure. We are accustomed to think about the abrupt changes in the baby's state from contentment to major distress. What happens if the mother's state of mind undergoes shifts of an equally violent, sudden, and unmodified nature? How is this overlay of phantasy and reality worked with and internalized?

This last baby seems to me be extremely alert and intelligent. He has needed to be. He has demonstrated very worrying states of despair and collapse, but over time these shocking states of collapse have become minimized in so far as they are restricted to small movements of head and hands in place of a fall or a collapse. He also seems to freeze and withdraw eye contact and actual physical proximity. He knows to play at a distance and not call on his mother in certain situations and to deal with falls and disappointments by becoming very still and not approaching her. He seems to do best when she is somewhat preoccupied and a bit withdrawn. At other times, when she is in a good frame of mind, he is happy to clamber on her and play with her. They are deeply attached to one another.

Discussion

We are left with the question of how the child makes sense of these experiences. Can it make sense? How does it defend itself? How might a child, on the receiving end of such an object, present to an analyst later on?

Grinberg (1962) has said that an experience of being heavily projected into in the countertransference should alert the analyst to the possibility that the patient may have been at the receiving end of massive projections. Some years ago, speaking about a case where there was a suspicion of child sexual abuse, Ron Brookes (personal communication 1990) made the comment that a penis was not necessarily the worst that could be intruded into a child, and that powerful projection could be equally damaging. I have always thought that this was very important advice and have often wondered how often this sort of experience is retrospectively interpreted as sexual abuse and how difficult it is to differentiate.

An adult patient in analysis described how, when ordinary reassurance did not help, she would have to steel herself to make herself impervious to her mother's panic and then, under more pressure, would not be able to protect herself anymore. She would then feel dirtied and invaded inside and would notice that her mother would become instantaneously calm and say things like *Why are you so upset or angry?* She would be left with indescribable feelings of intense rage and helplessness. What does this mean in terms of reparation? Because here is a clear way of *helping, healing* a state of panic in the object but at the cost of annihilation of separateness and integrity.

Gianna Henry (1997) describes that specific failure in the container–contained relationship that I am struggling with as follows:

> [the failure] goes beyond the experience of having projections rejected. [These] patients have not only lacked containment, but have also perceived themselves as receptacles of un-metabolized phantasies and experiences projected into them by their parents. [p. 927]

She suggests that patients may try to protect themselves in two ways: The first way is by developing what she calls *no-entry defences*; anorexic patients are an example of this. Autism might be another. In the countertransference, when working with such patients, she says that

> "No entry" patients can break and enter into me with powerful projections of an intensity that parallels their dread of being invaded. [p. 928]

The other possibility for such patients is that they stay *porous*—that is, open to parental and presumably others' projections. Such patients are more likely to be bulimic, she says, and she thinks that these *porous* patients have many features in common with those children who are described in the literature as being disorganized, disoriented, or D attachment (Main & Solomon, 1986). She sug-

gests that the countertransference response to such patients involves a disorganizing of the analyst's thinking, but she sees this as
being qualitatively different from attacks on linking, being, instead, a plea from the patient to help sort and differentiate what is
taken in. This leads her to suggest that what such patients introject
is not a containing object and alpha function, but what she calls a
dispersing projecting object and omega function—an object that
has a disorganizing impact in the internal world, which is different
from envy. The request of the patient in the countertransference is
something like

> Please help me to tidy up . . . to differentiate foreign bodies
> from nourishing [food] . . . and [help me to] internalize an
> internal filing system and an organizing system of my own. [p.
> 939]

Rosenfeld (1987a) also refers to maternal projection before and
after birth in *Impasse and Interpretation*. He writes about projective
processes possibly taking place *in utero* or shortly afterwards. He
cites June Felton's term *"osmotic pressure"* to describe the almost
passive transfer of psychic content from mother to foetus, which in
a mysterious way seemed to have seeped into the child. This continues after birth and prevents the child from forming a normal
relationship with the mother.

> Children of this kind are from the beginning of life phobic
> about the mother. They are terrified that they may at any mo-
> ment have to guard against something very frightening which
> is being forced into them. They need to block the mother's
> influence . . . this can be observed shortly after birth and gives
> rise to feeding disturbances and a tendency to turn away from
> contact with the mother. [p. 276]

He says that when the patient tries to

> communicate by projection something of this "osmotic pres-
> sure", they often transmit something which they themselves
> feel is alien and confusing to them. If the analyst tries to con-
> front them with what they transmit, they feel persecuted and
> believe that the analyst is projecting his own problems into
> them, not diagnosing something that coming from them. [p.
> 277]

There seems with such cases to be

an increased need to find the good mother inside the analyst, and they are preoccupied with trying to find a good internal space to dive into, but they then feel terrified that it may again be poisonous and bad and that they will have to escape from this. [p. 277]

CHAPTER TEN

Observing babies and supporting the staff

Margaret Cohen

Further on the theme discussed in chapter 5, in this chapter about infant observation in a neonatal intensive care unit where the babies are very premature or ill—for example, on drug withdrawal, as some of the mothers are heroin addicts—the focus is on one baby in particular, who is on methadone and possibly has AIDS. Powerful feelings are aroused in the nurses and in the observer. Margaret Cohen describes the gradual development in this baby of a sense of containment, the beginnings of exploration of her world and the rudimentary symbolic expression of a psychic conflict related to the experience of methadone.

This chapter was originally written for the doctors and nurses of the New Natal Intensive Care Unit (NNICU) where I work as a child psychotherapist. This Unit works mainly with very premature babies but also with very sick babies and those withdrawn from the drug their mothers were taking when they were *in utero*. The process of such a withdrawal is often very painful for the baby and taxing on the Staff's imagination and patience. The chapter is concerned with the connection between these two. The Unit is divided into a high-dependency nursery and a special-care nursery, which is less technological. Parents are encouraged to spend time beside their babies and to take on some of their care little by little. Attempts are made to keep the lighting low and the noise controlled, but this is an environment of intense medical involvement. I would like to thank the Staff for their generosity in allowing me to work in their midst.

Infant observation: "Jilly"

The atmosphere in the special care nursery of the NNICU one Autumn was bad. There were two infants withdrawing from heroin along with several other difficult babies. It was these two babies who created an atmosphere of irritability.

> One baby, "Jilly", was on methadone to help her with the withdrawal. Her mother was sick with AIDS, her father was unaware of her illness or of her drug problem, and because the parents were not married, the Staff were bound by confidentiality on these issues. The other baby, Debbie, was also on methadone. She was 3 weeks old, she was stiff, and there were worries about her long-term neurological state. Her parents were both drug users and seemed to drink much alcohol, so there were social work worries about whether these babies would go home with their mothers.

> Several times in the cool nursery I was aware of how irritable the nurses were, how near the end of their tether, how outspoken they were in their dislike particularly of Jilly, who screamed almost all the time that she was awake. I decided to spend more time in the cool nursery and to write up observations of Jilly.

> I had often heard Jilly's awful piercing scream, but when I came into the Nursery when she was 4 weeks old she was quiet. I learnt that she was now on methadone once a day, and she had had a very bad night. Jilly was in her pram on her tummy, face to her right, mouth and nose into the ruffled sheeting. She was making little mouth movements, her eyelids fluttered, and her eyes moved under her lids. Overall she

looked so still that I was amazed at the constant movement of her eyes and mouth. These little movements went on for some time, and then she nestled into the sheet with her head as if she were burrowing, struggling a bit and rubbing her nose. The nurses began to be worried about whether to feed her because it was now 5½ hours since her last feed. One nurse picked her up, and she immediately started crying. She put her down and got the feed ready. Jilly was crying and rubbing her eyes. Jilly took the offered bottle, and fixed her gaze on the two fluorescent light panels on the ceiling. The nurse complained that she had not wanted to wake her up, but it was unit policy, which was silly because the policy was for premature babies and Jilly was not premature. Jilly took the bottle without any interest; her hands, white with pressure, were placed on each other on her chest. The nurse commented that she was not really taking anything and took the bottle away to show me. The nurse continued complaining that she had had such a good feed at nine o'clock and that now she wanted to sleep, but that it was policy and so she had to do it. At this moment Debbie's father left the nursery, flicking on the radio as he went out of the door, so that we were all then subjected to the noise.

I thought that Jilly had found some peace from her internal torment, and that she was burrowing into the mattress trying to get even further from her tormentor. She had no interest in being fed, and the nurse knew this but could not take responsibility for having her own thoughts, so she followed Policy, who became the tyrant with power over both of them. Jilly gazed up at the light panels—an institutional baby who finds the physical surroundings more comforting than the procession of nurses passing through. I felt a wave of rage sweep over me as this all seemed to be symbolized by Debbie's father's action as he left the nursery.

I came into the Nursery the next day and it was quiet, but Nurse Nancy said that I should have heard both babies screaming just now. She was holding Debbie, feeding her, while a new nurse was feeding Jilly, holding her well away from her and talking to her in a distanced manner. Nurse Nancy talked about all the screaming, telling Debbie off, but saying that it was not really her fault. There was a feeling of anger and exasperation with the babies. Jilly began to scream; the nurse put her down, and she became frantic. Nurse Jean picked her up, got a sling, and asked me and the speech therapist to help her put Jilly into it. We did, and she laughed, saying that it took three people to look after her. Jilly was instantly quieted. Nurse Jean got on with looking after the other babies with Jilly strapped to her front.

The babies were being blamed for the situation, although there was some recognition by the nurses that it was not really their fault. It was some weeks before people would talk to me openly about their worries about Jilly's possible HIV status, but I think that we can see here how Jilly was kept at a distance. Nurses said that they just had to follow ordinary guidelines, but these did not allow for the fear and horror that people were feeling that a baby might be carrying this disease. The nurses were also very frightened that father did not realize that mother was ill and that they could not tell him because the couple were not married, and that he might become very angry with them when he found out. Some nurses even felt that he might come with a gun. So the feelings around Jilly were very raw. Nurse Jean, a mother herself, was confidently clear about Jilly's needs but seemed to want some emotional support in strapping her on, perhaps unconsciously acknowledging that one needs all the internal resources one can muster in looking after a baby as persecuted as Jilly.

The following day, when I came into the Nursery, Nurse Jean was about to put Jilly into the sling but could not do so because Debbie was screaming. She was torn in two directions and gave Jilly to me. She gave me the dummy, which I gave to Jilly, who had a fight with it, wanting it and not wanting it. She was screaming and writhing, and I felt tremendously incompetent. I put her up on my shoulder, and she quietened. She was facing away from me, and I could not see what she was doing, but she was hot and wet on my shoulder—sucking her hand, or was it my pullover? She was awake and moving, restless but quiet. Sometimes she became disturbed, and I would rock her or pat her. Whatever position calmed her did not seem to last for long. I put her on my lap, and she began to scream—with a voice like sandpaper, rough and coarse. I put her on my shoulder and walked with her, and she became quiet, although moving around and trying to find a comfortable place. Then she began to cry frantically. I wondered where the dummy was. I tried this and that, but she cried—awful screaming—legs and arms drawn in—face red. A nurse gave me a dummy that I held in for Jilly, and she calmed down immediately. She closed her eyes and nestled into me—sucked and rested, her hands clasped together. I watched her very intently while holding the dummy firmly in her mouth. She sucked and stopped, sucked and stopped, her face mostly clear but occasionally crumpling but not succumbing to disintegration. She became disturbed, and I rocked her while holding the dummy in, and she quietened. I reflected on the amount of minute-by-minute care she needed. She began struggling on the dummy, not wanting it but frantic without it. I devised a strategy of taking it away for a second and then returning it, my idea being that it had to be decontaminated, but that she needed it back quickly. This seemed to work, and we struggled on. Gradually she fell into deepish sleep. Any bit of peace had to be welcomed for itself rather than as a promise of a period of calm. Soon I put her down, and she lay just as I placed her without her dummy.

I wondered why Jilly was so constantly on the move. It seemed to me that wherever was good very quickly became bad, but I also thought that perhaps stillness soon felt like emptiness and had to be avoided, that moving constantly kept terror at bay. Her scream was awful and sounded as if she were in hell. She seemed to be able to get rid of some of the horror through her mouth. Perhaps she put anxiety into the dummy and got rid of it, but then needed the dummy back to take the next lot. It seemed to me that at this time the dummy was rather useful to her.

The following week I went to see Jilly, who was now 5 weeks old. She was crying, and Nurse Harriet picked her up. She carried her face down on her left arm. Both Jilly's hands were in fists. Her eyes were open, and Harriet was jiggling her. She looked around, and Harriet held her firmly, with hands clasped between her legs. Harriet talked to other parents, holding and jiggling Jilly all the time. Jilly looked around, her eyes closed and opened. Her left hand opened. Her eyes closed, and her left hand curled. Jilly yawned, and Harriet tried to give her a dummy. But she did not want it, and Harriet took it away. Jilly then opened her mouth several times. Her eyes were open, and her hands were fists. She looked around, moving her hands and opening her mouth. She seemed perhaps to be looking for something, perhaps to be yawning. Then she was crying, and Harriet very gently talked to her and put her over her shoulder. Then she began screaming.

Nurse Harriet held her sideways and took off her Babygro, saying that she was boiling. She was crying less frantically, quietened a little, and then cried more. Debbie began to cry, and Nurse Harriet looked perplexed about which baby to go to. I offered to hold Jilly and immediately noticed how smelly she was. I tried to put this out of my mind, but I could not understand why Harriet, who seemed an excellent nurse, had not changed her. But I also felt the brunt of Harriet's irritability as she asked me what I would do with these observations. I said that I wanted to write something about withdrawing babies. She brightened up and said yes, what it feels like. I said the babies and the nurses, and she said yes, like throwing the babies out of the window.

So I (or, rather, Jilly) was left with this dirty nappy, and I did not feel as if I could say anything. I tried putting Jilly over my shoulder, on my lap, walking, with a dummy, without. And she just screamed and screamed, sometimes a little less, but usually more, and at one point so much that she could hardly breathe, and I thought that she might die and I would stand guilty. I felt that there was general appreciation of the fact that I was having such a hard time: one or two of the nurses grinned. I gave her back to Harriet, who said that she was dirty and dismissed it. I plucked up the courage to say that perhaps Jilly did mind. She put her in her cot and undid her nappy. She remarked that she had the runs. Jilly stopped crying, and they looked at each other. Harriet spoke sweetly to her as she cleaned her up, saying that she did not like having a dirty nappy, did she, and that

that was better, wasn't it, and that she would dry her now. But then another nurse came over, and the two nurses started talking, and the moment of connection was lost. Jilly became upset, but in a more controlled way. Harriet said to her that she could not stay with her. She wrapped her in a sheet, saying that sometimes she liked this and sometimes she did not, but that anyway she liked to have her hands out. Jilly was screaming, and Harriet laid her on her tummy. Jilly worked herself right up against the right-hand corner of the cot. I came back later, and she was quiet, squashed up in the corner. Harriet had put a sheet over the cot to protect her from the light and noise.

Jilly had the runs, and Harriet seemed reluctant to clear up the mess. When she did, there were a few moments of intimacy between Harriet and Jilly. I think that the nurses were feeling that Jilly was half-abandoned to them. At times mother was so ill that she was hospitalized. There was an atmosphere of misery and blame. I certainly felt like rubbish—unable to comfort Jilly—and I imagine that that was often how the nurses were feeling. It was very hard to bear Jilly's inconsolability—and to see it as such and not to be tormented by it. I think that Jilly was living in a very frightening world—perhaps the jiggling that calmed her pushed the fear and pain out of her mind. When Harriet offered her the dummy, it seemed both to be and not to be what she wanted and to remind her that there was something that she wanted. This was a very fragmented world, where any meaning ran away, much as Jilly's insides did, so that it was hard for the nurses to hold on to what they knew (for instance, that babies tend not to like dirty nappies and want their carer's attention once they have got it). Jilly banged herself right up in the corner of her cot—maybe there was some hope of escaping from her tormentors. Nurse Harriet put the sheet over her to give her some peace from so much stimulation, but also maybe to protect Jilly from her own murderous impulses towards her. She had asked me what I did with the observations and talked clearly about murderous feelings. I thought the issue here was who would recognize and bear the nurses' feelings—provide a nappy, as it were—so that these feelings did not have to run away and be acted out.

That same week I went to see Jilly again. I had noticed that nurses were discussing her more: what ways did she like to lie, did swaddling help, did she like her arms in or out, her legs free or swaddled. It was half past twelve, and I was told that she had been screaming all the morning. I saw that a senior nurse had been feeding her. She was very firmly wrapped up, with her arms in, and put lying on her right side. She had her eyes closed and was very still. She wriggled a little, made some sucking movements and dribbled some milk out.

This observation continued with Jilly's eyes opening and looking around, and her mouth opening and her tongue moving inside it. I was very struck by the big hole of her mouth and her tongue inside. She began wriggling more inside the swaddling, and this sometimes turned more to struggling: Her left foot kicked out of the sheet and her arms seemed to be struggling to get out. Her mouth opened, and again I could see her tongue inside. She moved the sheet off with her arms. She put her mouth up against the sheet and mouthed it. She took her head away from the sheet and then back. She put the sheet over her face, then moved it away. Then she got completely free from the sheet. She seemed quite calm. She stretched and opened her eyes very wide. Her arms and legs were gyrating, and she was hiccuping. She was looking towards me but not into my eyes. She looked over to a crying baby, and her leg and arm movements seemed less. She was sucking. Her tongue went out, and she was making little noises. She stretched her arms up above her and then back down. Then she was gyrating. She looked towards the light. . . . She looked towards me. She stretched her right hand out in her field of vision, then looked up to another light in the ceiling. Then back towards me. Her mouth was open, and her tongue was out. She looked at me, hiccuped, and looked away to the left side, then up to the first light. Her hands went down for a second and then up to shoulder level in little loose fists. She was hiccuping. Her left index finger went to the thumb and went towards her mouth and away. She made little noises. Again her finger and thumb went to her mouth.

I was very intrigued by this observation. It seemed to me to be the first time that I had seen Jilly awake and exploring her

world. The nurse who had fed her was someone quietly confident who knew her own mind, and there was that look about
the way Jilly was lying in her cot. She seemed safely held and
from that base could go exploring. At first I felt struck by this
cavernous hole of her mouth and felt that it did not have a
proper grip, and that likewise her eyes would look in a direction but not fix. But this gradually changed as the mouth
seemed to focus more around the tongue, which became not
just something in the mouth but something that could move
and go in and out. She struggled out of her sheet like a moth
out of the chrysalis and could then put her mouth to the sheet
and then the sheet to her mouth. She was gaining considerable
mastery over her world, going after what she wanted, but also
able to bring it to her—all this with a new degree of calm.

This observation began with a sense of security. Perhaps we
need this before we can begin to have a sense of separateness
and therefore of self. In this observation Jilly did something—
she pulled the sheet away and back. She achieved something
rather than being done to. Perhaps we see here the precursors
of separateness. And then this exploration with her mouth and
what goes into it seems to remind her that there is a world out
there, and she looks towards the light, towards her fist, and
then to the person sitting with her looking at her. She then goes
on a voyage from the lights which she used to stare at when
she was being fed, to the person, backwards and forwards as
if getting to know the path. Then she makes the connection
between her thumb and index finger going to her mouth and
away. This is something we see premature babies in the intensive care nursery struggle to do, and here we see Jilly only
achieve it at 5 or 6 weeks. But it is very moving to see her
manage it. I think that she has at last been able to make these
basic connections against the blast and fragmentation of her
withdrawal. She has to work hard against the experience of her
extra-uterine and presumably her intra-uterine life as well.

I again went to see Jilly when she was nearly 7 weeks old. The
nurse in charge said that she was a bit better. Jilly was lying on
her tummy; her head was to the right, and her right hand was
to her mouth. She was well tucked in. I was struck by how

much bigger she looked. She was rather still, lightly sucking on her hand. She stretched slightly and sucked the side of her hand. Then her mouth opened on her hand and moved on it. Her mouth opened, and her hand was against her lower lip. Her eyes looked as if they were about to open. Her hand was very gently against her lower lip, her top lip pursed. Her lower lip sucked. Her top lip pursed. Her hand moved about half an inch away from her mouth. She was sucking, and her hand moved slightly. Her bottom lip—perhaps really her chin—was sucking, and then her top lip pursed. Her hand moved infinitesimally. Then there was stronger sucking of her jaw. Her eyes flickered, and her eyebrows went up, as if her eyes were going to open. Her mouth pulled back. Her lips closed very quickly, and there was some movement around her eyes. Her thumb moved and was almost touching her lower lip and then was touching it. Her top lip moved and then her bottom lip sucked. Her hand moved and touched her bottom lip very gently. Her lips came together for a second, and then her tongue came out between them. Her mouth was closing and opening a little with her tongue moving around inside. She moved her face into the sheet, nuzzling, then she rested with her mouth open, her hand away from her mouth and her fingers curled underneath. She was still, and her mouth was in a triangle. She sucked and pulled her mouth back.

I was amazed by this observation, by the disparate movements of her top and bottom lips. I tried to move my lips in the same way— not in unison—and found it very difficult to do anything approaching what Jilly was doing. This is how I made sense of it for myself. Earlier in Jilly's life it was very marked how she would go for the bottle and then fight against it. I thought that whatever was good quickly became bad. But there may also have been a fight in herself between going for what she needed and turning away from it. One might think of this as a healthy turning towards and a perverse turning away. Of course this is all complicated for Jilly, because her experience is so filled with ambiguity. Presumably even *in utero* she suffered the hell of withdrawal and the relief of the drug. Then in the first few weeks she had the relief of the methadone and then the hell of the lack of it. So the drug, which caused her misery, also gave her the relief from it. One nurse told me that Jilly never struggled against the methadone, even at the beginning. But the bottle—what we would see as the representative of maternity, comfort, nourishment, healthy dependency, the growing recognition of some source outside that she could relate to—was something she often fought against. So, earlier she had suffered from this terrible ambivalence. In this observation she seemed to have found a remarkable way of effecting a split. It seemed to me that the bottom lip supported by her jaw could get on with expressing a healthy wish to turn to nourishment and to suck. The top lip, the purser, expressed the wish to turn away—the wish that we would expect to find in a more developed form as contempt or even perversion. With Jilly this seemed a very helpful split, which lifted her conflict to a more symbolic sphere. All of this seemed to happen under the aegis of her hand, which gently came and went and which touched and supported her bottom lip. The internal world in which she was living seemed to be improving, as did the external world of the nursery.

The speech therapist and I had decided that at our Friday afternoon meetings we would show a video of Jilly for several sessions. These are meetings that anyone from the Unit is welcome to attend. We have a track of video and show quite small clips in sequence, stopping to discuss what we have seen. We ask participants to observe the baby, the environment, and their own feelings in watching the clip, all in the service of trying to understand better what is going on. This is our attempt to marry a NIDGAP (Neo-Natal Individualized Developmental Care and Assessment Programme) point of view and a more psychoanalytic baby observation view. We were motivated to show Jilly partly because she was having such a hard time, but also because we saw what an emotional toll this was on the nurses. We hoped that by offering a place to discuss all of this away from the heat of the nursery we might be helping the situation. This meeting, when Jilly was about 7 weeks old, was attended by a group of nurses, a play specialist (PS), the speech therapist, and myself. We showed a clip of Jilly crying and then being held by the PS.

In the discussion Shirley (a nurse) said that she thought that Jilly felt that she had something very bad inside her and that she was trying to get rid of it. We talked about how she was rubbing her legs together as if trying to scrape something off them. The PS said that adult addicts had told her that they felt as if they were crawling with ants. She added that Jilly does not like being stroked gently, she likes firm handling. It was remarked that she pushes herself up against the hard surface of the cot. It seems that she likes to come up against something. It is difficult for nurses to allow this to happen, as they would naturally position a baby in the middle of the cot. Rosie (a nurse) said that she was only speaking personally—and I interrupted her to say that that was all that any of us could do, that we can all only use our own thoughts and experience—but, she said, she could not bear the sound of the PS's music. It was too much. You felt bombarded. They all talked about feeling irritable. The PS said that you could not be any use to Jilly when you were irritated—she had felt like that the other day, she had to leave the room for five minutes to recover, otherwise you would upset her. I said that I thought we might think of it the other way round—that we pick up some of Jilly's feelings—that by examining our own feelings, we can learn something about Jilly's feelings. I thought that perhaps Jilly, too, felt bombarded when addressed by too many sensations at once, perhaps she, too, could only concentrate on one thing at a time. The nurses discussed this and their own feeling of irritability. I said that the PS had left the room to recover herself and that I wondered what the nurses did; that part of the point of this meeting was to discuss these things in the effort to recover. This led on to a discussion about whether there could be just one nurse for a baby like Jilly, so that you did not feel all the time that you ought to be with another baby. It was generally recognized that this was a good idea, but it was thought that the mothers of other babies might be jealous. Also, it would not work, because if Jilly was quiet you would feel you had to help with the other babies. This brought us on to the topic of mothers. Joanna (a nurse) said that Jilly would settle when her mother came in. The other nurses hotly disagreed, saying that it was just that when she came in they had settled her. Joanna stuck to her view that Jilly calmed down for her mother.

It seems to me that this discussion was very important. Shirley said clearly that Jilly feels as if she has something bad inside, and that in crying she is trying to get rid of it. There is a question about how when we feel bad, we try to get rid of it—evacuate it, scrape it off? Also there is a recognition of her need for something firm outside to get up against in this nightmare. The association of ants crawling all over one is a vivid one and makes one wonder about Jilly's experience of her skin. Perhaps it did not feel like an integrated membrane that held her together, but as something horrible in itself. Certainly her nappy rash, a breakdown in her skin, was very bad and prolonged and must have been painful.

Rosie then felt safe enough to voice her own feeling of irritability and her anger with the PS for aggravating this. The question then arises whether we hold on to these feelings and use them to understand what is going on, or do we too have to get rid of them. Can we cope with them by accepting them and thinking about them, being interested in them rather than just pushing them out? It is useful to acknowledge how irritable Staff can get with one another, and that this can then be seen as an inevitable part of the whole process and not turn into some personal dislike. It was then agreed that a baby needs one or two caretakers—people who know her intimately, help her to make sense of her world and provide continuity. This quite logically led us on to thoughts of her mother, who would be the natural person to fulfil this job. Quite a hot dispute followed about who could get Jilly to settle. There is a telling scene in Dennis Potter's *Blue Remembered Hills*, where the grown-up little girls quarrel about who is going to be mother and in the tussle the baby gets thrown on the ground. When a baby is very difficult, like Jilly, she can be thought of as a rubbish baby that nobody wants to look after, but once she becomes the focus of some interest I think our little-girl feelings of who is the best mother can be activated, so that we can become competitive with the mother and with each other—who is best with her, who understands her better, and so on. And particularly where the baby has suffered from the mother's behaviour, it is hard to think that Jilly might have a real and important link with her mother. When Jilly was tiny, she hated having her nappy changed. This was something the nurses thought about a great deal, partly from watching the video—how they could do it in a way that upset her less. And she began to like having her nappy changed. I think that she came to feel relieved to have the dirty nappy taken away and dealt with and to be cleaned up by a confident nurse who often talked to her while doing this, so that this was not just a matter of changing her nappy but also of processing and giving words to her feelings. In the same way I think that Unit Staff have messy feelings about the babies and that these need a place where they can be considered with tact and kindness. They turn out then to be feelings of some interest, which can help us and which, when seen as having a legitimate place, are in less danger of exploding.

At around 7 or 8 weeks, Jilly seemed to become more dependent on those around her. Once when I held the dummy in for her I spoke to someone else, and her hand flew on to my hand and held it in place with tremendous force. She would also clutch on to a finger, seemingly for security. Nurse Rosie told me that Jilly wanted to be held all the time. I wondered if the meaning of this had changed somewhat. At first she seemed to want continual movement perhaps, as I have suggested, to keep nightmarish sensations at bay, now perhaps she had some idea of something which at times took the torture away, something that could help, and she did not want to lose this. She was often discussed on the Unit, and people would boast about whether she had smiled at or talked to them. In the middle of the horror, people seemed to be getting glimpses of an ordinary beautiful baby.

The speech therapist and I had another video meeting. We showed a track of Jilly being bathed by Joanna. Several nurses attended. In the film Jilly was screaming, and whatever Joanna did seemed to make no difference. One participant said did we think that Jilly was ill with HIV—how could withdrawal go on for so long? Or was it that she had got used to crying, that this was all she knew? Harriet said that she was no longer comforted by her mother. Someone replied that they were glad because the mother would now know what she was taking on. But Harriet thought with despair that Jilly would then not even have her mother to comfort her. This led to a general worry about how mother would ever manage at home. The nurses said that they could not bear the screaming, even though they only had to put up with it for a shift at a time. Also, mother was an addict and so would have less patience. Someone added that she did not have somewhere like here to come to talk about Jilly and her own feelings. We looked at some more video where Joanna took off Jilly's nappy and put her in the bath. Jilly screamed throughout. Joanna said, "Oh, Jilly, you are so miserable" and looked as if she too might cry. As Joanna swooshed the water around her and spoke to her, saying that now she felt safe and comfortable, Jilly stopped crying. She put her hand down towards her raw nappy area. She began crying, and Joanna put her on her tummy over her arm.

There was a discussion about how we can know what babies are feeling, that they do not have the same concepts as we do. People talked about very primitive sensations such as falling or turning to liquid (going down the plug-hole). We talked about how, when you can give words to feelings or tell a story around them, they are less frightening, so Jilly was in a more unprotected state than we are.

We thought about the comfort that Jilly got from the water. But one nurse pointed out that even when she stopped crying, her hands were clenched. We noticed that her cry, once she was over J's arm in the water, had quite a different quality—it was more of a complaint, like when you go home and whinge about how dreadful the day has been. Harriet said that the frantic cry sounded like "get me out of this". I thought that what was so awful about it was that there was no belief that there was someone there, whereas the complaint was to someone.

The nurses began talking about how they might have looked after Jilly better. Would a more isolated room with less stimulation have been better. Others were worried that she would then have been left too much on her own. They talked about her need for darkness and to be wrapped up. Harriet said that if they tried isolation with another baby and he did better, they would never know whether it was better or if this baby was less ill.

We watched Joanna trying to feed Jilly. She kept the bottle in her mouth, although Jilly was screaming. One nurse laughed and said "You will take this bottle". People felt sympathy for the nurse but thought that she had persisted too long. We agreed that one just longed for Jilly's mouth to close around the teat. We talked about how hard it was to watch the video. Harriet said that she just comforted herself with the thought that Jilly would remember none of this. This began a by now familiar argument between those who agreed with that and those who did not. One nurse put it that she would not remember it, but she would be shaped by it. Another said that we generally think that the first few weeks of life are important so they must be for Jilly too. They acknowledged ruefully how keen they were to hand her on to someone else, and as a result how many she was handled by.

One nurse then said that she thought that the mother was evil. How could these addicts do these terrible things. The mothers talked about how awful withdrawal was without thinking what they were putting the babies through. Another nurse said that Debbie's father seemed proud of the methadone and the withdrawal, as if it made him special. They talked about AIDS and the risks and the split condom that mother said had produced Jilly. They laughed a little and said how boring their lives were. As they left, one nurse said how brilliant these sessions were.

The speech therapist and I hope that these sessions will give rise to practical improvements in the care of the babies. She is very good at holding on to these thoughts and putting up notes over a baby's cot with suggestions about practice. We also hope that by giving the Staff a space to reflect on their own observations, they will not only have practical ideas, but that these will have sprung from thinking about the baby's experience. So this session began with some concern for Jilly and her mother. We talked about the philosophical problem of knowing about anyone else's experience, and how this was even more difficult with a baby. To help our imagination, we had to rely on our most primitive fears, and we knew that Jilly would be even more vulnerable than most of us because of her immaturity. The nurses seemed to cope with their own feelings of vulnerability and to have an imaginative discussion about Jilly's crying. In the same way, Joanna coped with her sadness and went on to comfort Jilly. But the thought about whether care could have been better was a very painful one. Feelings were raw, and so then there was a wish to put Jilly away in isolation—a wish that had to be resisted. Then the torment of seeing Jilly unable to be comforted broke out in anxieties about what all this was doing to Jilly—would she be able to get away from it, or would she be stuck with it forever? I was struck by how one of the most sensitive nurses clung to the view that all this was just for the moment and would pass without a trace. I thought that my other view was too distressing for her and indeed for most of us.

There was a wish at this point to shift the blame onto mother and more generally onto addicts.

"Where do babies come from" is a very common childhood question, and it may be not just about the mechanics of intercourse but about what sort of union does a baby come from. I think that unconsciously such thoughts affect us all. With Jilly there was an idea that she was the product of a murderous intercourse, where any number of people might consequently have become infected; that she was the product of a split condom, a sort of bad joke, and perhaps to be thrown away like an old used condom. Furthermore, she had the nerve to prefer her mother—surely a sign of her bad taste in choosing this mother over the nurses? Gradually the mother in this woman had to be recognized and the Staff became concerned about her and about father, who was something more than merely a potential gunman.

Jilly came off her methadone and left the Unit quite quickly—or so it seemed to me. I saw her on a Thursday and when I came in the following Tuesday, she had left. I felt bereft. Her corner of the Nursery seemed terribly empty. I continue to wonder how she is and what her life will be like. It is the weight of such thoughts that sometimes drags us away from reflecting on our patients and our feelings about them.

CHAPTER ELEVEN

Projective identification: the analyst's involvement

Michael Feldman

Michael Feldman describes in detail a particular form of interaction between patient and analyst where the latter is enacting— without initially being aware of it because it is congruent with some view he has of himself—the role that the patient wishes him to play. What the patient has projected into the analyst is not so much a part of the self but an archaic object relationship, and it is in this that the patient hopes to coerce the analyst to play a part as opposed to thinking about it. In this way the frightening discrepancy between the patient's phantasy and the actual analytic situation can be reduced to comfortable proportions. But if this occurs, the pain remains imprisoned.

In Klein's original formulation of the mechanism of projective identification, she referred to an unconscious phantasy in which the patient expelled (usually) disturbing contents into

---

An earlier version of this chapter was given at a conference, "Understanding Projective Identification: Clinical Advances", held at University College London, October 1995.

another object. This object is partially transformed *in the patient's mind* as a consequence of the projection, being now possessed of qualities the patient has expelled. In addition to its use as a method of evacuation, Klein suggested that projective identification may fulfil a variety of other unconscious functions for the patient, such as leading him to believe that he possesses the object or controls it from within. These projective processes usually alternate with introjective ones. Thus the phantasy of forceful entry into the object by parts of the self in order to possess or control the object creates problems with normal introjection, which the patient may find difficult to distinguish from forceful entry from the outside, in retribution for his own violent projections (M. Klein, 1946, p. 11).

The exploration of these unconscious phantasies has increased our understanding of the functions and defensive needs these primitive mental mechanisms serve for the patient. While the elucidation of these processes has, in the past, often seemed to emphasize the analyst's role as a dispassionate observer, the impingement of the patient's phantasies and actions on the analyst has in fact been recognized from the earliest days of psychoanalysis. Following the early work of Heimann (1950) and Racker (1958), there has been increasing interest in the systematic investigation of the *way* the patient's phantasies, expressed in gross or subtle, verbal or non-verbal means, may come to influence the analyst's state of mind and behaviour. Fairbairn (1958) wrote, "In a sense psychoanalytic treatment resolves itself into a struggle on the part of the patient to *press gang* his relationship with the analyst into the closed system of the inner world through the agency of transference." We now recognize that while this conscious or unconscious pressure on the analyst may interfere with his functioning, it can also serve as an invaluable source of information concerning the patient's unconscious mental life—his internal object relations in particular. More recently, a number of authors have been concerned to elaborate the concept of countertransference into what is described as an "interactive" model of psychoanalysis, where the emphasis is on the significance of the analyst's own subjective experiences in his understanding of the patient and his method of responding to him or her. Tuckett (1995) has provided an excellent commentary on some of the interesting work in this area. Building upon the notions of Racker (1958), Sandler (1976), and Joseph

(1989a), he elaborates a model of the analytic situation in which both the patient and the analyst engage in unconscious enactment, placing more or less subtle pressure on the other to relate to them in terms of a present unconscious phantasy. He makes the point that ". . . Enactment makes it possible to know in representable and communicable ways about deep unconscious identifications and primitive levels of functioning which could otherwise only be guessed at or discussed at the intellectual level".

I want to focus here particularly on the nature of the involvement by the analyst that the patient seems to require as an essential component of the defensive use of projective identification. I will suggest that the projection of elements of a phantasied object relationship represents an attempt by the patient to reduce the discrepancy between an archaic object relationship and an alternative object relationship the patient might be confronted with, which threatens him. There are times when the analyst is used primarily as the recipient of projections by which he is transformed in the patient's phantasy alone. More commonly, as described above, it seems necessary for the patient that the analyst should become involved in the living out of some aspects of phantasies that reflect his internal object relations. I hope to illustrate some of the ways the patient's use of projective identification exerts subtle and powerful pressure on the analyst to fulfil the patient's unconscious expectations embodied in these phantasies. Thus the impingement upon the analyst's thinking, feelings, and actions is not an incidental side-effect of the patient's projections, nor necessarily a manifestation of the analyst's own conflicts and anxieties, but seems often to be a essential component in the effective use of projective identification by the patient. (I consider some of the defensive functions these processes serve further on.) Confronted with such pressure, the analyst may apparently be able to remain comfortable and secure in his role and function, involved in empathic observation and understanding, recognizing the forces he is being subjected to, and with some ideas about their origins and purpose. He may, on the other hand, be disturbed by the impingement and transformation in his mental and physical state, becoming sleepy, confused, anxious, or elated. Finally, it may become apparent to the analyst that he has unconsciously been drawn into a subtle and complex enactment that did not necessarily disturb him at first but can subsequently be recognized as the living out of important elements of the patient's internal object relationships.

We are concerned with a system in which both patient and analyst are dealing with the anxieties and needs aroused in each of them by the phantasies of particular object relationships. The disturbance in either the patient or the analyst or both arises from the discrepancy between the pre-existing phantasies that partially reassure or gratify, and those with which each is confronted in the analytic situation, which are potentially threatening. I am suggesting that this unwelcome discrepancy drives each to deploy either projective mechanisms or some variety of enactment in an attempt to create a greater correspondence between the pre-existing unconscious phantasies and what they experience in the analytic encounter. As I aim to illustrate, part of the analyst's struggle involves the recognition of some of these pressures, and the capacity to tolerate the gap between the gratifying or reassuring phantasies and what he is confronted with in the analytic situation, which includes the unconscious anxieties evoked by the patient's projections.

Rosenfeld (1971) describes a psychotic patient who, when confronted with interpretations he admired, was filled with envy and driven to attack his analyst's functions. In his phantasy, he wormed his way into the analyst's brain, like a parasite, interfering with the quickness of his thinking. This use of projective identification was often accompanied by the patient becoming confused, unable to think or talk properly, with claustrophobic and paranoid anxieties about being trapped in the analyst. Rosenfeld (1987b) describes the need for the analyst "empathically to follow the patient's description of both real and fantasized events, which are often re-enacted by being projected into him. . . . The analyst has to bring together the diffuse, confused, or split-up aspects of the patient's pre-thought processes in his own mind so that they gradually make sense and have meaning." When Rosenfeld was able to interpret the dynamics of the patient's state to him in a clear and detailed way, his anxiety about having completely destroyed the analyst's brain diminished, and the patient was able, with relief, to experience him as helpful and undamaged. When it became possible for the patient to introject this object in a good state, he could, for a while, recover his own capacities for clearer thought and speech.

Bion (1958) gives a complex description of the beginning of a session with a psychotic patient who gave the analyst a quick glance, paused, stared at the floor near the corner of the room, and then gave a slight shudder. He lay down on the couch, keeping his eye on the same corner of the floor. When he spoke, he said he felt quite empty and wouldn't be able to make further use of the session. Bion spells out the steps in the process by which the patient first used his eyes for introjection and then for expulsion, creating a hallucinatory figure that had a threatening quality, accompanied by a sense of internal emptiness. When he made an interpretation along these lines, the patient became calmer, and said, "I have painted a picture". Bion writes, "His subsequent silence meant that the material for the analyst's next interpretation was already in the possession of the analyst." Bion suggested that his task was to consider all the events of the session up to that point, try to bring them together, and discern a new pattern in his mind that should be the basis for his next interpretation.

Case study: "Mr P"

A patient of mine, a young man, "Mr P", arrived for the first session after a holiday, and I noticed that he was moving and speaking in an unusually clear and businesslike fashion. He said that when he arrived in the waiting-room, he had found another man there already (he occasionally sees the patient of my colleague there). He had not seen this particular person before, and he was disconcerted at first. He thought I might have made a mistake and double-booked two patients. He imagined me suddenly discovering my mistake, feeling terribly embarrassed, and not knowing how to cope with the situation. He speculated that I would probably ask my colleague to go to the waiting-room to call one of them out and explain the situation to him, and then I would see whoever remained.

He portrayed me, in his mind, as confused, embarrassed, and moreover unable to face the muddle I had created, sending someone else to deal with it on my behalf. After his brief discomfiture, the patient found himself in a position of calmly observing and imagining the situation, without a momentary thought that *he* might have made a mistake. Later in the session it emerged that in the course of the previous week, during my absence, he had got into a terrible mess; he had lost his watch, he had been very confused, and he had not known what was going on.

It seemed that the patient's knowledge and experience of his own state of confusion, his embarrassment about finding himself in such a mess during the holiday, and his difficulties over time (expressed in his loss of the watch) were projected, in phantasy, into me before he had actually encountered me. After a momentary sense of discomfort within himself on finding an unfamiliar person in the waiting-room, he cured himself of the unwelcome and disturbing thoughts and experience and behaved in an efficient and well-organized way, while (in his phantasy) his analyst had to summon help to rescue himself from confusion and muddle.

These examples illustrate the patients' unconscious belief in the effectiveness of a concrete process by which (usually) undesirable and threatening parts of the personality can be split off and projected. The motives for this projection vary, but the involvement of the object as a recipient of this projection is a defining characteristic of projective identification, as is the belief in the transformation of the object by the projection. This transformation may take place in relation to a delusional or hallucinatory object, an absent object, or a dream object, but central to our work is the investigation of the process in relation to the analyst in the room with the patient. In the examples quoted, the patients seemed to have no doubt about the effectiveness of the transformation of themselves that accompanied the transformation of the object. I think there was a general assumption, based on previous experience, of the sympathy, understanding, and receptivity of the analyst, but it is a feature of the projective processes manifested in these examples that they did not depend on concurrent evidence of the analyst's capacity or willingness to receive the projections.

Indeed, the noteworthy feature of these examples is the contrast between the picture we have of the analyst's actual mental state and the way this is represented in the patient's phantasy. As Bion has pointed out, patients vary in the extent to which they are able to take "realistic steps" to affect their object by projective identification and in their capacity to recognize and respect the actual properties of the object. Thus with some patients, the omnipotent phantasy is likely to have little counterpart in reality. While Rosenfeld and Bion have made important contributions to our understanding of the impact of the patient's projections on the analyst, in the situations I have quoted they both convey thoughtful, calm, benign attention, in marked contrast to the phantasy either of a persecutory object or an analyst whose mind has been invaded and damaged. When Rosenfeld talked to his patient in a clear, insightful, and empathic way, taking the phantasy into account but clearly demonstrating a state of affairs diametrically opposite to that which obtained in the patient's phantasy, the patient was relieved and was able to recover some of his lost ego functions.

With my own patient, Mr P, I found myself interested in and concerned about the patient's experience and the properties with which I had temporarily been invested in the patient's mind. I did not actually feel uncertain or confused, and I was confident I was seeing the right patient at the right time. What my patient said did not, on this occasion, discomfort me. On other occasions he could be more accurate about my state of mind and consciously or unconsciously select more effectively what to say or do to *affect* my state of mind, inducing me into impatience, uncertainty, or anxiety. The other feature of this brief example is that when I did talk to the patient in a way that conveyed that I was neither confused nor particularly anxious and gave him the impression that something was being understood, he was able to recall and integrate more of his own experiences. Later in the session he told me that during the holidays he had moved out of his office to a larger, more spacious office on a higher floor. The two people with whom he had shared the old office had been away, and when they returned they complained bitterly about the terrible mess he had left behind. Mr P said, in a rather indignant way, that there might have been a *bit* of untidiness and he had *intended* to clear it up, but he had been busy with other things. He went on to say how unreasonable and neurotic his colleagues were and described other examples of their childish behaviour. He began to sound like the confident and superior person in the larger more spacious office whom I had encountered at the start of the session.

What I think I had failed to question initially was why I should have felt *so* comfortable and secure when I was presented with the material at the start of the first session after a break. I suspect that I was, in part, enacting the object relationship that the patient subsequently made clearer to me. I was the confident, sane, sensible figure in a superior position, dealing with someone into whom almost all the disturbance and confusion had been projected. This projection and the slight enactment it gave rise to failed to disturb me or even to alert me at the time, since my role as the unruffled observing analyst in the office above was congruent with a version of myself with which I was reasonably comfortable, at least for a while.

Reflecting on this material, what I also failed to recognize initially was the patient's unconscious communication of a bitter complaint about my responsibility for having left him with such a mess during the holiday, defensively claiming that I had intended to do something about it, but largely denying my responsibility for the disorder. As I illustrate later, we have learnt to take notice not only of our feelings of discomfort as possible reflections of the patient's projective identification, but also to consider situations in which we find ourselves perhaps feeling a little too secure and comfortable, confident about where the pathology lies and who is responsible for the mess. I think this example illustrates that there is in fact a complex relation between the projection into an object in phantasy (even in the absence of the actual object) and what happens as soon as the patient and analyst encounter one another, when quite subtle, non-omnipotent interactions begin to take place, usually based on unconscious projections into the analyst.

Of course it is not difficult to see the advantages of projection into a hallucinatory, delusional, or absent object. Since it is an omnipotent process, there is no doubt about the object's receptivity and the consequent transformation. (There also seem to be no problems about the corresponding introjection of the object's valuable properties.) The patient is not confronted with the contrast between phantasy and reality, which is disturbing, nor with the differences between himself and his object.

What were the factors that allowed the more benign integrative process, which Rosenfeld describes, to take place, albeit temporarily? How can a patient sometimes tolerate, and indeed feel greatly relieved when confronted with, an analyst in a state quite discordant with their psychic reality at that moment? Why, on the other hand, do some patients feel driven to use other methods, more subtle or more violent, to involve the analyst through projective identification? While Bion's patient had split off and projected a dangerous persecutory version of the analyst into the hallucinatory object in the corner, he did at least have some conception of benign symbolic communication, which is implied in the belief that it was possible to paint a picture in the mind of a suitably receptive analyst. Other patients either seem to have no belief in this possibility or cannot tolerate such a configuration. Bion (1959) has vividly described how the infant, confronted with what seems like an impenetrable object, is driven to attempt to project into such an object with more and more force. The early experience of such difficulties with the object's receptivity may drive the patient to involve the analyst in such a way that his mind *is* actually disturbed, or *actually* to force him to become compliant or persecutory. It is as if the patient has such doubts about the possibility either of symbolic communication or the object's receptivity to *any* form of projection that he cannot relent until he has *evidence* of the impact on the analyst's mind and body. If this consistently fails, confirming an early experience of an unavailable, hateful object, he may give up in despair.

We tend to assume that once the patient has felt understood, in the sense of some important part of him being taken in, he would be relieved by the contrast between the more sane and benign imago of the analyst and the archaic one projected into him—to use Strachey's terms (1934). We sometimes assume that it is only the operation of the patient's envy that militates against this. However, it often seems that there is a different drive in operation, namely the pressure towards identity, which seems paradoxical and difficult to reconcile with the longing for a better, more constructive experience. It is as if the patient requires the analyst's experience or behaviour to correspond in some measure to his unconscious phantasy and is unable to tolerate or make use of any discrepancy, however reassuring we might assume that to be. On the contrary, as Sandler and Sandler (1978, 1990) have pointed out, the patient's attempts to "actualize" such phantasies can be regarded as a form of wish-fulfilment, serving a reassuring and gratifying function. Joseph (1987) describes a session in which an analyst interpreted a deprived child's reaction to the imminent end of a Friday session. The analyst interpreted the child's urgent wish to make a candle as an expression of her desire to take a warm object away with her. The child screamed, "Bastard! Take off your clothes and jump outside". The analyst tried to interpret the child's feelings about being dropped and sent into the cold, but the child replied, "Stop your talking, take off your clothes! You are cold. I'm not cold." While the projection into the representation of the analyst leads to the child saying "You are cold. I'm not cold", this will not suffice for the child. Her non-delusional perception of the analyst as being relatively warm and comfortable drives her to try to force the analyst *actually* to take off her clothes, so that she would indeed be cold, and there would not be the immensely painful and disturbing discrepancy between the internal representation and the figure she encounters in the external world. This dramatic scenario is reproduced in more subtle ways with many of our patients.

I am suggesting that this goes beyond, and seems to conflict with, the need to feel understood or reassured about the capacity of the object to take in and to "contain" the projections. The lack of this identity between the internal and external reality may not only stir up envy or doubts about the object's receptivity, it may also create an alarming space in which thought and new knowledge and understanding might take place, but which many patients find intolerable.

(I am assuming some familiarity with the way in which Rosenfeld and Bion have expanded and deepened our understanding of the use of projective identification as a means of communication and recognized the forceful or even violent use of projective identification in an attempt to get through an impenetrable, rejecting object. Clinically, of course, the patient's use of more forceful projection may be driven by his experience of the analyst as a non-understanding, non-receptive figure, which the analyst may not perceive.)

There have been important developments in our recognition and understanding not just of the ways the patient might need to project a feeling of confusion, inadequacy, or excitement into the analyst, but the more complex and subtle ways in which the *analyst* is induced into states of mind, sometimes accompanied by various forms of enactment, which are relevant to the patient's early history and his current anxieties, defences, and desires. I want to consider what functions these interactions serve for the patient and how he might succeed in involving the analyst. Sometimes the analyst will recognize that there is something slightly alien, disturbing, discordant with a view of himself that he can comfortably tolerate, and we have learnt to consider this state as a result of the patient's projective identification. This recognition can lead us to a better understanding of our own difficulties, as well as the important configurations in the patient's object relationships that are being lived out in the analytic situation. What writers like Joseph (1987, 1988) and O'Shaughnessy (1992) have described are the ways in which the analyst's involvement, which results from the projective identification, are not always easily or quickly recognized. On the contrary, the analyst may have the sort of comfortable, benign, dispassionate involvement I described at the beginning. What sometimes emerges is that this state represents the unconscious convergence of the patient's and the analyst's defensive needs and may militate against real progress.

Money-Kyrle (1956) has described the process taking place in the analyst as follows: "As the patient speaks, the analyst will, as it were, become introjectively identified with him, and having understood him inside, will re-project him and interpret" (p. 361). When there are particular difficulties in understanding or helping the patient, two factors may contribute to this: (1) the patient's projection and disowning of unwanted aspects of himself, (2) when these projections correspond to unresolved and not understood aspects of the analyst himself, he may have difficulty in appropriately re-projecting the patient. If he then "cannot tolerate the sense of being burdened with the patient as an irreparable or persecuting figure inside him, he is likely to resort to a defensive kind of re-production which shuts out the patient and creates a further bar to understanding" (p. 362). Money-Kyrle makes the point that for some analysts—for example, those who most crave the reassurance of continuous success—the strain of not being able to understand or help the patient is felt more acutely than others. He suggests that the extent to which an analyst is emotionally disturbed by periods of non-understanding will probably depend, in the first instance, on another factor: the severity of his own superego. If our superego is predominantly friendly and helpful, we can tolerate our own limitations without undue distress and, being undisturbed, will be the more likely soon to regain contact with the patient. But if it is severe, we may become conscious of a sense of failure as the expression of an unconscious persecutory or depressive guilt. Or, as a defence against such feelings, we may blame the patient.

While I find Money-Kyrle's descriptions familiar and convincing, what we have become more aware of is that when the analyst is confronted with the anxieties and strain he describes, he may be unconsciously drawn to diminish them by enacting a complex object relationship *with* the patient, which initially serves to reassure both. I believe this is achieved by the analyst striving to create a closer correspondence between a relatively comfortable or gratifying internal representation of himself and the way he experiences and interprets the external situation. Indeed, while I think Money-Kyrle is delineating the process by which the analyst disentangles himself from the patient's projection in order to understand and communicate, the re-projection he describes may actually be a form of enactment by which the analyst deals with an uncomfortable version of his relationship with the patient. Returning for a moment to the paper by Rosenfeld from which I quoted at the beginning, in which he described his work with the psychotic patient, he writes:

> One of the difficulties of working through such situations in the analysis is the tendency to endless repetition, in spite of the patient's understanding that very useful analytic work is being done. It is important in dealing with patients and processes of this kind to accept that much of the repetition is inevitable. The acceptance by the analyst of the patient's processes being re-enacted in the transference helps the patient to feel that the self, which is constantly split off and projected into the analyst, is acceptable and not so damaging as feared. [p. 180]

Why does Rosenfeld address his colleagues in this way? I think the point he is making is that unless the analyst recognizes the fact of, and perhaps even the necessity for, the repetition and re-enactment, he may become disheartened, confused, or resentful—

in other words, far from being able to feel reasonably confident in the representation of himself as a helpful, effective, patient analyst, he might be burdened by an intolerable version of himself, which he may then try to deal with very concretely. This could be enacted by the analyst blaming or accusing the patient in a hostile and critical way, entering into a defensive collusive arrangement, or terminating the treatment in despair.

What I am thus suggesting is that what is projected is not primarily a part of the patient, but a phantasy of an object relationship. It is this that impinges upon the analyst and may allow him to remain reasonably comfortable, or may disturb him and incline him to enact. This enactment is sometimes congruent with the phantasy that has been projected, so that the analyst becomes a little too compliant or too harsh. On the other hand, the enactment might represent the analyst's attempt at restoring a less disturbing phantasy to the fore (for example, having to distance himself consciously or unconsciously from an impotent or sadistic archaic figure). Finally, we must also be aware that the impulse towards enactment may reflect unresolved aspects of the analyst's own pathological internal object relations.

Some of these issues are addressed by O'Shaughnessy (1992) with great clarity and insight. She describes how a patient initially drew her into making denuded, undisturbing interpretations and offering what seemed like reasonable links with the patient's history. Thus, it seems, the analyst initially felt reasonably comfortable with her role and functions. After a period of time, however, she became uneasy and dissatisfied with such interpretations, which felt inauthentic and which did not seem to promote any change. The insight and work involved in the recognition of something in the patient's limited and over-close relationship with her, and her own denuded functioning with the patient, which needed exploration and thought, led, I believe, to a crucial transformation in the analyst's representation of herself and consequently in her ability to function. There is a convergence between the internal representation of herself as a thoughtful, reparative figure and the person who has now been able to recognize the degree of acting out which inevitably occurs, and this can be used to further understanding. This shift in internal perspective promotes the change from the situation in which the analyst is unwittingly involved in the enactment of the patient's problems, to the emergence of the potential for containment and transformation by the analyst, reflected in a shift in the style and content of the interpretations.

What O'Shaughnessy was then able to recognize was the function that this over-close, secluded, and denuded relationship served for the patient. The fact that the patient made a refuge of symmetry and over-closeness suggested that she was afraid of differences and distance between herself and her objects. The placation between analyst and patient was necessary because the patient feared either too intense erotic involvement or violence between them. I assume that she had unconsciously evoked corresponding versions of these disturbing phantasies in the analyst's mind, which resulted in her functioning in the way she initially described. O'Shaughnessy describes how, in sessions when acute anxiety threatened, the patient worked to rebuild her refuge, subtly and powerfully controlling the analyst to be over-close and to operate within its limits.

Thus, at the beginning of the analysis, the patient transferred her highly restricted object relations into the analytic situation. She must have communicated with words and non-verbal projections her intense anxieties about a fuller and freer object relationship, with the terrifying erotic and violent phantasies associated with this. I believe that the analyst's anxieties about being experienced both by the patient and by herself in these disturbing and destructive roles led her to function in the way the patient apparently required. While this may have served as a necessary temporary refuge at the start of the analysis, the analyst subsequently felt uneasy and dissatisfied with her role and was then able to think about it in a different way. I think the patient always finds this shift very threatening—it creates an asymmetry and may arouse envy and hatred, with powerful attempts to restore the status ante quo. This may be successful if the analyst cannot tolerate the uncertainty, anxiety, and guilt associated with the emergent phantasies of the relationship as a frightening, disappointing, and destructive one, and we sometimes need the internal or external support of colleagues to sustain our belief in what we are attempting to do.

Meltzer (1966) describes a somewhat similar dynamic, in relation to a group of disturbed patients who use extensive projective identification, which results in a compliant, pseudo-mature personality:

> The pressure on the analyst to join in the idealisation of the pseudo-maturity [is] ... great, and the underlying threats of psychosis and suicide [are] covertly communicated. The countertransference position is extremely difficult and in every way repeats the dilemma of the parents, who found themselves with a "model" child, so long as they abstained from being distinctly parental, either in the form of authority, teaching, or opposition to the relatively modest claims for privileges beyond those to which the child's age and accomplishments could reasonably entitle it. [p. 339–340]

The parental figure is thus faced either with the phantasy of being helplessly controlled or the phantasy of driving the child into madness or suicide.

I should like to illustrate in more detail first the way I believe a patient was able to use projection into the internal representation of the analyst (in his absence), to free herself from anxiety, whereas in the subsequent analytic sessions she needed to involve the analyst in different ways. I believe she achieved this through her projection of phantasies of disturbing object relations, which were not only reflected in her verbal communications, but also partially enacted by her in the sessions. I suspect that if the analyst is receptive to the patient's projections, the impact of the patient's disturbing unconscious phantasies, which concern the nature of his relationship with the patient, inevitably touch on the analyst's own anxieties. This may evoke forms of projection and enactment by the analyst in an attempt at restoring an internal equilibrium, which the analyst may initially be unaware of. The difficult and often painful task for the analyst is to recognize the subtle and complex enactments he is inevitably drawn into with his patient and to work to find a domain for understanding and thought outside the narrow and repetitive confines unconsciously demanded by the patient and sometimes by his own anxieties and needs. While the achievement of real psychic change is dependent on this process, it is threatening for the patient and liable to mobilize further defensive procedures.

Case study: "U"

The patient I want to speak about is a single woman, who has been in analysis for several years.

"U" arrived on a Monday morning and after a silence told me she was very involved in something that had occurred on Saturday, and which she hadn't thought about since—not until she was actually here. A friend, who works as a psychotherapist, told her about a young male supervisee who confessed to her that he had seduced one of his patients. My patient's friend told her not to tell anyone, and as soon as she said that, U immediately thought of me. She proceeded to give some details of the complicated connections between therapists, supervisors, and the patient involved. She seemed very concerned about who discussed what with whom and commented on how incestuous it all seemed. She added there was something almost sinister about all these people knowing about it. Then, after a silence, she said, "Thinking about it here, I was wondering *why* it should come to my mind here. I feel reasonably calm about it, it doesn't make me want to curl up in horror. I feel sufficiently removed from it, otherwise it would be horrific." There was a tense and expectant silence, and I felt aware of a pressure to respond quickly to what she had brought. When I did not do so, she commented that the silence seemed rather ominous.

When, on the Saturday, U was confronted with the disturbing image of a therapist's incestuous involvement with his patient and told not to tell anyone, I was conjured up in her mind, and I believe she projected the knowledge, the anxiety, and the disturbance into me. It was then not something she had in mind to tell me about— on the contrary, it had become unavailable to her until she actually encountered me on Monday. I suggest that we are thus dealing not with ordinary thinking or communication but, rather, with the omnipotent projection in phantasy not only of mental contents but also of the capacity to think about them. Since the process *is* an omnipotent one, the patient does not need to use symbolic means of communication. In this case, the phantasy involves an object immediately receptive to the patient's projections and apparently neither disturbed by them nor changed into something threatening. Involving the object in this way seems to have succeeded in completely freeing the patient from anxiety and discomfort.

When U encountered me at the beginning of the session on Monday and became aware that in reality I did not have possession of what she had got rid of, she recovered that part of her mind and its contents, which had in phantasy been projected. She was then driven to use verbal and non-verbal communication in a non-omnipotent way, apparently in order to achieve the same outcome. While telling me about all the incestuous connections between therapists, supervisors, and patients, it was striking that my patient wondered why all of this should come into her mind while she was with me, apparently failing to make the link between the story she reported and the phantasies connected with her own relationship with her analyst. I believe that by the combination of conscious and unconscious actions involved in this procedure, the patient was able both to communicate with, and to "nudge" the analyst into thinking about and taking responsibility for, the thoughts, phantasies, and impulses towards action that threatened her. The point I wish to emphasize is that the projective mechanisms served several functions: (1) They evidently allowed the patient to disavow the disturbing or potentially disturbing responses to what her friend had elicited. (2) They involved the analyst in the sense that it was now his function to make the connections and think about the significance of what she had communicated. (3) They served to draw the analyst into the partial enactment of some of the underlying phantasies that had been elicited, which had to be dealt with by the patient, in spite of the analyst's conscious attempts to avoid such an enactment and to find a working position with which he could feel reasonably comfortable.

In the session, I was made aware of the obvious role I was expected to play by the palpable pressure to respond quickly to what U had brought and make some half-expected comment or interpretation. My long experience with this patient suggested that if I had complied and directly addressed the material she had brought, offering some rather obvious answers to why it should come to her mind in the room with her analyst, there were a limited number of repetitive and unproductive scenarios. The first and most common one involved U relaxing and withdrawing, re-enacting with me the procedure that had taken place on Saturday when her friend had spoken to her, making it clear that the difficult and potentially disturbing material was no longer in her possession but in mine. The second involved a less complete projection, where the patient retained some contact with what had been projected but resisted the dangerous prospect of thinking for herself about these issues, insisting that it was my function to do so. The third scenario was one in which my interpretations were themselves concretely experienced as threatening and demanding intrusions.

In the session I have described, I was not aware of being disturbed by the contents of U's material, but I was troubled and disheartened by the prospect of enacting one of these repetitive and unproductive roles with her. However, when I remained silent for a while, attempting to find a way of understanding and approaching her, my silence *nevertheless* evoked U's phantasy of a disturbing archaic object relationship, in which she was involved with a threatening, "ominous" figure filled with unspoken, alarming things, potentially intrusive and demanding. I believe she had partially re-created an important archaic object relationship through the interaction of two powerful factors: (1) the phantasied projection into the analyst of some of these archaic qualities and functions, (2) by communicating and behaving in the way she had, she was indeed faced with an analyst whose mind was filled with thoughts about what she had told him, who did indeed want something from her and might make difficult and "intrusive" demands on her. When these expectations and experiences were coloured by the qualities projected into them, the patient was indeed living out an archaic, familiar object relationship.

In this session, and in those that followed, I felt the need to try to find a way of working that would, I hoped, partially avoid the repetitive interactions I have described. I remained silent at times, trying to understand what was taking place, or I made comments on what I thought U was doing with me or expecting of me. I also attempted to get her to explore what was making her so uncomfortable, and some of the links between her material, her family history, and the analytic situation, which I thought were available to her. I was made aware of the threat my efforts posed to the patient's equilibrium and her extreme reluctance to allow either of us to escape from familiar interactions that appeared, paradoxically, to be necessary and reassuring for her. I felt subjected to powerful pressure either to allow myself to be used in such a way that I had to hold, and take responsibility for, the disturbing material that U projected, or to enact some elements of the phantasy of a forceful seductive or intrusive relationship. I was thus confronted with painful and unwelcome representations of my role in relation to my patient and continued to struggle to find an approach that felt more constructive and with which I could be more comfortable.

There is always the idea that by remaining more silent, or speaking more, understanding the situation in a different way, taking a different tack, one can free oneself from such repetitive and unproductive interactions. Sometimes this is manifested in the thought (held by the analyst, or the patient, or both) that if the analyst changed or were a different kind of analyst, these problems would not arise. Of course, these considerations have to be taken seriously and will often have some element of truth. However, for much of the time in dealing with U, I came to believe that whatever I said or did was liable to be experienced in accordance with the limited, archaic phantasies I have briefly indicated, and that the repetitive living-out of these phantasies in the sessions served important and reassuring functions for the patient. There were brief periods of thoughtful reflection which were relieving to me, as I felt I could regain a sense of my proper function. However, it was evidently painful and difficult for the patient to be anywhere outside the familiar and reassuring enactments, and she would quickly withdraw again, or re-evoke the excited provocative relationship in which, paradoxically, she seemed to feel safer.

> For example, after a period of difficult work, U said, thoughtfully: "I can see . . . both sides . . . in what has been going on. I can appreciate you want me to look rather more closely at the things that have come up. After all, just putting them out in an extremely cautious way as 'ideas' doesn't get me any further." Her voice then became firmer and more excited: "At the same time it seems remarkable to me that I'm even prepared to men-

tion these things. In fact I'm amazed. I must feel very confident that I am not going to be pushed into anything more." Her excitement escalated, and she repeated how extraordinary it was that she had said as much as she had, what a risk she had taken that I would seize on the opportunity. U said that normally her main concern was to avoid saying things if she could foresee some sort of opening she might give me, so she has to make sure this doesn't occur.

Thus, having briefly and uncomfortably acknowledged the existence of an analyst who was actually trying to help her, and the recognition of the defensive processes she was so persistently caught up in, U moved into a state of erotized excitement, which gripped her for much of the rest of the session. She thus seemed compulsively driven to involve me in interactions where she either experienced a tantalizing, ominous withholding, or exciting demanding sexual intrusion. These were, or course, aspects of the powerful oedipal configuration that had been evoked in her mind by the episode her friend had originally reported to her, and which had important links with her early history.

While it is familiar to us, I find the recurrent pressure on the analyst to join the patient in the partial enactment of archaic, often disturbed and disturbing object relationships one of the most interesting and puzzling phenomena we encounter. With U, what functions did it serve to involve me, not as a helpful, benign figure, but a version of a disturbing archaic one? I suspect there are many answers to this. This interaction frees the patient from knowledge of and responsibility for her own impulses and phantasies: she is predominantly a helpless victim. It was very evident in the sessions that it provided her with a degree of gratification and excitement. It may have served as a means of making me recognize and understand aspects of her history, or her inner life, which I had thus far failed to address, although I am uncertain about suggesting this as her *motive*. What I want to add is the way in which it seems to serve a reassuring function if what is enacted in the external world corresponds in some measure with an object relationship unconsciously present. The alternative, when she is confronted with the discrepancy between the two, is painful and threatening.

From the analyst's point of view, I suspect that if he is receptive to the patient's projections, the phantasies of archaic object relationships must inevitably resonate with the analyst's own unconscious needs and anxieties. If these relate too closely to areas of conflict that remain largely unresolved, there is a danger that the analyst will be driven into forms of enactment that either gratify some mutual needs or defend him against such gratification. As Hoffman (1983) points out:

> Because the analyst is human, he is likely to have in his repertoire a blueprint for approximately the emotional response that the patient's transference dictates and that response is likely to be elicited, whether consciously or unconsciously.... Ideally this response serves as a key—perhaps the best key the analyst has—to the nature of the interpersonal scene that the patient is driven by transference to create. [p. 413]

As Joseph (1987, 1988), O'Shaughnessy (1992), and Carpy (1989) have suggested, we may have to recognize that a degree of enactment is almost inevitable, part of an on-going process that the analyst can come to recognize, temporarily extricate himself from, and use to further his understanding. Indeed, in the clinical situation I have just described, it seemed important to recognize the pressure towards enactment within the patient and the corresponding pressures felt by the analyst. The recognition of the compulsive and repetitive nature of these interactions may have important consequences. As Rosenfeld and O'Shaughnessy have indicated, it may allow the analyst to recover some sense of his own proper function. This diminishes the discrepancy between his own phantasies of his role and what is manifested in the analytic situation. If the analyst is also more able to tolerate whatever discrepancies exist, he will be less driven to use projective mechanisms and the forms of enactment I have been describing. In the space thus created, he may be able to think differently about his patient.

* * *

I have tried to emphasize in this chapter that what is projected into the analyst is a phantasy of an object relationship that evokes not only thoughts and feelings, but also propensities towards action. From the patient's point of view, the projections represent an attempt to reduce the discrepancy between the phantasy of some archaic object relationship and what the patient experiences in the analytic situation. For the analyst, too, there are impulses to function in ways that lead to a greater correspondence with some needed or desired phantasies. The interaction between the patient's and the analyst's needs may lead to the repetitive enactment of the painful and disturbing kind I have described. It may be very difficult for the analyst to extricate himself (or his patient) from this unproductive situation and recover his capacity for reflective thought, at least for a while.

As I have indicated, the difficulty is compounded when the projection into the analyst leads to subtle or overt enactments that do not initially disturb the analyst but, on the contrary, constitute a comfortable collusive arrangement, where the analyst feels his role is congruent with some internal phantasy. It may be difficult to recognize the defensive function this interaction serves both for the patient and for the analyst, and the more disturbing unconscious phantasies it defends against.

The analyst's temporary and partial recovery of his capacity for reflective thought, rather than action, is crucial for the survival of his analytic role. The analyst may not only feel temporarily freed from the tyranny of repetitive enactments and modes of thought himself, but he may believe in the possibility of freeing his patient, in time. However, such moves are likely to provoke pain and disturbance in the patient, who finds the unfamiliar space in which thought can take place frightening and hateful.

Summary

This chapter emphasizes that what is projected into the analyst is a phantasy of an object relationship that evokes not only thoughts and feelings, but also propensities towards action. From the patient's point of view, the projections represent an attempt to reduce the discrepancy between the phantasy of some archaic object relationship and what the patient experiences in the analytic situation.

For the analyst, too, there are impulses to function in ways which lead to a greater correspondence with some needed or desired phantasies. The interaction between the patient's and the analyst's needs may lead to the repetitive enactment of the painful and disturbing kind I have described. It may be very difficult for the analyst to extricate himself (or his patient) from this unproductive situation and recover his capacity for reflective thought, at least for a while.

This difficulty is compounded when the projection into the analyst leads to subtle or overt enactments that do not initially disturb the analyst, but, on the contrary, constitute a comfortable collusive arrangement, where the analyst feels that his role is congruent with some internal phantasy. It may be difficult to recognize the defensive function this interaction serves, both for the patient and the analyst and for the more disturbing unconscious phantasies it defends against.

CHAPTER TWELVE

Psychic turbulence

Patricia Daniel

*Patricia Daniel describes the complicated changes in the trans-
ference of a lonely, cut-off young man whose desperate need to
be understood was repeatedly negated by various manoeuvres,
such as ambiguity and falseness, by which he quickly moved
away from genuine contact. He feared being shattered by contact with his own shattered internal objects. Images of glass are
drawn on to convey qualities, especially of ambiguity—reflection with transparency, fragility, and shattering. With the gradual
analytic dismantling of this combination of manic and obsessional defences, the psychic equilibrium that kept his pain imprisoned, was upset resulting in a turbulent, confused state. At
the same time his dreams reflected greater stability.*

This chapter is about defensive structures and the anxiety
and psychic pain in changing them. I shall start by describing defences that were mobilized during the first part of an
analysis and how these protected an ego felt to be extremely
fragile, and which also sought to evade contact with an object felt

to be shattered. These psychic structures were formed from a complex interlocking between schizoid and manic mechanisms. As the analysis proceeded, there was a change to a different structure in which a tie to an object was established and the patient began to experience conflict and anxiety, but the loosening of defences brought other problems associated with the movement towards more fluid but also more turbulent states.

Case study: "Mr V"

A young man, "Mr V", came to analysis because he felt stuck in his life, both in personal relationships and in his work, and felt lonely and miserable. While he described others as seeing him coping adequately, he conveyed a contradictory sense of himself as cut off from life and yet deeply pained by he knew not what. He told of his early life having been difficult. In infancy he had been so acutely ill that he had had to spend time in hospital and was cut off from contact with his mother and family. His father and sister had suffered from chronic ill health, and his mother had struggled to support the family. The emotional atmosphere at home was usually fraught. Mr V thought that as a small boy he had felt attached to his mother and rather fearful of his father, whose moods were unpredictable—sometimes leading to outbursts of temper and at other times to silent withdrawal. In boyhood and adolescence Mr V felt increasingly isolated, and his success in academic work only served to increase his isolation from his peers. He gained qualifications in his chosen field but struggled with panic attacks in his first job.

> There was an unreal quality to the early stages of the analysis. His experiences, whether presently or in the past, were described with a kaleidoscope of ever-changing emotional tones—sometimes it was as if he felt I would be appreciative of his sensitivity, and at other times I thought he expected me to be rather intrigued by what he told me. My speaking seemed either to disturb him or to excite him, and the content of interpretations was frequently passed over, so that I would feel I had

missed the point; on occasion I would notice that what I had said had been absorbed into the material he reported in quite a subtle and disguised form. There was a desperate quality to what was occurring, and I thought he was terrified, unconsciously, of the analytic situation. I felt I was unable to contact him and it seemed as though I was being experienced as a distant and unpredictable object. Experiences in the present and in the fragile home environment in the past seemed to have left Mr V without any sense of orientation: he seemed to be unconnected and disconnected from his objects.

Psychic structure

Slowly the structure of his internal world began to emerge, and in the third year of analysis he had a dream that, I think, encapsulates key elements of his internal object relationships. Later on and very gradually these were to become manifest in the transference. The dream showed an internal system that included a false idealization surrounding a façade of a structure, which, in turn, concealed a terrible claustrophobic situation.

In the dream "*he is in an idyllic village, surrounded by idyllic countryside. Tourists are being shown around an historic building, and he joins them because he wants to see what it is like inside. But then the historic exterior turns out to be a façade: inside it is a holiday camp full of people who cannot get out because there is wire all around and no one is allowed out. The person showing them around is doing so in order to show them how awful it is. The holiday camp then turns into a concentration camp, and he is crying for the children. He feels very upset.*"

Unusually, Mr V was silent for quite some time; he seemed uneasy, and I felt him becoming increasingly remote while I was having ideas about the dream. Later in the session he referred back to a number of matters he had spoken of in recent days, but in a way that seemed thin and unconvincing, as if he felt he was filling out the time to the end of the session. I interpreted that he felt disturbed by the dream and upset by the approaching holiday, and so was now erecting a false façade to conceal his need to keep us away from some much more desperate and frightening situation, like the concentration camp in the dream. He made no verbal response and remained tense and emotionally distant to the end of the session. The material and dynamic in subsequent sessions leading up to the break became more openly false, fuelled, I thought, by his increasing anxiety about the analysis exposing something dreadful and his then being abandoned during a long holiday break.

Within the analytic encounter, a false object relationship was emerging in which patient and analyst were both involved. The analyst was being experienced as narcissistic and engaged in falsely purveying a pseudo analysis, and the patient projectively and introjectively identified with this false object. The analysis began to expose a double thread—that is, two sorts of relationships: an apparently ordinary one between patient and analyst, which had to be kept smooth and friendly, and another secret relationship in which the patient believed he had inserted himself into the analyst's mind by means of projective identification, and could from there omnipotently observe their interactions and relationship. Each, he believed, reflected and deflected the other, for, as he once told me, there is an ambiguity about glass: you can see through it, but it also throws off a reflection. Beneath the ambiguity and falseness there seemed to lie a profound dread of some appalling situation within his own mind, from which he believed there could be no escape, and to which he feared the analysis would cruelly expose him.

Imperceptibly, this state of affairs gave way to one of extreme ambiguity. It became increasingly difficult to distinguish between what I sensed to be genuine and what I felt to be false, whether in the emotional quality of the transference or in the external situation being described or a memory being recalled. During this phase there was a mercurial quality to the transference. There were moments of what seemed genuine contact with me or with aspects of himself, and immediately these would be cut off by another elaborate description, another emotive account, and a different affective tone. These elaborate descriptions had a hollow emotional tone and usually occurred after what I felt were moments of real contact. They formed part of a defensive structure that he used as a retreat from disintegration and persecution, as described by Steiner (1993). The falseness followed the severing of connections—both of affect and of thought—and working with this structure was like trying to follow quicksilver. Never was there sufficient time for a sufficient connection that might allow another connection or a further link, and our relationship was characterized by this repetitively shattering process.

Internal world

Mr V's internal world was peopled with remote, fragile, and preoccupied objects interacting with unpredictable violent ones. For example, he frequently felt I was in some way emotionally distant from him and if he thought he detected a change in my appearance or manner or heard unusual sounds about the place, he believed I was distracted and probably unwell.

To protect himself from the pain of such tenuous contact, he had constructed an idealized but brittle object that appeared in his material and dreams as fine pieces of glassware. These were felt to be in danger of being smashed. It was difficult to tell when he was identified with these idealized, fragile objects and anxious to protect them and when his hostility towards them was being expressed in the phantasy of shattering them. There was a different, more schizoid defence, which, he felt, protected him from dangerous, violent aspects of his objects, as well as from his own hostile impulses projected into them. This took the form of breaking off from the genuine contact, whether with his objects, including myself in the transference, or from aspects of himself. These various defences were interwoven and formed a kind of shell that left him isolated from objects in his inner world and alone and lonely in his actual life.

In the course of the analysis I came to learn of the combination of internal forces and external events that had led to such a depleted world. It is easy to imagine the difficulties at home while the infant was becoming established within a fragile emotional environment, with an ill and volatile father and a mother preoccupied with illness and having to work. Mr V told me his care during babyhood had had to be shared by several female relatives. Again and again in the transference we experienced the psychic trauma for the infant, and the different women involved in his care made me think (and feel) the lack of a consistent object available and able to contain his infantile anxieties—anxieties intensified by early life spent in hospital. It appeared that experiences such as these had contributed to the development of the shattered object that emerged in the transference. The analyst was experienced as distant, preoccupied, and liable suddenly to become hostile, intrusive, and vindictive towards him. When he believed I had become this hostile figure, he felt interpretations as cruel and exposing him in a way he felt to be terrifying. Another feature, which I have already mentioned, was the transitory nature of genuine contact, for it was momentary and would be followed by Mr V becoming either disconnected and remote or, alternatively, excited. A striking feature of the transference was its unpredictability, especially at the beginning and near the end of sessions, when his anxiety increased regarding his perception of my attitude towards him, as did my uncertainty as to his feeling and thinking state. The tenuous quality of genuine contact suggested a desperate internal situation where contact with objects perceived to be shattered was believed to be a shattering experience for the self, but to be cut off from objects was felt to be equally terrifying. The severing of contact defended Mr V from the pain of involvement with such an object, but this defence left him diminished and more deprived.

What had emerged was an intricate defensive structure to protect the patient from contact with a desperate persecutory inner situation (the concentration camp) that imprisoned him. On the surface Mr V identified with and sought to maintain a smooth relation with an idealized object, which was inevitably experienced as unstable (the idyllic countryside and village). Behind lay manic mechanisms to shield him from an object believed to be false and narcissistic (the false façade of the holiday camp and building). All were enmeshed and re-enforced each other. At the core of this imprisoning system was an object felt to be remote and shattered, and a disconnected self also felt to be damaged. Gradually we came to understand Mr V's great fear and reluctance to experience awareness of the meaning and consequences of these defensive structures, since it faced him, on the one hand, with anxieties of psychotic intensity with fears of disintegration and breakdown and, on the other, with facing the acute pain of conflict and psychic turbulence, as we shall see.

Movement towards unlocking the defensive structure

For a long time these defences continued to re-enforce each other: they were interlocked and barred the way to a genuine contact with a needy part of the self, but as the analysis proceeded, the mockery and falsity became less prominent, and the character of the patient's dreams began to change. Where previously they lacked coherence and structure and were often reported in a broken-up fashion, now they appeared more sharply defined and with some sequence of action. Yet at the same time Mr V's associations to the dreams seemed to become more ambiguous, even misleading, as though there was latent content that had to be hidden. Gradually the ambiguity intensified and then was replaced by a very real confusion. Mr V began to experience depersonalized states during sessions when he would be unable to hold onto or connect his thoughts; even though I tried to keep interpretations short and simple, he had difficulty in hearing and understanding them. He told me that the sound of my voice seemed to come from a great distance, and he could not make out what the words meant, although it was apparent to me that he was struggling to keep contact through the sounds, since he was unable to grasp meanings.

Rosenfeld (1950), in his work on confusional states, describes how under certain internal and external conditions aggressive impulses become temporarily dominant, and loving and hating and good and bad aspects of objects become mixed up in the subject's mind. He suggests that these infantile states of confusion are states of disintegration, and he emphasizes that they are accompanied by extreme anxiety because destructive feelings threaten to overwhelm loving ones and the self is felt to be in danger of being destroyed too. Rosenfeld stresses the need for the ego to be helped to regain its capacity to differentiate, so that normal splitting can be restored and loving impulses be strengthened. I think Mr V's confused and depersonalized states, which were mostly confined within sessions, came about as a result of the analytic work, which loosened the rigidity of his schizoid defences. The tight, claustrophobic, "concentration-camp" structure began to give way, but what followed made him feel very anxious. He became disconnected from what he felt and what he thought, as well as confused as to what was doing him good and what he felt to be harming him. When some of these problems could be worked through, the confused states occurred less frequently, and he was able to recover from them more quickly.

Around this period Mr V had a dream that indicated a changed internal situation, for in this dream he was now in a relationship to an object. In the dream *he was on an ocean-going sailing yacht that was moored to a landing stage: there were a lot of people on board, none of whom he knew. Someone was inviting him to come away, but he refused.*

In his associations he first said he thought it may have been a drugs and drinking party, but later in the session he said he knew he was trying to suggest this to me. He did not see (in the dream) who it was who was urging him to leave, and he did not sound convinced about wanting to leave the yacht, nor about wishing to go with the person who was trying to lead him away.

I understood this element in the dream as a part of him that did want to lead him and his analyst back to the false defence, but in the dream and in associating to it he could recognize this wish and resist it, for in the dream he refused to leave the yacht and in his associations he told me he knew what he was doing with his "suggestions". I thought the ocean-going yacht represented a more resilient self, though its large size indicated some grandiosity too. The landing stage showed he was now attached/moored to an object, and he and his internal world (all the people on the yacht) were clearly differentiated from it. But the dream also conveyed the dilemma for the patient when he faced this new situation. There was the pull to return to pseudo relations and grandiose views of himself, and the lure away from new and potentially more lively relationships, but he was now able to resist the part of him that tried to entice him back to these defences. Joseph (1989a) stresses the anxiety and panic patients feel when they experience the disequilibrium associated with every small change in the way they relate to their objects, and she emphasizes the hold of the regressive pull to previous ways of relating. I think we can see, too, how his internal object was now experienced differently, although he perceived it as a new, or different, object: instead of an idealized or broken inanimate object (glassware), it was represented as manifestly human—the many people on the yacht.

The contrast between the two dreams occurring at different stages in the analysis highlight the changes in the defences and in the relationship to objects. Early on, Mr V's contact with his object was repeatedly shattered, and he felt himself to be an amalgam of aspects of self and objects. The difficult circumstances of his infancy and the fragile home environment had contributed to the formation of massive defences to protect the self, as I have described. The unlocking of these defences led to severe states of confusion, and though these were contained within the analysis, they were experienced by Mr V as shattering to his precarious sense of identity. By the time of the second dream, a "mooring" to a firmer object had been secured. But then he felt acute claustrophobic and agoraphobic anxieties whenever he felt the relationship to be threatened. He also began to experience conflict, as when he knew there was a pull away and he wanted to resist it. While the analytic work led to a gradual increase in Mr V's capacity to differentiate the quality of his experiences, internally and externally, it also led to considerable intra-psychic disturbance as he struggled to free himself from the defensive structures that had constricted him, and then face the pain of guilt and the psychic effort of repair and restoration of his objects.

The analytic process increases as well as relieves anxiety, and any movement towards change involves psychic turbulence and the pain of facing internal reality, including the pain of guilt for one's part in it. Defences build structures and when analysis of defences leads to changes in object relations, the structure of the ego also changes. Mr V had a complex structure of defences behind which lay a shattered ego. I have tried to show some change in object relations as the analysis proceeded which led to change in the ego too. It was no longer felt to be shattered, although still liable to become so.

CHAPTER THIRTEEN

The concept of
the envious/jealous superego

Leslie Sohn

Leslie Sohn explores the concept of the envious or mad super-ego, its hypnotic quality, and its inevitable jealous component, illustrating this in the analyses of both non-psychotic and extremely disturbed psychotic patients, including murderers, all of whom had experienced considerable deprivation in childhood. Once the rest of the ego is in thrall to this envious/jealous superego, emotional pain will remain imprisoned—one might say embedded—in hallucinatory voices and delusions.

In the conclusion to her monograph, "Envy and Gratitude", Melanie Klein (1957) says:

> I have described in other connections the impact of the earliest internalized persecutory object—the retaliating, devouring and poisonous breast, I would now assume that the projection of the infant's envy lends a particular complexion to his anxiety about the primal and later internal persecution. The "envious superego" is felt to disturb or annihilate all attempts at reparation and creativeness. It is also felt to make constant and exorbitant demands on the individual's gratitude. For to

persecution are added the guilt feelings that the persecutory internal objects are the result of the individual's own envious and destructive impulses which have primarily spoilt the good object. The need for punishment, which finds satisfaction by the increased devaluation of the self, leads to a vicious circle. [p. 231]

This chapter attempts to look at the facts of the envious superego and presents clinical material to confirm its reality in the clinical practice of psychoanalysis. Whilst immediately wondering why it is the superego that takes on these characteristics, particularly as the above quotation is followed by a statement of the "ultimate aim of psychoanalysis is the integration of the patient's personality", Freud's conclusion that where id was ego shall be is a pointer in that direction. In other words, the effect of such envious assaults would be experienced within the ego itself, and the deficits of such pathology would be expected in the ego itself. To clarify, let us turn in Klein's monograph to earlier references to the superego:

> When the infant reaches the depressive position and becomes more able to face his psychic reality he also feels that the object's badness is largely due to his own aggressiveness and its ensuing projection. This insight as we can see in the transference situation, gives rise to great mental pain and guilt when the depressive position is at its height. But it also brings about feelings of relief and hope which in turn make it less difficult to reunite the two aspects of the object and the self and to work through the depressive position. . . . Through mitigation of hatred by love the object improves in the infant's mind. . . . The internal object acquires a restraining and self-preservative attitude and its greater strength is an important aspect of its superego function. [M. Klein, 1957, pp. 196]

This is followed by a note that such positive development, either intrinsically produced in the normal development of the child or later via psychoanalytic treatment, could be temporarily or more permanently undone. In Klein's paper there is an emphasis on such undoings. The essence, however, of what Mrs Klein seems to be saying is that what has been termed superego is in reality an ego that has been suffused with the most pernicious, cruel, and pretentious forms of superego controls and behaviours—so that if this idea is correct, the psychoanalytic intention would be not only integration, but a re-distribution and re-orientation of ego and superego activities.

Another reference to superego in the Essay is the statement that

> envy of creativeness is a fundamental element in the distur-
> bance of the creative process. To spoil and destroy the initial
> source of goodness soon leads to destroying and attacking the
> babies that the mother contains and results in the good object
> being turned into a hostile, critical and envious one. The super-
> ego figure on which strong envy has been projected becomes
> particularly persecutory and interferes with thought processes
> and with every productive activity, ultimately with creative-
> ness. [M. Klein, 1957, p. 202]

Again there seems to be no good reason to differentiate the situation as a superego figure: the ego has become projected into with
such frequency that it contains all the biting, pernicious quality of
the initial envious attack. One of the patients to be described is in a
long-term stay in a maximum-security hospital and will be shown
to epitomize the above views with a set of psychotic experiences in
which the new superego/ego is not only cruel and implacable but
contains all the hypocritical pretentiousness felt by the patient's
juvenile ego's view of his object, but which now poses as his new
and permanently installed good object.

The final reference to the superego in "Envy and Gratitude"
has a particular significance for the patient just mentioned.
Melanie Klein says: "I have tried to show in various connections
how destructive impulses, the expression of the death instinct, are
first of all felt to be directed against the ego" (M. Klein, 1957, p. 72).

This chapter, whilst not being able to give a great amount of
historic detail because of confidentiality, will attempt to examine
why, in some patients, the expression of the death instinct is not
simply a believed-in fantasy felt to be directed against and to have
affected the ego, but is enacted in a truly physical assault upon the
total ego of another—in this case, of the original good object—
whereas in the first two cases to be described it remains a fantasy,
albeit acted out in a relatively harmless way, except to their own
ego's.

It seems too easy to ascribe such differences to genetic structures—there is no history of mental disorder in either of the families of the two psychotic cases to be described—or to the amount

of innate aggressive potential within the patient, both of which seem extremely important. I think I can come to the conclusion that what is of desperate importance in the differentiation is the undoing previously referred to by Melanie Klein. After listening to and treating various patients who have enacted violently and who contain all the elements of envy we have referred to, I feel that the undoing, whether it be of the positive elements that may be present or more usually of the wild idealization that actual bad objects produce, leaves the developing child unable ever to experience or integrate any form of mitigation. The idealization, in these cases of their original objects, seems to me to be almost always present and is an invitation to dissolution and undoing, with full wild hatred being present, leaving the mental field free for enactment and horror.

Unfortunately, there is a very subtle transferential danger present. In a hospital setting where all the patients receive good, decent psychiatric care, proper and appropriate medication is given, which may or may not be meaningful but which in its tranquillizing quality makes patients available for psychoanalytic/psychotherapeutic intervention. But what happens in the patient's mind if a proper analysis takes place and not simply an attenuated form of love via the routine system of a good psychiatric hospital? One hopes that the continued use of major antipsychotic medication, which certainly attenuates the degree of psychotic anxiety, will be able to hold the fort. It's a question that has to be asked. If Mrs Klein is right—and the author of this patient feels she is—the absence of reintegration leaves the patient constantly open to this form of undoing and therefore of destructiveness enacted.

Case study: "S"

The first clinical reference is to a woman, "S", who was hospitalized because she behaved in an intolerable way at home, which included attacking her aristocratic mother. Interestingly, her sophisticated family only became aware of her illness because she kept on falling over and fracturing her arm, as if she had to demonstrate her fractured mind concretely to them. Gradually, S, too, became aware of her madness. Listening to her, one had the feeling that there was something much more than what one was hearing about, but she either dealt with it as though it were perfectly normal or as if she was enjoying keeping something secret.

S's mother could not understand how anyone could spend long periods of time with her daughter—it was too painful. Presumably either the mother had minimal capacity to cope with projections, or else those coming from her daughter were so painful that she could not bear them. The patient seemed to be enacting this relationship with her mother when she behaved as if there were something absent. At this time, S started to talk about jealousy. She also spoke about social situations such that if she were in place A, she would always be wondering about what she could be doing if she were at place B, even if place B was merely a very exciting delusional idea. She also spoke of her envy of other people's ability to walk around without falling and breaking their arms.

S would be accompanied to the consulting-room by a nurse who would greet me, but the patient did not and, instead, looked confused. When the nurse had gone, my patient would say "Hello" in a friendly way—that is, she would not speak to me in front of the nurse. It turned out that the nurse had actually said to the patient about me: "I wouldn't mind putting my slippers under his bed." The patient in her posh voice said to me, "If you think that I would say hello to you in front of her, you are bloody mad"—that is, she concretely felt the jealousy and the relationship that was being jealously attacked, but equally she was aware of the bond between us that could be attacked by the nurse. Thus, despite the intensely psychotic quality, this patient could protect the link between herself and me by behaving as if it didn't really matter. Unfortunately, she idealized this capacity to deny the seriousness of what she was feeling.

S had become friendly with the ward sister who was French, and she and this ward sister spoke French to each other. As a result of this friendliness, the sister lent her some French magazines, which she did not read; instead, she tore the magazines into bits and pieces, peed on them, and then swallowed them, and only then did she feel that she had a clear and concise understanding of the contents of the magazines, which she had not read. The sister was an extremely important, provocative figure of jealousy to her, but once she had urinated on the sister's productions she could feel totally satisfied. It was a highly idealized, omnipotent psychotic triumph over her object in which her urine was so much more meaningful than the sister's. It took some time to work through this phase of the brilliance of her urine—and, for that matter, of any excremental product—against which the ward sister's books/breast or my ordinary interpretative work were forced to compete. This led on to the beginning of an understanding of what was going on, because she started to smell badly and was clearly, by her indications, drinking her own urine and, at the same time, from the stains on her face, was also coprophilic.

S came into the room one day, falling all over the place and unable to make up her mind whether she wanted to kiss me, hug me, or hit me, and I simply tried to protect myself by holding up my left arm, whereupon she grabbed it, turned a somersault, and landed on her feet. She spent an enormous amount of time, many hours, admiring not my interpretative capacities but my circus acrobatics, and it took some time for my mind's capacity to maintain its own balance instead of being mad listening to her admiration. Gradually one was able to stabilize this girl's internal world and deal with it in a particular way because the work that followed centred upon the core problem of her schizophrenic illness.

When S started to tell me her history, it was that she was the first viable child of this aristocratic family, the other children having died of some congenital disorder. She was kept under constant surveillance by day and night nurses as well as by the doctors who watched her to see whether anything untoward was going to happen. Fortunately, in her case it did not. After she had reached a certain stage of development, when it was clear that she was now going to live safely, the watchfulness stopped. Coincident with this was her father's return from the war. The nurses were withdrawn, and she was given a nanny.

Meanwhile her mother, following the father's return, became pregnant and had another two babies—twin girls. S was on her own, but she did not envy the two sisters; what she envied was her mother's "bloody dog", who was allowed into the mother's bed. Then we could see that in the coprophilia she was identifying herself with her mother's faeces, so that she could get right inside her mother's body through her mother's intestines.

This girl, despite her fractured character, could still enact her schizophrenic view of her envious mind and its results. She could tolerate the triumph of turning the internal object/ the ward sister/ the breast/ her analyst into a pretty wet (=wimpish, drippy) affair. In addition, she often described her father as a rich wet.

In this material we can see that the envious superego is potentially jealous as well—that is, jealous of the link between the patient and the new good object in the transference. This is manifested in the jealousy situation between nurse and patient and between sister and patient.

Clinical vignette: "X"

The second patient is a homosexual man, "X", who, in describing a new friend, says to me, "He is so beautifully girlish, I find him so attractive". This paradoxical statement is in fact an attack on the analyst's mind. Here is a man who avoids any contact with women or girls admiring a new male friend for his beautiful girlishness. The statement is such that it invites the analyst's mind to feel split or to feel attacked so that it cannot see or understand. It is an attack on my awareness of the paradox, or else, if he could be thought of as a man who is possibly thinking of a woman or girl as attractive, he approaches this aggressively, destructively and dishonestly.

X would not be thought of as psychotic, and he is gainfully employed full-time. But this statement was an envious attack on the analyst's mind/breast. What he envied was my mind's capacity to reject a compromise by not being homosexual. Nor did he feel I was excited by a pretty, girlish young man, be it himself or any idea that he would present that would symbolize the pretty girlish young man. There was in fact a split-off version of that in the pretty–pretty presentation of the deceptive material. This also occurred in other sessions.

But gradually we became aware that X's life was punctuated by disastrous experiences of total unhappiness and impoverishment of his natural talents. At an early age he had been separated from his mother; during this time he was well and carefully fostered by a neighbouring family, who happened to be Jewish. In addition, in adult life he kept a secret list of Jewish restaurants throughout the world, which he promised he would publish in book form when he was well enough to tolerate sharing his secrets. The same situation was true in the transference and externally. But the trouble was that what he was talking about was not as clear as this. All these facts remained as unintegrated, separate, split-off entities. The integration and therefore the truth of all this was prevented by the massive splitting, which kept these entities apart whilst he was secretly enjoying the breast's envy of the multiple surrogate breasts/Jewish restaurants throughout the world. Obviously centrally and therefore perversely this also occurred in the transference. His collection of the Jewish restaurants is his attempt to render an intolerable situation of envy and jealousy tolerable. It is a projection of envy into the internal object, which was itself originally the envied object. The list of restaurants represents a secret triumph over the analyst/internal object that is much more easily tolerated. Again we can see that the envious superego is potentially jealous of the new relationship in the analysis as well. His triumphant secret defence broke down during breaks in the treatment when he would be faced with an unanswerable question—"What about me?" which would immediately be followed by homosexual cavortings.

The importance of these two cases is about the role of the envious superego, which is potentially jealous, as well of the link between the patient and the new good object in the transference.

Clinical vignette: "L"

The third patient is a man, "L", whom I see three times a week in hospital.

During a session I suddenly became aware that he was behaving as if he were simply at a party, drinking or eating and simply absorbing everything. I said to him: "You're not thinking", and he said: "I do not have to think, I've got you. Since I have known you, you have done all the thinking for me." He was living in an idealized situation that had not been available to him as a child.

L told me that his aggressive life started at the age of 4, when the organization "War and Want" came into his life and gave him a pair of real boots with which he could freely kick anybody and everybody. This followed the sudden death of his father in a railway accident, which was clearly the fault of his employers, but they never paid the compensation that they had promised, and this led to his mother becoming psychotic. She would not feed the children and hid the food under the bed. They had to find the food when she was actually asleep or was feigning sleep. Here in my sessions with him everything was "up front", as he put it, everything—that is, constant food—was available, and he could take his choice.

At this time L has no psychotic features to see whatsoever. He can pass as a perfectly normal man, but one who has this almost psychotic quality of a relationship to his therapist, as he puts it. Without actually discussing his index offence, I would like to describe something that led up to his first offence. L was in the throes of a psychotic illness in which he was in communication with the Devil, and whilst in this he got a command hallucinatory instruction to go and kill, so he walked out, stole a car, and drove, looking for somebody to kill. He saw a woman and a child, both totally unknown to him, and the voice told him to kill the mother of the child, but he said "No". He said "No" to some mad—what he called devilish—aspect of himself and in which voice a countervoice said, "Were you to kill that woman, the child would become an orphan". In other words, there still existed in this man's mind a part that was available for sane and constructive use. He was aware of what the fate of that child would be. This related to the whole quality of his childlike feelings in his situation with me, in which situation his deprived superego was murderously jealous. But there was still something in his mind—a normal part of his ego, albeit momentary—that could oppose this jealous impulse.

It is not uncommon, following the murder of a particular person, for their livers to be eaten by the murderer. To these people, the liver seems to be the most important organ, perhaps because of its very name and the associated fantasies about its continuous involvement in the inner bodily life-giving processes. This is a parallel to the above patient's feeling that there is a total absorption in my thinking about and for him. I am his liver. But this also links to the constant mental feeding that enlivens the envy/jealousy of his dead mother.

Clinical vignette: "J"

The fourth and last patient, "J", is also in hospital. He grew up in a weird world—a world where he jealously regarded his mother's step-children in one of whose houses she lived. He would regard them with considerable jealousy because of the palatial houses that they lived in. His mother would meet him periodically and regale him with stories of her exciting underworld rich life. His adolescence was punctuated by care-orders, residential schools, drug-taking and selling, and he is consistently aware of his jealousy of what he feels to be "the rich ones". His mother had abandoned the family to take up with a very undesirable though extremely rich man.

During the course of his ongoing treatment, J is now free of all manifest signs of psychosis, and the treatment situation is even more dubious than before. He is frequently irritable and condescending in the extreme. His attention darts away impulsively to any outside noise or fantasied event. The treatment itself is felt to be intrusive, demanding, and persecutory, and his peculiar identification with his delinquent mother heightens such behaviour patterns. His hatred of being anywhere near the depressive position manifests itself in sleepiness and the wish to be left alone to his own devices. J feels I am against all his previous preoccupations and "intellectual" pursuits, which unfortunately matches fantasies of interfering with my interest in him and his mental state.

This simply mirrors J's mind's view that he was responsible for his mother's strange behaviours and abandonings. At the moment, the split in the midst of his threatened depression is expressed through him and his brother having totally differing views of his mother— the good mother being at the moment ensconced in his brother's mind. This is primarily defensive in that the brother experiences the greater sense of loss but also relates to the feeling of unworthiness that his mind has no entitlement to miss his mother. This latter is related to a phase of delinquent behaviour and drug-taking that preceded the psychotic breakdown. The combination of inattentiveness that is so linked to the idealization of the absent mother also heightens the missing of his previous interests in the occult and mysticism that permitted him never to think, only to listen and wait.

The phase I want to talk about is where J forms a relationship with "H"—a girl who, in some peculiar way, tolerates his weird behaviours. He became preoccupied with books on the Occult. She watches the way he reads these strange books. She seems able equally to tolerate his phases of clearly psychotic behaviour, and the relationship somehow or other stumbles along. On a particular day she changes and she says, "We are supposed to be attached to each other". At this stage the hallucinatory experiences in this man's mind are well established, and the pattern of the hallucination is singularly simple: "Do this", "Do that", "If you don't do this or that"—usually some particularly violent act—"you will die!"

To return to the girl, she says: "You have been messing about with all your private ruminations for days now. Isn't it time we behaved as if we were having a relationship, and make love?" J refuses, but then he changes his mind. Then, following the apparently successful sexual act, J meaninglessly, according to some of the statements he makes—that is to say, it has no meaning for him—strangles the girl. Later, whilst on remand in jail because he presents himself to the police and confesses that he has killed "H", he decides to present to a lawyer and to the court that he and "H" had been engaged in a sexually enhancing game, and that he had semi-strangled her to enhance her sexual responses, at her request. His plea was accepted, and he was given a short sentence. From the material it was clear that the act of making love was interpreted by what was then a psychotically envious part of his mind, as if it were being replaced by H. That is, the envious superego madly and jealously viewed his relationship to H, and terminated it by getting him to kill her.

The second phase of the mental drama, when J decides to present her as being sexually demanding (his words), had been preceded by a depressive sorrow in which he actually missed the girl, so he had to present her to the envious/jealous superego as being sexually abnormal and thus to appease it. Again we see that the envious superego can also feel jealous.

The telling of this story was matched by an experience that was going on in his mind, which J then managed to tell me about, and I interpreted it to him. Namely, that the lady consultant who had referred him for treatment would feel extremely and threateningly jealous about our relationship in the treatment situation, where he felt that our involvement was much deeper than that which he and the lady consultant had experienced. In fact, his relationship to her was predominantly one that related to altering his medication as necessary. He said that on two occasions he had actually lied to her about the absence or presence of certain symptoms of madness, and that he was absolutely convinced that she would do to him what had happened to him previously—that he would be abandoned again. His telling me this was punctuated by periods of considerable reticence about coming to sessions and tremendous persecutory anxieties about such possibilities until the appropriate interpretations were made.

To go back to Melanie Klein's introducing the envy of the superego, I find that she suggests it arises by either introjective identification with an enviously attacked breast, or projective identification, which I prefer, following memoried previous assaults upon the breast. For this patient, the envious attacks upon the breast are associated with experiences of tremendous jealousy of the peculiar world in which his mother moved and of the stepchildren who would be given that which he was never given. So the fantasies invariably taking place in this man are the enrichment of these strange and undeserving stepchildren, by both the presence and the symbolic version of his mother's breast. In other words, in my patient's case, the envy of the breast is penumbrated by the jealousy issue that later took its shape in this whole hallucinatory experience in his psychotic illness, which led to this dreadful end of his girlfriend. What is interesting is the function of the envied/ jealous breast in J's mind, and how it began to create a situation of such destructive and violent experience in his life and in the lives of others connected with him. In the sessions we can clearly see his powerful re-enactment of the relationship. The envious assaults on the breast are represented in the hallucinatory experience, namely that the envious superego is there, totally consistently. He is never left by it, and it is present even now in this heavily sedated world in which he lives, and in which there is no sign of the original psychosis except, episodically, highly split-off versions of it. His- torically the envious superego superseded the actual presence/ absence of the original mother figure, or mother, and was always present. As such, any relationship to his own mother would be manifested by two things: (a) she would obviously be extremely envious of this internal situation that has come up over and over again in the sessions we have played out in the transference, and (b) the whole quality of the peculiar, albeit persecutory assault of the breast would create a situation of a need to impersonate it in his mother. At one stage J got a gift from his mother of money that had accumulated in some strange way, and despite this man's very peculiar premorbid history, he could not touch the money that was given to him by his mother, to be used for whatever purposes he may find necessary.

The difficulty with this man is that which arises from the phobic avoidance that occurs in those patients, previously manifestly dis- turbingly psychotic, whose lives were totally devoted to the main- tenance of a psychotic illness. When they come into treatment, albeit in this caring situation called a hospital, they phobically consistently avoid—and unfortunately the environment encour- ages this—any contact with the psychotic experience.

Fortunately, with this particular patient there are beginnings of signs of his being able to tolerate these episodic returns of the seductive quality of the psychosis manifesting itself in competition.

* * *

The similarity between the two patients whom I described, L and J, as being in care at the moment is that they have both enacted and put into practice the character of their psychotic behaviour.

It is to be hoped that I have made clear the ubiquity of the so-called envious superego, which is able to enact both envy and jealousy, without really knowing their proper Kleinian definitions. I hope I have restored the significance of the envious/super jealous/superego to its rightful place in psychoanalytic thinking.

CHAPTER FOURTEEN

Frozen pain

Joan Symington

This chapter outlines Bion's relinquishment of the term superego and his expansion of the concept to include a ubiquitous "god" hostile to growth of the mind. This god arises from a primitive search both for the "cause" of the obstruction and for those morally responsible. This search interferes with the development of thought (selected fact and Ps ↔ D move), as illustrated in the analysis of a deprived woman whose pain was imprisoned in a frozen depression. Fear of this "god" resulted in persistent evacuation of the contents of her mind until the god could be confronted through an inner strengthening of the parental couple.

Sydney Klein has always been interested in Bion's work and thinks that much of it has not been understood. One aspect of this is Bion's idea of the superego.

Bion viewed the transformation of emotional experience towards O or the ultimately unknowable reality as the pivot of analytic work, elaborating the L, H, or K link necessary for this transformation and the minus links against it. Related to the latter is his expanded view of the superego. This is revealed in his writings as he moves from the idea, expressed in his early paper, "Attacks on Linking" (Bion, 1959), of an ego destructive superego, associated with perceived imperviousness of the object to a god hostile to the acquisition of knowledge of emotional experience—that is, hostile to transformations in O. This "god" is a ubiquitous anti-growth component of social life, seen in myths and embodied in groups and institutions (Bion, 1970, p. 112). Melanie Klein did not agree with Bion's use of the term "superego", which she thought should be reserved for internal objects (H. S. Klein, personal communication, 1996). In fact, Bion practically abandoned the term, saying in 1978 that in his experience he had found little evidence for the ego, superego, and id; rather, the self that has the capability of being a good father or mother is kept under (Bion, 1978).

In questioning how this arises in mankind, he wrote, "Primitive levels of thought are stimulated to discover the 'cause' of the obstruction" (Bion, 1965a, p. 63). This search for a cause and for "moral" responsibility interferes with the development of insight (selected fact and Ps ↔ D move). It is important to note that Bion is talking about the pervasive moralistic component in life, "the envious assertion of moral superiority without any morals" (Bion, 1962a, p. 97) that interferes with growth of the mind. He postulates that this unscrutinized moralistic quality, together with the idea of causation that is imposed unchallenged onto the thought, develops as part of the severe restriction to which thoughts without a thinker are subjected by their passage through a thinker (Bion, 1990, p. 70).

On every thought, feeling, or event a moralistic causal link can be imposed rendering life and being opaque and inaccessible. This empty superiority versus inferiority adds a sense of doom and punitiveness to the recognition of one's destructive actions (this recognition being the normal conscience). Thus anxiety about relinquishing a masochistic position may be related to fear of precipitating god's punishment or fear of loving to a dread that the god will send death to the loved one.

Viewing events from a god vertex, submission to –K may appear the expedient policy. Opposition to this god implies, at the least, permanent exile from paradise. Alvarez says in chapter one that "there was an idea around, which was a parody of Melanie Klein, that 'people got the bad objects they deserved'". I think this idea is one of the moralistic "god" who is linked with the idea of causality.

Thus in clinical work, for example, the following ideas will be in some sort of association—an object experienced as impermeable or out of touch, moralistic judgements, searches for a cause, and restrictions or prohibitions on getting to know the self and the other.

Some of these ideas are explored in the following clinical material of a middle-aged mother, long since divorced, who came to analysis with the hope of finding a fulfilling partnership, having enacted a repetitive pattern of disastrous relationships with men. She had very little knowledge about analysis except that she should "stick with it through thick and thin".

Case study: "W"

History

At the age of 4 years, W had been taken away by her mother from her family home to a far-distant city, never to see again her mentally disabled brother, nor did she see her father until adulthood except on one brief occasion. Shortly after this, she was placed in a boarding convent where she did not know from one Sunday to the next whether or not her mother would turn up to visit. It was completely unpredictable, so she would sit waiting while the other girls were collected by friends and family, only to realize finally when left alone that her mother would not be coming that day. The nuns were aloof and unsympathetic and cruelly shook off any of this little girl's attempts to find comfort or understanding. In addition, her mother moved her from one convent to another at whim. At the age of 6 years at yet another convent, she wet the bed. The wet sheet was then displayed at assembly to the whole school by the disgusted nun, thus publicly humiliating W. She remembered as a little girl how she had looked longingly at the soft breasts of the older girls, wanting to touch, as though carrying

within her mind a belief or memory of another sort of experience, of softness, caring, and warmth.

W's mother was an exceedingly immature and narcissistic
woman who gave no maternal support or comfort to her
daughter, prematurely expecting her to be responsible but at
the same time violently angry if she showed any independence.
She praised herself for any of her daughter's good qualities but
publicly humiliated her for any defects. She also vilified the
patient's father. As a young and no doubt attractive young
woman, my patient was told by her mother to move out of their
home, because the mother had a new *de facto* husband who, she
feared would find her daughter more attractive than herself.
Although W had visited her regularly in hospital, she repeatedly, emphatically, and monotonously said how much she
hated and would never forgive her mother, who had died after
seven years of aphasia following a stroke.

Feeling stifled in her own marriage, she, too, walked out on
her bewildered husband, taking her children with her. She
then sought out men to use them for sexual satisfaction. Often
she was attracted to cruel men who abused her emotionally.
An older man cared for her as a child, and this was gratifying
except that he was very controlling and mean. Finally she met a
man of her own age whom she loved but who died tragically
while recovering from a serious illness.

Given this history, it is not surprising that the analysis revealed W
to be in a dilemma as to whether she wanted to proceed with
emotional development or whether this was too risky in terms of
unbearable pain—in other words, could the hostile god be chal-
lenged without bringing down on her head yet another disaster.
This chapter displays this dilemma and its working through.

Fear of the god who forbids intimacy

W's walk was like that of a little girl but had a slightly wooden
quality to it. She attended regularly and punctually and poured
out a mass of fragmented material, each bit coming from a

different voice. Before and after every session she poured out, into the toilet, urine or diarrhoea, as though she could never have enough of pouring out. It was my job to make sense of it. She did not want to think about herself or my interpretations. She found relief in pouring out, pouring out, and yet more pouring out. The first term was a honeymoon, the first holiday a shock, a punishment for pouring out. She then felt frightened when she used the toilet at home. A terrifying, cruel, violent force gripped her. She called it the Gestapo. This fear in the toilet, which soon disappeared, was an hostility to the pouring out that brought relief—the analysis—and was a reappearance of the cruel and disapproving nun.

In the first year on three separate occasions W told me that sitting in a warm bath on the previous evening she had suddenly felt coldly, cruelly suicidal, capable of carrying this out without care or concern for her children—just like her mother, who had had no qualms about abandoning her little son. She thought with satisfaction that it would ruin my reputation, dwelling on my public humiliation, imagining how I would read about it in the newspaper while having coffee with my husband. The newborn awareness of not being inside me in a special place had to be murdered. The warm bath had changed from security and specialness to urine to be discarded, and her with it.

Having found the breasts at last, it was unbearable to have to wait yet again for their return, so the comforting, warm experience was interrupted by a deadly, cold, negating force: insight—"I don't own the breasts after all"—became meaninglessness. It reminded me of an episode in the film of "Lawrence of Arabia" when Lawrence, accompanied by an Arab, was travelling through the desert and came to a well. The desert stretched for miles endlessly around them. There was not a soul to be seen. The Arab dipped a container into the well, and both drank. Immediately on the horizon a small cloud of dust appeared, which steadily grew and moved towards them until, some minutes later, the owner of the well materialized and shot dead the Arab, who, as the owner said to Lawrence, knew better than to steal his water. As soon as W had had a drink at my breast, this Arab appeared and threatened death. Rushing to the toilet after a session was an attempt to get rid of the evidence before this menacing force arrived.

In the following months dreams were filled with terrifying images of the Gestapo. In one dream, *as she was about to board a train, a Gestapo officer warned her, "You watch it".* She felt terrifyingly uncertain about going ahead. This dream brings out the moralistic poisoning of life's spontaneity and flow. In another dream *she was in the front passenger seat of a car, telling the woman driver that the Gestapo were no good. At that moment, a Gestapo man hidden in the back seat of the car tapped her warningly on the shoulder.* Here the hostility against the analysis, the moralistic –K quality, is combined with the normal conscience, the father hostile to being left out and criticized.

I knew how lacking in love and attention her childhood had been and the cruel experiences that had been her lot, but on one occasion I suddenly became aware of a lived feeling of profound deprivation. I spoke to her of this, and she felt deeply held and emotionally moved. The next day, W came late—something that had never occurred before. I met her in the waiting-room only to find her adamant that she was never coming again. She accused me of having microphones in the room, saying that this was why I was able to remember so much about her. A couple of days later, however, she returned, although she remained suspicious. She said that I taped her sessions and listened to the tapes while I was doing the dishes. This was a strikingly violent retreat from what had been a very profound moment of understanding between us.

The Gestapo, the microphones, the suicidal thoughts captured for her the quality of this deadly negating force, Bion's –K.[1] The meaningfulness of our attentive listening to each other, the profound experience for both of us, was denuded, converted into

---

[1] Bion's –K is "backward looking" (Bion, 1965, p. 77) and "violent, greedy, envious, ruthless, murderous and predatory, without respect for the truth, persons or things" (Bion, 1965, p. 102) against very existence.

secret, inanimate microphones taping her—that is, turned back into moralistic but emotionally meaningless beta elements, the live experience killed. This reversal is achieved by cutting her capacity for auditory perception. Here she tries to reassure the god that our interaction is not becoming emotionally real and powerful but that it is merely a mechanical matter. (At the same time she has me totally preoccupied with her words as I do the dishes.) Emotional intensity can be easily reduced to a superficial recording of events.

W's basic mode of coping with emotion was by discharge. For a long time she ignored interpretations, changed the subject, mocked any reference to reliance on me. She did not want any of this evacuated persecutory stuff back again. She often took offence, sat up haughtily, and refused to speak. Sometimes she stomped out of the session but would return within five minutes. It seemed to occur no matter how carefully I worded my interpretation; it bruised her fragile skin. Otherwise it bounced off her tough skin. But sometimes an interpretation would go straight in and be understood. A later dream showed her *waiting for a bank to open its doors, but when it would do so was completely unpredictable.* She felt at the mercy of an unpredictable object, an analyst who might or might not understand. Similarly, her tough second skin might unexpectedly and suddenly melt. I was reminded also of the autistic either–or: either an impenetrable object or an utterly open one.

Sometimes, totally unexpectedly, I would open the door to a completely different person, or so it appeared at first sight. Normally W had an attractive, feminine face. This person's face looked completely different—hard, ugly, and malicious. The flesh around her lips looked swollen, as if suffused with poison. Sunglasses contributed to the impression of unrelenting hardness. She sat opposite me on a chair instead of lying on the couch and contemptuously lashed me with her tongue for daring to speak to her like that and pulverizing me (the diarrhoea) for my gross inadequacies as an analyst. On the previous day, some time after the session, an interpretation would start to get under her skin. It became something that stuck in her mind,

threatening change, and which could not be discharged immediately, a persecuting foreign body that had to be forcefully
evacuated, another baby in the bath that had to be killed.

But this vitriol was bursting out of her under great pressure, a
release of pent-up fury against the impenetrable mother/nun.
This decimating and evacuative attack on me was done with
such finesse, such dramatic intensity, that I wondered, too,
if it expressed not only the attempt to get through the impene-
trability but also an ability to throw herself into activities, including the analysis, without holding back. For example, W
was a good mimic. I felt I knew very well what her contempo-
raries sounded like, and myself as well. In this way she used
her own investigatory "microphones" in the service of humour.
As this attention-riveting virago, she not only attacked and
evacuated but also deeply expressed her liveliness, her talent
for humorous mimicry. Perhaps this was something that had
helped her through all the desolating experiences she had en-
dured. This is an aspect H. Sydney Klein brings out in his paper
on manic states (1974).

The suicidal feelings diminished and were controlled by W
keeping a bottle of anti-depressants in her bathroom cupboard,
together with my phone number, neither of which she used
except on one occasion, when she angrily took a tablet a few
hours before her session to "show me". Now she would occasionally report a very distressing occurrence, usually on a
weekend, to which she referred as involuntary crying. She
would suddenly find herself weeping, numb with depression,
like a helpless, hopeless child, gazing mutely into space, unsee-
ing, frozen. This state would persist for several hours.

Once she described a film depicting the Allies freeing the inmates of concentration camps. A train of inmates had been
abandoned in the snow, all the prisoners being locked in cattle
trucks. But one woman, starving, emaciated, frozen, but still
alive was found hiding under one of the trucks. In some almost
superhuman way she had managed to get out of the truck. I
could visualize this scene clearly from her description—the ut-

ter horror and the shock of finding this barely alive woman, who had escaped from the wagons full of frozen corpses. W suddenly grew suspicious again, saying that I must have seen the film. Again she refused to return the following day but then changed her mind. As with the microphone episode, the process of understanding was interrupted because it is so powerful and threatening. She could not tolerate a sign of life in her own frozen mind, a survivor of the usual evacuative procedure. She was also closer to her fear of what would be revealed for which she was responsible. The moralistic quality of the god interferes with going forward.

During the first year or so she brought dreams of *semi-detached houses, one already renovated and the other in a damaged state, needing repair*. These dreams described her mental life. She lived in a state of semi-detachment from her psychic reality by maintaining a wall that separated her from her mental problems. This detachment depended on partially splitting off her perceptual equipment, as with the microphones. The wooden quality of her walk showed this semi-detachment from emotional life, her second skin (Bick, 1968). The many voices and fragmented material represented the house needing repair. She was also semi-detached in the sense of being partly separate from me and partly living inside me, as in the house already renovated. Whatever might reveal this as a delusion had to be bypassed or discharged or interrupted. For example, five minutes before the end of each session she would sit up and begin putting on her outdoor clothes and gathering her things together. Her idea of renovation at this stage was discharge, cleaning out everything.

If, however, W penetrated into the house needing repair, she was faced with suicidal feelings, the victim and perpetrator of murderous rejection, or else with frozen, despairing depression. Much later in the analysis, when she referred back to the microphone episode, she said that she resented that I had penetrated into her private area. In a similar way contact with the concentration camp victim was like a breach in the wall that had kept hidden the cruelly neglected object.

Rebellion against the god

W stuck to the analysis, as she had been determined to do. She became less intimidated by the god. Rebellion and a more deliberate interference with proceedings were evident. Against my god-like tyranny she left me an angry note, saying "You can stick the analysis up your arse if demi-gods have them".

Whereas earlier in the analysis she had poured out for sheer primitive relief, as though getting rid of potential emotional experience solved life's problems, now the spilling-out was a defiant gesture, a deliberate throwing away part of her mind, a positive refusal to tolerate any discomfort. "I'm buggered if I'll tolerate it", she said on one occasion—that is, should she wish to do so, she could tolerate it, but, identified with her internalized mother, she was not going to attend to this "child"— her mind—which she did not value. It was merely a nuisance, periodically causing pressure, which required the immediate relief of abandoning it. Lucas (1998) describes a manic–depressive patient who repeatedly surrendered herself to an internal tyrannical mother figure rather than take care of herself represented by a baby. The self that had "the capability of being a good . . . mother (was being) kept under" (Bion, 1978). In saying "I'm buggered if I'll tolerate it", W expresses the belief that what she evacuates out in words and diarrhoea comes back through her bottom, and therefore to tolerate it is to be buggered. To her, this is what tolerating frustration feels like.

A dream captures this throwing-away phase: *"A plumber was inspecting her toilet and indicated his disapproval of an extra pipe leading away from the bowl."* Some of the basic substance of the analytic emotional experience was still being thrown away, but now a plumber–father was on the scene. In contrast, she was also a reparative scavenger, retrieving from the gutter dropped articles of clothing. These rescued babies she would lovingly wash and repair.

Gradually, dreams of the Gestapo lessened, and a baby appeared instead—sometimes her baby, sometimes a baby she was looking after for someone else. These babies were well-nourished and content, all they needed was a change of their wet nappies. In other words, further attention was required to her deliberate pouring out and greedy wasting. This included getting up at night at least twice to urinate.

One of her sexual fantasies was of being a young girl who was asked, by his wife, to give sexual pleasure to an old man. This showed the beginnings of working through—being able to have a man with the mother's agreement rather than her murderous jealousy. But a dream revealed something less benign: *She dreamed of being in a motel-room. While waiting for a woman companion to finish her shower, she answered a knock on the door to a man who raped her at knife-point. She enjoyed this.* Having to wait could trigger in her a turning-away from me, a masochistic collusion with having her mind raped.

At this time she began a weekend sexual relationship with a man who was attentive but obsessional and mean. She decided not to have orgasms with him in case she would then be stuck for life with him—that is, she, too, withheld. This affair plugged the hole left by the weekend and reinforced her phantasy of living inside, albeit with the concurrent restrictions. A rash on one of her breasts, which developed every Friday and vanished on Monday, gave the lie to the fantasy that her being with the father was just what the mother wanted.

After a couple of years this man found another woman who suited him better. My patient felt betrayed, but was not too upset. She felt a certain release from bondage. The rash on the breast that held imprisoned the vitriolic attack on and contemptuous abandonment of the breast–mother disappeared.

Pain suffered and the coming together

Having returned the father to the mother, she now began to be persecuted by noises in the night, in particular an endlessly running toilet, about which she could do nothing but impotently complain in various letters. Now the hostile listening was not in my "microphones". The wall that up to now had enabled her to be semi-detached from the damaged object was now becoming permeable. The parents were together, the analysis moved on relentlessly. Although threatened by this, there was a suggestion that she could tolerate it. She began to feel neglected at work and threatened to cut herself off from people to "show them". There were different complaints about me: that I didn't smile at her and say how nice she looked—that is, a more direct expression of her offended little-girl self, now fully detached, who felt so left out from the "night noises" of separateness.

Together with recognizing me as a separate person, she began to be interested in her analysis. The virago had shrunk to a few threats to leave and complaints about analysis being "no bloody good". She began to give quick, accurate, brief associations to dreams. Although she periodically tried to stop insight-threatening material from building up, the plumber father was installed in her mind to point this out, the normal conscience not the moralistic Gestapo god. There was a change in her orientation from a superego (god) vertex to an ego vertex, hence interpretations started to become interesting facts to her, not threats from the Gestapo.

As she poured out potential emotionality less, she could observe its effects. Thus on one occasion she was moved by something I said and began to cry. She observed that as soon as she began to cry, her wish to go to the toilet disappeared. On another occasion she noted that if she had a dream, she did not have to get up to the toilet at night. This going to the toilet at night finally ceased after an interpretation about her greed, an interpretation she did not like but accepted without the usual abuse of me the next day. Recognition of her greed stopped the liquefaction of her mind (Neville Symington, personal communication, 1998), and there was no longer any need to spill out.

She continued to sit up or refuse to speak when some interpretation offended her. In this she created a very powerful atmosphere of someone superior who had been outrageously insulted. On one occasion I felt more than the usual need of courage to speak. I found myself feeling strongly that to interpret now would be to crush an already deprived child. Nevertheless I continued and spoke to her about something I had observed about her meanness even though she expressed her fury and outrage that I was continuing. She finally left in a huff, but the following day she reported that she had had feelings of sexual excitement at work, and she was convinced that this had arisen out of our conversation of the previous day.

At the same time she developed a sore anus, an indication that her narcissistic grip that kept the bank closed and her treasures intact resented the fact that life and development depended on a vigorous and fruitful intercourse between us. On this occasion, when I described that state of mind which chose to close down anally on her treasures, she said to me, "I don't feel offended", indicating that she recognized that normally she would have been offended but that now she could take in and understand. The bank was open! Her view of intercourse as plugging a hole or as one discharging into another had been transformed.

Very late in the analysis she told me that her mother had never cuddled or kissed her. I think this only emerged late because previously the pain of it had been imprisoned in her frozen depression and could only be experienced after she had internalized an adequate maternal figure to lead her through it. This imprisoned pain contributed to the repeated interruptions of any developing intimacy. The pain was experienced but not suffered (Bion, 1970, p. 19). So while she longed for understanding and intimacy, she almost equally dreaded the pain it would bring, much as she might dread Gestapo torture. Having found the breasts at last after waiting so long for them rendered further separation intolerable. This desperate feeling is then managed by the god, as in the rape-at-knife-point dream, where she turns away to masochism.

As the analysis approached its ending, something different began to occur in her dreams. These were dreams in which she noted actually smelling or really tasting something or really hearing a noise. This was a coming alive or a retrieval of each discarded sense (not only hearing) integral to emotional experience, a melting of her frozen prison and her semi-detachment, reversing that process which interrupted intimacy. I began to say to her that the coming together of these senses was like an orgasm, but as I began, she joined in, saying, "that thought crossed my mind just as you started to speak". Thus our thinking the same thought at the same time was like an orgasm between us. There was a coming-together in her senses and her emotions, the acknowledgement of her relationship with me as a person. With this came regret about what she had done to her husband. Her coming-together with me represented the integration of sexuality, emotion, and thought.

REFERENCES

Abraham, K. (1924). *A Short Study of the Development of the Libido, Viewed in the Light of Mental Disorders.* In: *Selected Papers of Karl Abraham, M.D.* (pp. 418–501). London: Hogarth, 1927 [reprinted London: Karnac Books, 1988].

Alvarez, A. (1992). *Live Company: Psychoanalytic Psychotherapy with Autistic, Borderline, Deprived and Abused Children.* London: Routledge.

Alvarez, A. (1995). Motiveless malignity: problems in the psychotherapy of psychopathic patients. *Journal of Child Psychotherapy, 21* (2): 167–182.

Barrows, K. (1999). Ghosts in the swamp: some aspects of splitting and their relationship to parental losses. *International Journal of Psychoanalysis, 80:* 549–561.

Barrows, P. (1999). Facing reality: work with a four-year-old and a thirty-four-year-old. *Psychoanalytic Psychotherapy, 13:* 213–231.

Bick, E. (1964). Notes on infant observation in psychoanalytic training. *International Journal of Psycho-Analysis, 45:* 558–566.

Bick, E. (1968). The experience of the skin in early object relations. *International Journal of Psycho-Analysis, 49:* 484–486. Also in: E. Bott Spillius (Ed.), *Melanie Klein Today, Vol. 1.* London: Routledge, 1988.

Bick, E. (1986). Further contributions on the function of the skin in early object relations. *British Journal of Psychotherapy, 2:* 292–299.

227

Bion, W. R. (1950). The imaginary twin. In: *Second Thoughts*. London: Heinemann, 1967 [reprinted London: Karnac Books, 1987].

Bion, W. R. (1957). Differentiation of the psychotic from the non-psychotic personalities. *International Journal of Psycho-Analysis 38*: 266–275. Also in: *Second Thoughts*. London: Heinemann Medical Books, 1967 [reprinted London: Karnac Books, 1987].

Bion, W. R. (1958). On hallucination. *International Journal of Psycho-Analysis, 39*: 341–349. Also in: *Second Thoughts* (pp. 65–85). London: Heinemann, 1967 [reprinted London: Karnac Books 1987].

Bion, W. R. (1959). Attacks on linking. *International Journal of Psychoanalysis, 40*: 308–315. Also in: *Second Thoughts* (pp. 93–109). London: Heinemann, 1967 [reprinted London: Karnac Books, 1987].

Bion, W. R. (1962a). *Learning from Experience*. London: Heinemann [reprinted London: Karnac Books, 1984].

Bion, W. R. (1962b). A theory of thinking. *International Journal of Psychoanalysis, 43*: 4–5. Also in *Second Thoughts: Selected Papers on Psycho-Analysis*. London: Heinemann, 1967 [reprinted London: Karnac Books, 1987].

Bion, W. R. (1963). *Elements of Psycho-Analysis*. London: Heinemann [reprinted London: Karnac Books, 1984].

Bion, W. R. (1965). *Transformations*. London: Heinemann [reprinted London: Karnac Books, 1984].

Bion, W. R. (1967). *Second Thoughts. Selected Papers on Psycho-Analysis*. London: Heinemann [reprinted London: Karnac Books, 1990].

Bion, W. R. (1970). *Attention and Interpretation*. London: Tavistock [reprinted London: Karnac Books, 1984].

Bion, W. R. (1978). Tavistock Lecture.

Bion, W. R. (1990). *A Memoir of the Future*. London: Karnac Books.

Birksted-Breen, D. (1996). Phallus, penis and mental space. *International Journal of Psycho-Analysis, 77*: 649–657.

Bott Spillius, E. (1983). Some developments from the work of Melanie Klein. *International Journal of Psycho-Analysis, 64*: 321–332.

Bott Spillius, E. (1993). Development in Kleinian thought: overview and personal view. *British Psycho-Analytical Society Bulletin, 29*: 3.

Bowlby, J. (1988). *A Secure Base: Clinical Applications of Attachment Theory*. London: Routledge.

Bremner, J., & Meltzer, D. (1975). Autism proper—Timmy. In: D. Meltzer, J. Bremner, S. Hoxter, D. Weddell, & I. Wittenberg (Eds.), *Explorations in Autism*. Strath Tay: Clunie Press.

Brenman, F. (1993). Review of Freud's "On Narcissism: An Introduction". *International Journal of Psycho-Analysis, 74* (3): 627.

Britton, R. (1989). The missing link: parental sexuality in the Oedipus complex. In: J. Steiner (Ed.), *The Oedipus Complex Today*. London: Karnac Books.

Britton, R. (1994). The blindness of the seeing eye: inverse symmetry as a defence against reality. *Psychoanalytic Inquiry, 14*: 365–378.

Britton, R. (1995). "Second thoughts on the third position." Paper read at a Clinic Scientific Meeting, The Tavistock Clinic, London.

Britton, R. (1998). Subjectivity, objectivity and triangular space. In: *Belief and Imagination*. New Library of Psycho-Analysis. London/ New York: Routledge.

Bruner, J. (1968). *Processes of Cognitive Growth: Infancy*. Clark University Press and Barre Publishers, USA.

Carpy, D. V. (1989). Tolerating the countertransference: a mutative process. *International Journal of Psycho-Analysis, 70:* 287–294.

Collis, G. M. (1977). Visual co-orientation and maternal speech. In: H. R. Schaffer (Ed.), *Studies in Mother–Infant Interaction*. London: Academic Press.

Daws, D. (1993). *Through the Night*. London: Free Association Books

Deane, S. (1997). *Reading in the Dark*. London: Vintage.

Fairbairn, W. R. D. (1958). On the nature and aims of psychoanalytical treatment. *International Journal of Psycho-Analysis, 39 (5)*: 374– 385.

Fonagy, P., Steele, M., Moran, G., Steele, H., & Higgitt, A. (1993). Measuring the ghost in the nursery: an empirical study of the relationship between parents' mental representations of childhood experiences and their infants' security of attachment. *Journal of the American Psychoanalytic Association, 41* (4): 957–989.

Fonagy, P., Steele, M., Steele, H., Moran, G. S., & Higgitt, A. C. (1991). The capacity for understanding mental states: the reflective self in parent and child and its significance for security of attachment. *Infant Mental Health Journal, 13* (3): 201–218.

Fonagy, P., & Target, M. (1995). Understanding the violent patient: the use of the body and the role of the father. *International Journal of Psycho-Analysis, 76, 478.*

Fraiberg, S. (Ed.) (1980). *Clinical Studies in Infant Mental Health*. London: Tavistock.

Fraiberg, S., Adelson, E., & Shapiro, V. (1975). Ghosts in the nursery: a psychoanalytic approach to the problem of impaired infant–mother relationships. *Journal of the American Academy of Child Psychiatry, 14*: 387–422.

Freud, S. (1905d). *Three Essays On Sexuality. S.E., 7.*

Freud, S. (1909b). Analysis of a phobia in a five-year-old boy. *S.E., 10.*

Freud, S. (1909d). Notes upon a case of obsessional neurosis. *S.E., 10.*

Freud, S. (1911b). Formulations on the two principles of mental functioning. *S.E., 12.*

Freud, S. (1914c). On narcissism: an introduction. *S.E., 14.*

Freud, S. (1917e[1915]). Mourning and melancholia. *S.E., 14.*

Freud, S. (1919h). The Uncanny. *S.E., 17.*

Freud, S. (1920g). *Beyond the Pleasure Principle. S.E., 18.*

Freud, S. (1923b). *The Ego and the Id. S.E., 19.*

Freud, S. (1930a). *Civilization and Its Discontents. S.E., 21.*

Garland, C. (1991). External trauma and the internal world. In: J. Holmes (Ed.), *Textbook of Psychotherapy in Psychiatric Practice.* London: Churchill Livingstone.

Gomberoff, M. (1990). The autistic object: its relationship with narcissism in the transference and countertransference of neurotic and borderline patients. *International Journal of Psycho-Analysis, 71* (2).

Grinberg, L. (1962). On a specific aspect of countertransference due to the patient's projective identification. *International Journal of Psycho-Analysis, 43:* 436.

Grotstein, J. (1981). Wilfred R. Bion: the man, the psychoanalyst, the mystic—a perspective on his life and work. In: *Do I Dare Disturb the Universe? A Memorial to W. R. Bion.* Beverly Hills: Caesura Press. [Reprinted London: Karnac Books, 1988.]

Grotstein, J. (1983). Review of Tustin's *Autistic States in Children. International Review of Psycho-Analysis, 10:* 491–498.

Haag, G. (1985). La mère et le bébé dans les deux moitiés du corps. *Neuropsychiatrie de l'Enfance 33* : 107–114.

Haag, G. (1991). Nature de quelques identifications dans l'image du corps (hypotheses). *Journal de la Psychanalyse de l'Enfant, 4* : 73–92.

Heidelise, A. (1982). Towards a synactive theory of development: promise for the assessment and support of infant individuality. *Infant Mental Health Journal, 3* (4, Winter): 229–243.

Heimann, P. (1950). On countertransference. In: *About Children and Children-No-Longer.* London: Routledge, 1989.

Henry, G. (1997). Reflections on some dynamics of eating disorders: "no entry" defences and foreign bodies. *International Journal of Psychotherapy, 78:* 927–994.

Herbert, Z. (1977). The envoy of Mr. Cogito. In: *Zbiegnew Herbert: Selected Poems.* Oxford, Oxford University Press.

Hoffman, I. Z., (1983). The patient as interpreter of the analyst's experience. *Contemporary Psychoanalysis, 19, 389–422.*

Innes-Smith, J. (1987). Pre-oedipal identification and the cathexis of autistic objects in the aetiology of adult psychopathology. *International Journal of Psycho-Analysis, 68* (3): 405–413.

Joseph, B. (1978). Different types of anxiety and their handling in the analytic situation. In: E. Bott Spillius & M. Feldman (Eds.), *Psychic Equilibrium and Psychic Change: Selected papers of Betty Joseph* (pp. 106–115). London: Tavistock/Routledge, 1989.

Joseph, B. (1986). Psychic change and the psychoanalytic process. In: M. Feldman & E. Bott Spillius (Eds.), *Psychic Equilibrium and Psychic Change: Selected Papers of Betty Joseph* (pp. 192–202). London: Routledge.

Joseph, B. (1987). Projective identification: some clinical aspects. In: J. Sandler (Ed.), *Projection, Identification, Projective Identification* (pp. 65–76). Madison, CT: International Universities Press, 1987. Also in: M. Feldman & E. Bott Spillius (Eds.), *Psychic Equilibrium and Psychic Change* (pp. 168–180). London: Tavistock /Routledge, 1989.

Joseph, B. (1988). Object relations in clinical practice. *Psychoanalytic Quarterly, 57,* 626–642. Also in: *Psychic Equilibrium and Psychic Change. Selected Papers of Betty Joseph* (pp. 203–215). London: Tavistock/Routledge, 1989.

Joseph, B. (1989a). Psychic change and the psychoanalytic process. In: *Psychic Equilibrium and Psychic Change. Selected Papers of Betty Joseph* (pp. 192–202). London: Tavistock/Routledge, 1989.

Joseph, B. (1989b). *Psychic Equilibrium and Psychic Change. Selected Papers of Betty Joseph.* London: Tavistock/Routledge.

Kernberg, O. (1969). A contribution to the ego-psychological critique of the Kleinian school. *International Journal of Psycho-Analysis, 49:* 317-33.

Klein, H. S. (1965). Notes on a case of ulcerative colitis. *International Journal of Psycho-Analysis, 46* (3): 342–351.

Klein, H. S. (1973). Emotion, time and space. *Bulletin of the British Psycho-Analytical Society, 68.*

Klein, H. S. (1974). Transference and defence in manic states. *International Journal of Psychoanalysis, 55:* 261–268.

Klein, H. S. (1980). Autistic phenomena in neurotic patients. *International Journal of Psychoanalysis, 61* (3): 395–402. Also in: J. S. Grotstein (Ed.), *Do I Dare Disturb the Universe?* Beverly Hills, CA: Caesura Press, 1981.

Klein, H. S. (1984). Delinquent perversion: problems of assimilation: a case study. *International Journal of Psycho-Analysis, 65:* 307–314.

Klein, H. S. (1985). The self in childhood: a Kleinian point of view. *Journal of Child Psychotherapy, 11* (2): 31–48.

Klein, M. (1932). *The psycho-analysis of children. The Writings of Melanie Klein, Vol. 2.* London: Hogarth, 1975.

Klein, M. (1935). A contribution to the psycho-genesis of manic-depressive states. In: *Love, Guilt and Reparation and Other Works 1921–1945* (pp. 262–289). London: Hogarth, 1975.

232 REFERENCES

Klein, M. (1946). Notes on some schizoid mechanisms. In: *The Writings of Melanie Klein, Vol. 3: Envy and Gratitude and Other Works 1946–1963* (pp. 1–24) London: Hogarth, 1975.

Klein, M. (1952). Some theoretical conclusions regarding the emotional life of the infant. In: *Melanie Klein: Envy and Gratitude and other Works 1946–1963* (pp. 61–93). London: Hogarth, 1975.

Klein, M. (1957). Envy and gratitude. A study of unconscious sources. In: R. Money-Kyrle with B. Joseph, E. O'Shaughnessy, & H. Segal (Eds.), *Envy and Gratitude and Other Works. The Writings of Melanie Klein, Vol. 3 (Writings, Vol. 3,* Chap. 10), 1975. London: Hogarth Press [reprinted London: Karnac Books, 1993].

Kohut, H. (1971). *The Analysis of the Self.* New York: International Universities Press [8th printing 1985].

Kundera, M. (1982). *The Joke.* Harmondsworth, Middlesex: Penguin Books.

Kut Rosenfeld, S., & Sprince, M. (1965). Some thoughts on the technical handling of borderline children. *Psychoanalytic Study of the Child, 18:* 495–517.

Laplanche, J. & Pontalis, J.-B. (1983). *The Language of Psycho-Analysis* (trans. D. Nicholson-Smith). London: Hogarth [reprinted London: Karnac Books, 1988].

Laufer, M., & Laufer, M. E. (1984). *Adolescence and Developmental Breakdown.* New Haven, CT/London: Yale University Press.

Laufer, M. E. (1997). Developmental breakdown in adolescence and psychotic functioning. *The British Psycho-Analytical Society Bulletin, 33* (8): 2–11.

Lucas, R. (1998). Why the cycle in a cyclical psychosis? An analytic contribution to the understanding of recurrent manic-depressive psychosis. *Psychoanalytic Psychotherapy, 12* (3): 193–212.

Main, M. (1991). Metacognitive knowledge, metacognitive monitoring, and singular(coherent) vs. multiple (incoherent) models of attachment. In: C. M. Parkes & J. S. Hinde (Eds.), *Attachment Across the Life Cycle.* London: Routledge.

Main, M., & Solomon, J. (1986). Discovery of an insecure–disorganized/disoriented attachment pattern. In: T. B. Brazelton & M. W. Yogman (Eds.), *Affective Development in Infancy* (pp. 95–124). Norwood, NJ: Ablex.

Meltzer, D. (1966). The relation of anal masturbation to projective identification. *International Journal of Psycho-Analysis, 47:* 335–342. Also in: E. Bott Spillius (Ed.), *Melanie Klein Today, Vol. 1* (pp. 102–116). London: Routledge, 1988.

Meltzer, D. (1975). The psychology of autistic states and of post-autistic mentality. In: D. Meltzer, J. Bremner, S. Hoxter, D. Weddell, & I. Wittenberg (Eds.), *Explorations in Autism*. Strath Tay: Clunie Press.

Meltzer, D. (1994). *Sincerity and Other Works*. London: Karnac Books.

Meltzer, D., Bremner, J., Hoxter, S., Weddell, D., & Wittenberg, I., (Eds.) (1975). *Explorations in Autism* (pp. 209–222). Strath Tay: Clunie Press.

Mitrani, J. (1992). On the survival function of autistic manoeuvres in adult patients. *International Journal of Psycho-Analysis*, 73 (3): 549–558.

Money-Kyrle, R. (1956). Normal counter-transference and some of its deviations. *International Journal of Psycho-Analysis*, 37: 360–366. Also in: D. Meltzer & E. O'Shaughnessy (Eds.), *The Collected Papers of Roger Money-Kyrle* (pp. 330–342). Strath Tay, Perthshire: Clunie Press, 1978.

Money-Kyrle, R. (1977). On being a psychoanalyst. In: D. Meltzer & E. O'Shaughnessy (Eds.), *The Collected Papers of Roger Money-Kyrle* (pp. 457–465). Strath Tay: Clunie Press.

Morra, M. (1991). The ease of a young university student from "Fifteen clinical accounts". *International Journal of Psycho-Analysis*, 72 (3): 487– 498.

O'Shaughnessy, E. (1992). Enclaves and Excursions. *International Journal of Psycho-Analysis*, 73: 603–611.

Paul, C., & Thompson-Salo, F. (1997). Infant-led innovations in a mother–baby therapy group. *Journal of Child Psychotherapy*, 23 (2 August): 219–244.

Racker, H. (1958). Classical and present technique in psycho-analysis. In: H. Racker, *Transference and Counter-Transference*. International Psycho-Analytical Library No. 73. London: Hogarth, 1968 [reprinted London: Karnac Books, 1982]..

Racker, H. (1968). *Transference and Counter-Transference*. International Psycho-Analytical Library No. 73. London: Hogarth, 1968 [reprinted London: Karnac Books, 1982].

Rey, H. (1986). The schizoid mode of being and the space–time continuum (before metaphor). *Journal of the Melanie Klein Society 4*. Also in: H. Rey & J. Magagna (Eds.), *Universals of Psychoanalysis in the Treatment of Psychotic and Borderline States*. London: Free Association Books, 1994.

Riesenberg-Malcolm, R. (1996). How can you know the dancer from the dance. *International Journal of Psycho-Analysis*, 77 (4): 679–688.

Rosenfeld, H. A. (1950). Notes on the psychopathology of confusional states in chronic schizophrenia. *International Journal of Psycho-Analysis*, 31: 132–137.

Rosenfeld, H. A. (1971). Contribution to the psychopathology of psychotic states: the importance of projective identification in the ego structure and the object relations of the psychotic patient. In: P. Doucet & C. Laurin (Eds.), *Problems of Psychosis* (pp. 15–128). The Hague: Excerpta Medica. Also in: E. Bott Spillius (Ed.), *Melanie Klein Today* (pp. 117–137). London: Routledge, 1988.

Rosenfeld, H. A. (1978). The relationship between psychosomatic symptoms and latent psychotic states. *British Psycho-Analytical Society Bulletin, 4*: 27.

Rosenfeld, H. A. (1987a). *Impasse and Interpretation*. London: Tavistock. New Library of Psycho-Analysis.

Rosenfeld, H. A. (1987b). Projective identification in clinical practice. In: *Impasse and Interpretation*. London: Tavistock.

Sandler, J. (1960). The background of safety. *International Journal of Psycho-Analysis, 41*: 352–365. Also in: *From Safety to Superego*. New York: Guilford; London: Karnac Books, 1987.

Sandler, J. (1976). Countertransference and role-responsiveness. *International Review of Psychoanalysis., 3*: 43–48.

Sandler, J. (1987). *Projection, Identification, Projective Identification*. London: Karnac Books; Madison, CT: International Universities Press.

Sandler, J. (1990). On internal object relations. *Journal of the American Psychoanalytic Association, 38*: 859–880. Also in: J. Sandler & A. M. Sandler, *Internal Objects Revisited* (pp. 121–140). London: Karnac Books, 1998.

Sandler, J., with Freud, A. (1985). *The Analysis of Defence*. New York: International Universities Press.

Sandler, J., Sandler, A.-M. (1978). On the development of object relationships and affects. *International Journal of Psycho-Analysis, 59*: 285–296.

Segal, H. (1957). Notes on symbol formation. *International Journal of Psycho-Analysis, 38*: 391–397. Also in: *The Work of Hanna Segal* (pp. 59–60). New York/London: Jason Aronson.

Segal, H. (1964). *Introduction to the Work of Melanie Klein*. London: Heinemann.

Segal, H., & Bell, D. (1991). The theory of narcissism in the work of Freud and Klein. In: J. Sandler (Ed.), *Freud's On Narcissism: An Introduction* (pp. 149–174). New Haven, CT: Yale University Press.

Sodré, I. (1994). Obsessional certainty versus obsessional doubt: "from two to three". *Psychoanalytic Inquiry, 14* (3): 379–392.

Steiner, J. (1993). A theory of psychic retreats. In: *Psychic Retreats: Pathological Organizations in Psychotic, Neurotic and Borderline Patients* (pp. 1–13). London: Routledge.

Steiner, J. (1993). Problems of psychoanalytic technique: patient-centred and analyst-centred interpretations. In: *Psychic Retreats: Pathological Organizations in Psychotic, Neurotic and Borderline Patients* (pp. 131–146). London/New York: Routledge.

Stern, D. (1977). *The First Relationship: Infant and Mother*. Cambridge, MA: Harvard University Press.

Stern, D. (1985). *The Interpersonal World of the Infant*. New York: Basic Books [reprinted London: Karnac Books, 1999].

Stolorow, R. D., & Lachmann, F. M. (1980). *Psychoanalysis of Developmental Arrests*. Madison, CT: International Universities Press.

Strachey, J. (1934). The nature of the therapeutic action of psychoanalysis. *International Journal of Psycho-Analysis, 15*: 127–159; reprinted in *International Journal of Psycho-Analysis, 50*: 275–292.

Symington, N. (1996). *The Making of a Psychotherapist*. London: Karnac Books.

Trevarthen, C., & Hubley, P. (1978). Secondary intersubjectivity: confidence, confiding and acts of meaning in the first year In: A. Lock (Ed.), *Action, Gesture and Symbol: The Emergence of Language* (pp. 183–229). London: Academic Press.

Tuckett, D. (1995). Mutual enactment in the psychoanalytic situation. *Bulletin of the British Psycho-Analytical Society, 31* (10): 1–12.

Tustin, F. (1972). *Autism and Childhood Psychosis*. London: Hogarth Press.

Tustin, F. (1981). *Autistic States in Children* (revised edition). London: Routledge, 1992.

Tustin, F. (1986). *Autistic Barriers in Neurotic Patients*. London: Karnac Books.

Tustin, F. (1990). *The Protective Shell in Children and Adults*. London: Karnac Books.

Tustin, F. (1991). Revised understanding of psychogenic autism. *International Journal of Psycho-Analysis, 72* (4): 585–587.

Winnicott, D. W. (1965). *The Maturational Process and the Facilitating Environment*. London: Hogarth Press.

Wittenberg, I. (1975). Primal depression in autism—John. In: D. Meltzer, J. Bremner, S. Hoxter, D. Weddell, & I. Wittenberg (Eds.), *Explorations in Autism*. Strath Tay: Clunie Press.

INDEX

Abraham, K., 122–124, 127
  anal character, 122
  melancholia, 123
Adelson, E., ghosts in the nursery, 74
adolescence, rebellion and
      reparation, 72
affects, withdrawal of and
      obsessional neurosis, 99–100,
      104–111
alphabet, autistic child's use of, 82,
      92–94, 97
alpha function, 133
Alvarez, A., viii, ix, 5–22, 89–90, 130,
      214–215
  borderline children, 5–22
ambivalence:
  in analyst–analysand relationship,
      192
  in infant observation, 158–159
anal erotism, 127
anal meanings, 124
anal organization of instincts, 118–
      127
anal–sadistic stage, 125–126

analyst:
  –analysand relationship:
    false object relationship, 192
    projective identification, 167–
      188
    sexualization of, 60–62
  -centred interpretations, and
      patient-centred
      interpretations, 113
  recognized by infant as ally, 131
Anna Freud Centre, 12
anorexia, parental projections and
      failure of containment, 146
anxieties:
  autistic child's, 82–97
  Freud's view of, 119, 120
  as god's punishment for
      relinquishing masochistic
      position, 214
  maternal failure to respond to, 55
  as result:
    of changed object relations, 197
    of dismantling defences, 189–
      198

236